Bio-Inspired Computational Paradigms

Smart cities with various technological innovations have played an important role and influenced society as well. Due to voluminous data transactions within smart cities, security and privacy concerns need to be dealt with. Though taking care of safety and privacy is challenging, it is essential for a smart city to understand the bio-inspired computing paradigms. This book discusses the utilization of bio-inspired computing procedures for effective computational devices. This book:

- discusses real-world usage of bio-inspired computations;
- highlights how bio-inspired computations hold the potential to significantly increase network security and privacy;
- talks about how society can avoid consequences of cyber security breaches;
- examines the combination of bio-inspired computational methods with IoT, AI and big data.

This book is primarily aimed at graduates, researchers, IT and industry professionals.

Bio-Inspired Computational Paradigms

Security and Privacy in Dynamic Smart Networks

Edited by
Vijayalakshmi S, Gayathri SP, Samiksha Shukla,
Parma Nand and Balamurugan Balusamy

CRC Press
Taylor & Francis Group
Boca Raton London New York

CRC Press is an imprint of the
Taylor & Francis Group, an **informa** business

Designed cover image: ShutterStock

First edition published 2024
by CRC Press
2385 NW Executive Center Drive, Suite 320, Boca Raton FL 33431

and by CRC Press
4 Park Square, Milton Park, Abingdon, Oxon, OX14 4RN

CRC Press is an imprint of Taylor & Francis Group, LLC

ISBN: 9781032164298 (hbk)
ISBN: 9781032164335 (pbk)
ISBN: 9781003248545 (ebk)

DOI: 10.1201/ 9781003248545

Typeset in Times
by Newgen Publishing UK

Contents

Editors

Vijayalakshmi S earned a Bachelor's degree in computer science in 1995 and a Master of Computer Applications in 1998 from Bharathidasan University, Trichy, India. She completed her Master of Philosophy in 2006. Mother Teresa Women's University, Kodaikanal, India, awarded her with a PhD degree in 2014. She has served as an assistant professor from 1998 to 2013 in the Department of Computer Science and Applications, Gandhigram Rural Institute–Deemed University, TN, India, and in the School of Computing Science and Engineering, Galgotias University, Greater Noida, from 2013 to 2021. She is currently an associate professor in the Data Science Department in Christ University (Deemed to be University), Pune, Lavasa Campus. She has many academic portfolios associated with her current position. Her research area is in image processing and IoT. She has contributed to many international and national conferences and reputed journals. She has published many book chapters and has several books in progress. She is a member of many academic bodies such as IFERP. Other than teaching, she also guides students in research as well as academic-related activities.

Gayathri SP earned her PhD from the Department of Computer Science and Applications in Gandhigram Rural Institute (DU), Dindigul, India, and is currently a guest lecturer in the Government Arts College for Women, Nilakottai. She has 15 years of teaching experience in the field of computer science at various colleges and in Gandhigram University. She has published many research articles in reputed journals and contributed book chapters. Her research interests are in digital and medical image processing. She has also published patents and a few books.

Samiksha Shukla is an Associate Professor and Head, Data Science Department, Christ University (Deemed to be University), Pune Lavasa Campus. Her research interests include computation security, artificial intelligence, machine learning, data science and Big Data. She is a certified AWS educator. She has presented and published several research papers in reputed journals and conferences. She has 16 years of academic and research experience. She serves as a reviewer for Inderscience journals, Springer Nature's *International Journal of Systems Assurance Engineering and Management*, and IEEE and ACM conferences. Dr Shukla is an experienced and focused teacher who is committed to promoting the education and well-being of students. She is passionate about innovation and good practices in teaching. She constantly engages in continuous learning to broaden her knowledge and experience. Her core expertise lies in computational security, artificial intelligence and healthcare-related projects. She is skilled at adopting a pragmatic approach in improvising solutions and resolving complex research problems. Dr. Shukla possesses an integrated set of competencies that encompass areas related to teaching, mentoring, strategic management and establishing a center of excellence via industry tie-ups. She has a track record of driving unprecedented research and development projects with international collaboration and has been instrumental in organizing various national and international events.

 **Parma Nand** holds a PhD in computer science and engineering from IIT Roorkee and MTech in computer science and engineering from IIT Delhi. Professor Parma Nand has more than 27 years of experience both in industry and academia. He received various awards such as the best teacher award from the union government, the best students project guide award from Microsoft in 2015 and the best faculty award from Cognizant in 2016. He had successfully completed government-funded projects and spearheaded the past five IEEE International Conferences on Computing, Communication & Automation (ICCCA), IEEE students chapters, Technovation Hackathon 2019, Technovation Hackathon 2020, and the International Conference on Computing, Communication, and Intelligent Systems (ICCCIS 2021). He is a member of the Executive Council of IEEE UP section (R-10), a member of the Executive Committee of IEEE Computer and Signal Processing Society, a member of the Executive Council of Computer Society of India, Noida section, and has acted as an observer at many IEEE conferences. He holds active memberships in ACM, IEEE, CSI, ACEEE, ISOC, IAENG and IASCIT. He is a lifetime member of the Soft Computing Research Society and ISTE.

 **Balamurugan Balusamy** is a professor in the School of Computing Sciences and Engineering at Galgotias University, Greater Noida, India. His contributions focus on engineering education, blockchain and data sciences. His academic degrees and 12 years of experience working as a faculty in a global university like VIT University, Vellore, have made him more receptive and prominent in his domain. He has high-impact factor papers in Springer, Elsevier and IEEE. He has done more than 50 edited and authored books and collaborated with eminent professors across the world from top QS-ranked universities. Professor Balusamy has served up to the position of associate professor in his 12 years of experience with VIT University, Vellore. He completed his bachelor's, master's and PhD degrees from top premier institutions of India. His passion is teaching and adapting different design thinking principles while delivering lectures. He has published 30-plus books on various technologies and visited 15-plus countries

for his technical courses. He has several top-notch conferences on his resume and has published over 150 essays in quality journals, conferences and book chapters combined. He serves on the advisory committees for several startups and forums and does consultancy work on industrial IoT. He has given over 175 talks at various events and symposiums.

Contributors

Jeevarekha A
MVM Govt. Arts College for Women
Dindigul, India

Subramaneswara Rao A
Madanapalle Institute of Technology &
  Science
Madanapalle, India

Karpagam C
Dr N.G.P. Arts and Science College
Coimbatore, India

Somsak Chanaim
International College of Digital
  Innovation, Chiang Mai University
Chiang Mai, Thailand

Xavier Chelladurai
Christ University
Bangalore, India

Ahmad Yahya Dawad
International College of Digital
  Innovation, Chiang Mai University
Chiang Mai, Thailand

Chokkanathan K
Madanapalle Institute of Technology
  and Science
Madanapalle, India

Ezhilarasan K
Gandhigram Rural Institute (Deemed to
  be University)
Dindigul, India

Joseph Varghese Kureethara
Christ University
Bangalore, India

Kalaichelvi N
Fatima College (Autonomous)
Madurai, India

Naveen Kumar N
Madanapalle Institute of Technology
  and Science
Madanapalle, India

Palaniappan N
Gandhigram Rural Institute (Deemed
  University)
Gandhigram, India

Preethi Nanjundan
Christ University
Lavasa, India

Chitra P
Dhanalakshmi Srinivasan University
Trichy, India

Aniwat Phaphuangwittayakul
International College of Digital
  Innovation, Chiang Mai University
Chiang Mai, Thailand

Siva Shankar Ramasamy
International College of Digital
  Innovation, Chiang Mai University
Chiang Mai, Thailand

Vijayalakshmi S
Christ University
Pune, India

Savita
Galgotias University
Greater Noida, India

Praveenkumar Somasundaram
Qualcomm Technologies Incorporated
San Diego, CA

Gayathri SP
Govt. Arts College for Women
Nilakottai, India

Charanya Nagammal T
Fatima College (Autonomous)
Madurai, India

Mageshwari V
Fatima College (Autonomous)
Madurai, India

Jaisingh W
VIT Bhopal University
Bhopal, India

1 Ant Colony Systems-Enabled Wireless Network Communication

Preethi Nanjundan and Jaisingh W

1.1 INTRODUCTION

WMNs (multi-hop wireless mesh networks) have been rising in popularity due to their ability to offer efficient services that are QoS-friendly. These networks also offer multiple hops, automatic configuration, self-healing and scalability. Relays, or WMN nodes, typically pass traffic between network nodes or provide localized wireless access to mobile and universal plans (such as processors, desktops and other web customers) (MCs) [1]. They serve as both the backbone and backhaul for fixed and mobile networks. Nodes in the WMN can act as routers by sending packets between themselves. It is possible for a node without access to the backbone network to find a joining by direction-finding packets through neighbors with admission to the backbone. Gateways, which are acting as relays for MCs in WMNs, connect the MCs to cyberspace, as shown in Figure 1.1

In Figure 1.1 Mesh Router (MR) has limited mobility in the network because of its WMN configuration [3]. Routers such as these can also serve as internet gateways that connect directly to the web. In Figure 1.1, we can see the basic components of a virtual private network: Entry Layer (GL), Mesh Router Coat (MR Layer) and Web Customers Coat (MC Layer). Connecting MCs to the internet is done via both gateways and MR nodes. It is the responsibility of MRs to handle traffic coming from and leaving mesh routers to the internet, while gateways deal with traffic coming from and leaving the internet. A similar omnidirectional antenna to IEEE 802.11 b/ g provides communication between neighboring nodes. A hybrid WMN is proposed whereby mobile computers are connected by gateways and bridges, i.e., mobile computers connect to a network infrastructure through gateways, and gateways relay internet communications to the mobile computers.

It gets to be challenging, be that as it may, to supply quality benefits to every single client. Cleverly calculations that take after organic standards have gotten to be progressively valuable in understanding complex building issues over a long time [2]. Modeling the swarming behaviors of ants, bees and other social creepy crawlies may be utilized to illuminate complicated issues, such as activity rerouting, stack adjusting

DOI: 10.1201/9781003248545-1

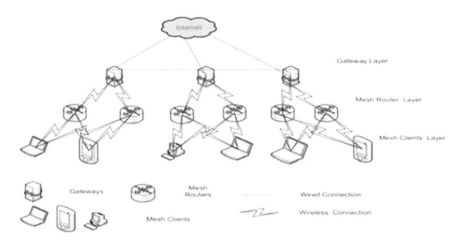

FIGURE 1.1   A typical scenario of a mobile mesh network [2].

and channel scheduling [6]. One of the foremost vital calculations within the category is Subterranean insect colony optimization (ACO). This calculation can involve complex combinatorial optimization issues.

Researchers have recently taken a look at the topic of a long QoS-aware provision collection using ACO. In particular, the network and user perspectives have been less considered on the topic of service selection except for the proposal in [6]. In [6], we analyzed wireless service selection algorithms, in which QoS is taken into account. A QoS-aware service selection problem was formulated for package arrangement, and two approaches were suggested to solve it: local exploration best service collection (LOSSA) and limited broadcast (LOSSA-k).

1.2   RELATED WORK

Many researchers have used an ant colony algorithm [7] to solve numerous engineering problems over the years, in particular the optimization of routing in multi-constrained networks [4]. Using the movement of ants as a heuristic, the basic ant colony algorithm is developed. In [5], two well-known ant colony algorithms are described. An ant agent is sent randomly to its destination by each node in the network at regular intervals in both algorithms. According to these ants, quality is assigned to routes, and the routing table is maintained. Every destination is listed in the routing tables, along with the goodness of the route to it. These values are called pheromones. Insects and data packets are routed using this pheromone information. High pheromone values indicate a quality product path. This pheromone value indicates packet routing with a higher probability. A node participating in routing keeps track of the pheromone values of the best paths. Thus, ant colony algorithms would be very appropriate for dynamic wireless networks on account of features such as multipath routing, adaptive tolerance for packet loss and packet failure and load balancing [4].

1.3 PROTOCOLS FOR ACO-BASED ROUTING

The optimal routing decisions in WMNs are being taken using a variety of ant colony-based algorithms. In the current literature, many routing algorithms based on these algorithms can be found. These algorithms will be discussed next.

1. One of the key aspects of ASAR is that it selects optimal routes according to the number of QoS requirements. This includes:
   - Asynchronous service is used in R mode; there is no tolerance for delays or errors. A low signal-to-noise ratio and low bandwidth are the main advantages of this method.
   - The service mode D is query-driven, and error tolerance is intolerant, but delay tolerance is tolerable. For this service, congestion may exist and the signal-to-noise ratio might be high.
   - Mode S: stream query service. A low-traffic path with a low signal-to-noise ratio would make sense since delay and error are intolerant of one another.

     Agreeing to the new convention, which is based on cluster-based engineering, there's a direct plot between cluster heads and sink hubs. Radio wires are produced for each sort of benefit (R/D/S) to recognize service-aware ways that meet an assortment of activity necessities and are consistent with QoS prerequisites. Based on the pheromone esteem of the ways, a probabilistic run of the show is characterized to decide the way to the following hub. Pheromone esteem is calculated based on a few variables, such as delay, parcel misfortune rate, transfer speed and vitality utilization. Each cluster head will have three ideal way tables, and the pheromone values and move probabilities for another jump will be in real time. As a result of re-enactment, the proposed convention changes in viability based on the sort of benefit, with a few getting great QoS in certain measurements, whereas others endure, particularly in terms of vitality utilization and delays. In addition, hierarchical models have some drawbacks, such as bottleneck problems and optimal path setup problems, which require extra calculations and slow down the network.

2. Rahman et al. [8] optimize execution measurements, counting delay, jitter, power use and parcel survival rate using the concept of insect colony optimization. The state of sensor hubs does not have to be kept up by a convention. Steering choices are based on neighborhood data alone. Both the segment from the current hub to another jump, as well as the remaining segment to the sink, are considered as part of the routing decision. To discover the briefest way with the specified QoS, the proposed convention employs two sorts of ants. By utilizing the likelihood equation, the following bounce will be decided by selecting the sending hub with the most noteworthy likelihood. The source sends a forward subterranean insect, which calculates the likelihood of each neighbor hub and advances the bundle to the hub with a better likelihood; this preparation is rehashed until the parcel comes to the goal. In the forward ant, if more than half of the nodes are visited, the path is looped or not convergent. The probability of a backward ant being generated after a forward ant has

successfully reached its destination is increased once it has achieved its goal. Both acknowledgment-based and non-acknowledgment-based configurations are available for the proposed protocol. In the acknowledgment-based configuration, forward ants acknowledge the path chosen by backward ants. Upon failure of the earlier packet or upon failure to receive the acknowledgment within a given period, a new routing node will be sent by the source. Even though the future procedure shows good performance in terms of jitter and delay, its simulation results are not compared to similar protocols. Furthermore, it finds the shortest path the majority of the time, leading to lower energy consumption. If some nodes deplete their energy earlier than others, then holes can form due to the lack of load balancing between them. As a result, deployment costs increase since precise geographic information about the node is necessary. The overhead of the protocol also increases as the network scales up, causing problems with scalability.

3. Alcolbr [9], in expansion to stack adjusting, addresses QoS prerequisites for WMN through insect colony optimization. We propose using insect colony optimization algorithms to establish intra-cluster routing via a minimal crossing tree, aiming to identify both optimal and suboptimal paths. A hierarchical routing tree to cluster heads is constructed using the Minimum Spanning Tree (MST) algorithm. Inter-cluster directing distinguishes ideal and imperfect ways by utilizing the ACO calculation. Imperfect ways will result when information volume surpasses the edge for way stream. The ponder presents forward and reverse ants. As the forward ants reach their limit, they will kick the bucket. As it moves from one forwarding node to the next, each forwarding node updates the pheromone based on its own pheromone update rule. Another likely forward hub will be another trust hub. Once a second and third suboptimal path is established, the process is repeated. According to the global pheromone rule, backward ants release more pheromones along these paths to reinforce their optimal paths. When the transmission commences, it continues to the destination. Node failures will result in an error message being delivered to the source node, which will then disable transmission on the node failure path and enable an alternate path. A protocol monitoring end-to-end delays between source and destination is used to determine whether congestion has occurred. When the threshold is exceeded, congestion messages are sent to the source. Once the source node receives this message, it reduces the amount of data sent along this path and enables an alternate path that is more reliable. Simulation results demonstrate that this protocol has superior latency and node life expectancy, as well as scalability and reliability, compared to other protocols. The proposed work has a drawback related to its hierarchical structure, which introduces issues such as bottlenecks and optimal path selection, which may move the presentation of the network.

4. A routing protocol based on ant colony theory and an ant colony procedure for wireless multimedia sensor networks are proposed. The standard game theory considers three elements: players, payouts and strategies. A study claims that players attempt to maximize their profits at the expense of minimizing costs.

In a sensor network, the routing path is determined based on residual energy and the outcome of the game. Using ant routing, the route to the destination node is discovered using a forward ant algorithm. An ant tracks its route based on pheromone trails. The residual energy, the delay and the bandwidth are all considered when calculating the probability. Following the path to the sink, the forward ants produce a backward ant that follows the path to the source.

5. A steering calculation is displayed by Alzubra Hiba et al. to discover the most limited way with the least fetched. The taken-a-toll work calculates interface vitality utilization, interface quality and connect unwavering quality. Vitality utilization is calculated by including the transmission vitality and hub vitality of the recipient. Connect unwavering quality within the taken-a-toll work is characterized as the rate of time when the connection is working appropriately, whereas connect quality alludes to the bit mistake rate on the connection. The pheromone value deposited on a link and the cost of the link determines the probability of forward ants traveling from one node to the next. Heuristic values for links are equal to the inverse of their costs at the beginning, and the initial pheromone values will be the same for all links. Almost all ants update their pheromone value when they find a link. As the pheromone value is updated, the link cost function will also be updated. In addition to pheromone evaporation rates and weights for cost functions, ACO performance can differ from model to model based on various factors, such as transition probabilities. The computation time doubles when the number of ants is doubled, according to a study. This means there's a greater chance of getting a good answer. The experiential worth must be given higher priority than the pheromone worth when determining the optimal path. Increased transmission rates will reduce queueing delays and loss percentages, as shown by simulation results. Also, they studied the effects of updating the video encoding rate to find that average queuing delays will increase with the increased frame encoding rate and large loss percentages will increase. The increase in event generation rate causes the average queuing delay to increase, which delays many packets beyond the set deadline and increases the packet loss percentage.

6. Beleghachi et al. proposed a routing protocol [10] that aims to find the path with the least delay, the most bandwidth and the shortest number of hops. There are two phases to the protocol: discovery and maintenance of routing information. Source nodes will begin the route discovery phase when they want to send data. Transfer of data begins once a path is discovered. The routing protocol uses four control messages: hello packet, route request, route reply and route error. All neighbors are periodically sent hello packets. Packets are replied to by ACKs from neighboring nodes. The current node calculates the bandwidth of outgoing links based on the time it takes to send hello packets and receive acknowledgments. The route request packet is broadcast, and the node will increase its hope count and enter its ID in memory once it receives a route request to a destination. End-to-end delay is obtained from the time of sending and the arrival time of route request packets, which are then converted into parameters. The node that receives

route request packets will subsequently convert them into route reply packets. Upon receipt of the route reply packet, the source node will receive it singularly. When the intermediate node cannot reach a specific destination, it sends an error message. After the intermediate stations receive this message, they will update their routing tables and probability tables for the unreachable destination. Measures employed for the objective function are delay, pheromone value, bandwidth and hop count. The distance between nodes is calculated by adding up the bandwidth of all links along the path. In the absence of a neighbor relation, pheromone values start at zero. Pheromone values increase by 0.1 in response to neighbor node greetings. Evaporation reduces the pheromone value if there is no data to send. Whenever a link between two nodes fails, the pheromone value on that link will be zero. Energy is exhausted on the optimal path if the load on it increases. By reducing this probability, alternate paths can be used more often and the preferred path is less likely to be chosen. According to simulations of various scenarios, the proposed protocol is more scalable and has a lower routing control cost than AODV. In addition to the protocol's disadvantages, energy consumption is not considered, and a variety of control messages are used during the route discovery process.

7. Wenyu et al. adjusted the ACO approach to unravel the QoS steering issue of remote sensor systems with delay-compelled most extreme vitality left-over proportions (DCEERRs). The proposed convention, named ACO-QoSR, points to discovering the most excellent way that equalizes QoS prerequisites and complexity to meet the QoS necessities of WSNs. In the investigation, transmission delay and energy preservation ratios, including energy balancing factors, were considered as QoS metrics. A directing preparation consists of three steps: a forward-ant stage, a backward-ant stage and an upkeep stage. From the source hub, the forward insect generates several forwarding ants; as they advance toward their goal, these ants record their way data. Once a node obtains an onward association for the primary period, a best is created in the direction-finding table and a random national is selected as the next hop. Using pheromones and heuristic values, the next hop is selected if a record can be found in the routing table. According to the heuristic calculation, the value of a link is determined by the ratio between the residual energy of its neighbors and that of the current node. An Ant ID is assigned by the source node to uniquely identify the forward ant, thus allowing it to distinguish duplicate packets. The forward ant is killed as soon as it reaches its destination. Using the address of the source node, the path information and the value for the pheromone update, an ant is created. The backward ant can calculate the increment in pheromone value using the energy residual ratio and hop count gathered by the forward ant. Paths for hormone updates will meet the requirements for delay and power. Routing table entries are allowed to expire for a specified period during the route maintenance phase. After the expiration time has passed, it will be time to begin the discovery phase again. In periodic hello messages, the network maintains updated information about neighbor node connectivity. In the case of a pheromone, the setting is set to zero, and

the node will automatically find another node in the neighbor table in case the link fails during data transmission. A pheromone value limit is proposed to avoid the situation of a dominant path. The proposed protocol has a lower average delay than the AODV and DSDV protocols based on simulations. In addition, there is less routing overhead and better path-normalizing energy.

8. As proposed by Adamu Murtala et al. [11], the proposed protocol is an improvement to the EEABR protocol. The routing decision considers not only the node's available power but also its energy consumption. Reducing the routing table will reduce memory usage. The memory of an ant contains only two visitations to the same node in the past two years. Also, routing tables must be updated only for neighbor nodes when forward ants are directed directly to sink nodes. A node's memory keeps track of all ants it receives and sends. An Ant memory record contains the previous node, the forward node, the Ant ID and the timeout value. This work modifies the EEABR protocol to enhance energy efficiency and improve protocol performance by (1) intelligently initializing the routing tables of nodes, (2) prioritizing neighbors of a source or route that falls under the destination route and (3) finally by reducing ant flooding. Initialize the routing table with uniform probability distributions using the proposed algorithm. Next, each node forwards to find the best path to the destination at regular intervals. Nodes can launch a maximum of $k*5$ ants at a time, and information about visited nodes is stored in memory and carried by the ants. Forward ants assign a greater probability to the neighboring node that falls to be their destination when they visit a node. Identical probabilistic rules were used by the forward ants to select the next hop in the ACO metaheuristic. A probability rule is established by taking into account energy consumption and pheromone values. In general, when forward ants reach their destination, the ant routing protocol generates backward ants to update the pheromone value of the route selected by the forward ants. The destination node calculates how much pheromone value the ant will deposit in advance of the ant returning. The amount of pheromone deposited depends on energy consumption and distance. By dividing the calculated pheromone value by the hop count number, nodes that are close to the destination will receive more pheromone value, forcing remote nodes to find better paths. A backward-moving ant will be eliminated once it reaches the source of the problem. As soon as the ant itself is destroyed if it is unable to reach, a loop is detected. The Routing Model Simulation Environment (RMASE) evaluates delays, energy efficiency and success rates in two scenarios: static sinks and dynamic sinks. Using the static scenario as a comparison, the proposed protocol has the shortest delay and a success rate of 96%. Additionally, the protocol has good energy efficiency and performs well when the network grows. Despite the dynamic scenario, the protocol still has a high success rate and is highly energy-efficient. The proposed protocol outperforms the BABR, SC, FF, FP and EEABR protocols in both scenarios.

9. The hierarchical structure routing protocol proposed by Luis Copo et al. complies with QoS requirements and supports power-efficient multipath video

packet scheduling based on, first, how the nodes are divided into clusters and then how routes between clusters are established. Forward ants transmit network traffic based on routes they have discovered. Multimedia sensors (nodes with a lot of resources) and scalar sensors are among the sensors in the network. Four metrics are taken into consideration: packet loss rate, memory availability, queue delay and remaining energy. Data transmission power is determined by the distance between nodes. When a network is clustered, its lifetime can be extended, its performance can be enhanced, and its scalability is also improved. The T-ant algorithm can be used to cluster networks. Rounds of clustering are performed successively. Cluster establishment and stabilization are usually included in the process. In this phase, group heads are chosen and their bunches are positioned about them. The sensors continue to send data to sinks during this phase. The cluster ants determine where the cluster heads will be located. The cluster head node is the only one with cluster ant, while the other nodes join the cluster head that is closest to them. Each node's pheromone value determines the cluster head. It is determined by memory and energy. During the sink's activity, an ant crawls randomly through the network releasing a fixed number of ants. The ants cause every node to increment its TTL. An ant leaves the sink by choosing a neighbor at random founded on the likelihood purpose, which combines the gathering pheromone value and the total pheromone value. To avoid being selected again, the pheromone value of a node that has been selected as the cluster head is reduced. A nominated protuberance must receive a group ant from another cluster head or the sink to become the cluster head. The maximum number of hops that ants are capable of performing is indicated by this value. Nodes that are three hops or farther away are notified by cluster heads. For a better CH distribution, the cluster head selects the neighbor on that node's path. There is a proposal for a packet-scheduling policy that takes into account the different priorities among the different classes of traffic. An ant route discovery process consists of three phases: the forward ant phase, the backward ant phase and the route maintenance phase. During the forwarding phase, the cluster head finds the best route to the sink using the information field and forwards the information based on a probability calculated by adding all the QoS metrics collected by the ants. There are several metrics to consider, including energy, delay, bandwidth, packet loss rate and memory. A sink evaluates forward ant information against QoS metrics and then starts the backward ant phase. An Ant is discarded if it does not follow application requirements. If a forward ant that meets the requirements of the application is received, a backward ant is generated and sent back using the reverse path of the forward ant. As the pheromone value reaches the sink, it is updated by all intermediate cluster heads. In the case of congestion and broken links, the routing maintenance phase is triggered. When data must be transmitted urgently, data ants transmit it. Traffic from data ants is prioritized over other classes. Their behavior is similar to that of forwarding ants. Using AntSensNet, a video stream can be sent between source nodes and sink nodes.

The mechanism used by [12] is efficient multipath video packet scheduling, which minimizes video distortion. To process the video, an ant is employed. For each intermediate node, the process is identical to finding a multipath, except that duplicate video ants are not discarded. Simulation results indicate that the proposed protocol extends cluster head lifetimes by more than twice those of T-ANT. Compared with ASNS and AODV, AntSensNet multimedia performs better than both protocols after a few seconds. The packet delay for ASN and ASNM is less than that of AODV. AODV uses fewer ants, which results in a lower overhead than this protocol. Pretend consequences indicate that the audiovisual eminence is higher than other similar hypermedia protocols like TPGF and ASAR.

1.4   PROCESS OF AODV ROUTING

Multi-hop directing is empowered by switches that utilize the Advertisement hoc On Request Separate Vector (AODV) convention, known as a receptive steering convention. It may be in the shape of on-demand steering, in which the source hub does not start the course revelation handle until the course to the goal is required. Moreover, proactive steering conventions keep up a course between a source and an endpoint indeed on the off chance that it isn't fundamental to the course to the endpoint. AODV's directing convention comprises two phases: (i) course revelation and i(i) course support. To put through with a goal hub, a sourcing hub to begin with counsels its directing table. A course will start communicating instantly if it is found. In the absence of a route, the discovery process will begin. Routing request messages (RREQs) are broadcast during the discovery process. The intermediate node can respond with an RREP message when it receives an RREQ message from the destination node. The RREQ message is something else broadcast through the middle-of-the-road hubs until it comes to the goal hub. The bounce check esteem in RREQ bundles is augmented by one at whatever point the middle of the road hub handles RREQ. By calculating the jump check for the goal hub, the jump tally is calculated. During expansion, the middle hubs make a section within the directing table that includes the IP address of the source hub, the number of bounces obligatory to reach the basis and the IP speech of the next hub, the hub from which the message originated. Amid the lifetime of a steering table entry, if it isn't utilized, it'll be expelled from the steering table. An RREP message is created when the source hub is made mindful of the hub.

Routing tables identify the source node for RREQ messages, which are broadcast to the next hop to the message originator. The hop total arena in the direction-finding table is incremented whenever a middle node receives an RREP packet. The hop count field in RREP packets represents how many hops it will take to spread the terminus node from the basis node. There is one more step left in route discovery. Once route discovery is completed, route maintenance must occur. In such cases, the source node performs the movement of the intermediate or destination node. In such cases, the source node receives the route error message (RERR). Intermediate nodes that receive RERR messages update their routing table entry for the destination as well as provide an infinity hop count. As soon as the source node obtains the RERR, it starts a new wayfinding.

1.5 FORMULAIRE FOR MESSAGE

1.5.1 REQUEST FORMAT FOR FORAGING ANTS

The following fields are included in the foraging ant control message as illustrated in Figure 1.2.

Defining types	A pair
Number of hops	Based on how many hops there are between a node that receives foraging ants and the node that initiated the request
Life expectancy	Control packet lifetime is limited by a counter mechanism
RREQ ID	Taking the originating node's IP address into consideration, this uniquely identifies the foraging ant.
IP address of destination	A destination IP address
IP address of the originator	Source nodes are identified by their IP addresses

1.5.2 FORMAT FOR REPLYING TO AN ANT MESSAGE [13]

In Figure 1.3, you can see the format of a reply ant control message, which contains the following fields [13]:

Defining types	The three
Number of hops	Amount of hops between a destination node and the node receiving a reply message
Life expectancy	Control packet lifetime is limited by a counter mechanism
IP address of destination	Destination node's address
IP address of the originator	The IP address of the basis node from which road discovery was started

```
 0                   1                   2                   3
 0 1 2 3 4 5 6 7 8 9 0 1 2 3 4 5 6 7 8 9 0 1 2 3 4 5 6 7 8 9 0 1 2
+-+-+-+-+-+-+-+-+-+-+-+-+-+-+-+-+-+-+-+-+-+-+-+-+-+-+-+-+-+-+-+-+
|      Type       |  Hop Count   | Time to live  |   Void        |
+-+-+-+-+-+-+-+-+-+-+-+-+-+-+-+-+-+-+-+-+-+-+-+-+-+-+-+-+-+-+-+-+
|                            RREQ ID                             |
+-+-+-+-+-+-+-+-+-+-+-+-+-+-+-+-+-+-+-+-+-+-+-+-+-+-+-+-+-+-+-+-+
|                      Destination IP address                   |
+-+-+-+-+-+-+-+-+-+-+-+-+-+-+-+-+-+-+-+-+-+-+-+-+-+-+-+-+-+-+-+-+
|                      Originator IP address                    |
+-+-+-+-+-+-+-+-+-+-+-+-+-+-+-+-+-+-+-+-+-+-+-+-+-+-+-+-+-+-+-+-+
```

FIGURE 1.2   Image of a foraging ant [13].

```
0                   1                   2                   3
0 1 2 3 4 5 6 7 8 9 0 1 2 3 4 5 6 7 8 9 0 1 2 3 4 5 6 7 8 9 0 1 2
+-+-+-+-+-+-+-+-+-+-+-+-+-+-+-+-+-+-+-+-+-+-+-+-+-+-+-+-+-+-+-+-+
|      Type      |   Hop Count    |  Time to live  |    Void    |
+-+-+-+-+-+-+-+-+-+-+-+-+-+-+-+-+-+-+-+-+-+-+-+-+-+-+-+-+-+-+-+-+
|                     Destination IP address                   |
+-+-+-+-+-+-+-+-+-+-+-+-+-+-+-+-+-+-+-+-+-+-+-+-+-+-+-+-+-+-+-+-+
|                     Originator IP address                    |
+-+-+-+-+-+-+-+-+-+-+-+-+-+-+-+-+-+-+-+-+-+-+-+-+-+-+-+-+-+-+-+-+
```

FIGURE 1.3 Response message format [13].

```
0                   1                   2                   3
0 1 2 3 4 5 6 7 8 9 0 1 2 3 4 5 6 7 8 9 0 1 2 3 4 5 6 7 8 9 0 1 2
+-+-+-+-+-+-+-+-+-+-+-+-+-+-+-+-+-+-+-+-+-+-+-+-+-+-+-+-+-+-+-+-+
|      Type      |  Time to Live  |    Hop Count   |    Void    |
+-+-+-+-+-+-+-+-+-+-+-+-+-+-+-+-+-+-+-+-+-+-+-+-+-+-+-+-+-+-+-+-+
|                     Destination IP address                   |
+-+-+-+-+-+-+-+-+-+-+-+-+-+-+-+-+-+-+-+-+-+-+-+-+-+-+-+-+-+-+-+-+
|                     Originator IP address                    |
|-|-|-|-|-|-|-|-|-|-|-|-|-|-|-|-|-|-|-|-|-|-|-|-|-|-|-|-|-|-|-|-|
|                   Residual Energy (32 bits)                  |
+-+-+-+-+-+-+-+-+-+-+-+-+-+-+-+-+-+-+-+-+-+-+-+-+-+-+-+-+-+-+-+-+
|                   Lifetime    (32 bits)                      |
+-+-+-+-+-+-+-+-+-+-+-+-+-+-+-+-+-+-+-+-+-+-+-+-+-+-+-+-+-+-+-+-+
```

FIGURE 1.4 Format for the Hello message [13].

1.5.3 MESSAGES TO HELLO [13]

Following is the format for a hello control message (see Figure 1.4) with the following fields [13]:

Defining types	There is one
Count of hops	Null
Life expectancy	Control packets are limited by a counter mechanism. The counter initially reads 1.
IP address of destination	An IP address for the node
Originator's IP address	A list of neighbors' IP addresses
Energies remanences	The residual vigor of the node from which the hello communication was received
Throughout one's lifetime	A link between two neighbors is active for as long as it remains active between them. Once the node has not received a Hello message from a national for a certain old of time, it assumes that the link is no longer active

1.6 WIRELESS AD HOC NETWORKS: METHODS FOR ENERGY-EFFICIENT ROUTING

Even in a wireless ad hoc network, you can reduce energy consumption if you carefully design the system layers. This includes (a) selecting a radio that is energy-efficient and implementing it in a way to provide an energy-efficient radio, (b) developing protocols for optimizing radio turn-on time at the medium access control layer, (c) mechanisms for reducing power consumption of radio links, error control and flow control are implemented, (d) network and transport layers – where energy consumption is considered integral to developing an efficient routing strategy. Throughout this chapter, we will be focusing on the latter. Studying energy consumption in radio ad hoc systems needs an examination of the coupling among the sheets. Considering the fact that energy is consumed not only during transmission but also during processing, it is necessary to conduct this study. The study of upper layer designs becomes much more complex when energy efficiency is taken into consideration in routing operations at the network layer, as well as when choosing the transmission power (which is related to the MAC and physical layers). Minimal energy consumption at each node is vital to minimizing energy consumption. Multihop routing schemes that account for the trade-off between broadcast control, energy outflow and route selection have been proposed, referred to as energy-aware multihop directing arrangements. Network energy consumption can be minimized by minimizing both network delay and throughput.

1.7   THE OPTIMIZATION CONCEPT FOR ANT COLONIES

The behavior of bee colonies and ants is found to be similar to the characteristics of dynamic distributed systems in terms of complex management and collective behavior [14,15]. Meta-heuristics is a framework for the analysis of problems using a variety of heuristic algorithms (called ACO algorithms) provided a mathematical model is properly defined. ACOs learn the problem space iteratively, building multiple solutions based on stochastic search policies and controlling the solution construction process. It is the goal of this strategy to develop solutions to problems that are optimal.

1.8   MOBILE AD HOC NETWORKS SHOULD UTILIZE ACO TECHNIQUES FOR DEVELOPING LOW-ENERGY ROUTING PROTOCOLS

In recent years, the use of mobile wireless ad hoc networks has gained considerable admiration due to new developments in radiocommunication technology and their correctness in scenarios with no pre-established infrastructure. Despite these characteristics, utilizing them can present several challenges, some of which may be in conflict. Among these challenges are: (a) ensuring data is effectively distributed and forwarded between nodes, (b) balancing the load between nodes, (c) lowering the power consumption, (d) making data routing efficient, (e) eliminating congestion, (f) ensuring minimal latency while maintaining reliability and (g) providing fault tolerance and scalability.

Several existing protocols handle the routing of a network as well as the management of the system overall. However, their effectiveness in dynamic environments was not always guaranteed. Based on ACO-based experiential techniques' ability to solve a wide range of still, unceasing and lively optimization difficulties, ACO-based approaches are a normal method to achieve optimal results for targeting trials or a mixture of trials. Vigor consumption is a key consideration when scheming routing conventions for radiocommunication ad hoc nets using pheromone trails, which provide a foundation for ACO-based algorithms.

1.9 SMART SWARMING FOR MOBILE WIRELESS IOT DEVICES

A key challenge of solving NP-hard problems is that their complexity levels (e.g., memory and time) grow exponentially. In such cases, the exact algorithm (i.e., the algorithm that finds the exact solution) does not work well. Particularly in NGN, a large number of linked plans, base stations (BSs), station conditions, varied capitals, etc. makes it difficult to determine the optimal algorithm. The following are some examples of ultra-dense networks: mobility-aware user association, sign discovery and station approximation and steering in the Internet of Things networks.

Systems intelligence is concerned with studying the behavior of complex systems composed of many individual components, which are capable of interacting with each other and their surrounding environment. An ant colony optimization method (ACO) mimics the behavior of ants in their search for food sources quickly, and particle swarm optimization models the behavior of birds in flocks. Nature-inspired algorithms have several advantages over conventional algorithms such as gradient-based algorithms and game-theoretic algorithms:

1. Make no assumptions about the optimization problem;
2. Ability to combine exploration and exploitation to find high-quality solutions;
3. Gradient information is not required for the optimization of the problematic (i.e., gradient-free);
4. Ease of implementation and simplicity.

In the subsequent years, SI proved to be an effective strategy for a wide range of issues in various spheres of inquiry, and it has been associated with a growing amount of issues in NGN. ACO is utilized to make strides in portability direction in domestic robotization frameworks, PSO is utilized to optimize radio wire situation in conveyed MIMO frameworks, and Firefly calculation (FA) is utilized to secure key upgrades amid handovers. According to Harris Hawk's optimizer (HHO), UAV-assisted visible light communication is based on the channel model. Algorithms based on HHOs, such as those described in [16], are capable of solving optimization problems by simultaneously finding multiple variables, so they are not necessarily convex as are the methods frequently employed. In [17], SI is applied to solve a deep neural network scheduling problem using PSO.

Research on SI mechanisms has shown several promising results, such as high reliability, high performance and convergence guarantees. As a result, SI is increasingly used as an important tool to deal with emerging NGN issues.

1.10 STOCHASTIC OPTIMIZATION AND SWARM INTELLIGENCE FUNDAMENTALS

The term "swarm intelligence" was first used to describe cellular robotics systems that benefited from the intelligence of swarms. Multicellular organisms are groups of organisms in which different individuals interact locally without a single point of control. A colony of ants, for example, consists of a queen as well as workers, soldiers and babysitters. As well as laying eggs, the queen builds the nest, raises larvae, defends the colony, collects food, etc. In spite of her lack of military experience, the queen manages to coordinate tasks and achieve goals. SI demonstrates its relevance. Ant colonies communicate locally through pheromones and resolve compound problems to guarantee their existence.

However, stochastic optimization algorithms fall under this heading as well, despite their differences from other kinds of metaheuristics like evolution, physics-based and event-based ones. Contrary to deterministic algorithms, this lesson includes some randomness, even when there is no random module. A stochastic algorithm generates random solutions at the beginning of the optimization process. Depending on the algorithm, the set will be improved until the end condition is satisfied.

A candidate solution set contains potential solutions to a given problem, so it is often referred to as a set of solutions. When there is only one solution in the set, then the algorithm is single solution. The algorithm used when more than one solution can be found is called population-based multiresolution.

Two questions naturally arise when the comparison between stochastic and population-based algorithms and deterministic and individual-based algorithms is conducted. Because deterministic algorithms produce the same results every time, they are computationally cheaper. Nevertheless, they have a habit of getting stuck in nearby ideal answers and require incline data. Probabilistic algorithms avoid local optimum despite this through their stochastic component. The downside of single-solution algorithms is that each step of optimization uses the same solution, and they are computationally cheaper than population-based algorithms. Single-solution algorithms also tend to have rapid convergence. Local optima are common with them, however. Despite being computationally expensive, population-based algorithms avoid locally optimal solutions. Population-based algorithms have been demonstrated to solve complicated engineering problems as quickly as possible.

As population-based stochastic algorithms and optimization algorithms continue to advance, one might wonder whether such methods need enhancement. Physicists have long believed that no algorithm can solve every optimization problem, which means an algorithm may be better at solving one set of problems and worse at solving another. This is known as the No-Free Lunch theorem. Researchers have improved algorithms by using the no-free lunch theorem. To improve the performance of stochastic algorithms, hybridization has been popular. There are a variety of hybrid algorithms, such as borrowing algorithms, sequentially applying more than one algorithm, adding chaotic maps, etc. These various methods increase computational costs but produce more accurate results.

SI methods have been widely adopted for solving inspiring practical difficulties in discipline and manufacturing because of their simplicity, gradient-free mechanisms, high local-optima avoidance and accurate estimation of worldwide answers. Black-box optimizers are often referred to as such because of their characteristics and applicability. We can estimate optimal solutions without having to understand the internal mechanisms of a problem by tuning the contributions and nursing how they change the output. SI methods must consider real-world design constraints when evaluating candidate solutions derived from real-world problems. Solutions that violate the constraints cannot be implemented. These are termed infeasible solutions because they satisfy the constraints but are optimal. Different methods can be used to handle constraints. This area is dominated by penalty functions, which penalize incorrect solutions so that they don't show a higher objective value than others. As a result, SI methods do not recommend them as solutions. Several swarm algorithms have recently been proposed. Throughout the following subsections, we analyze the most recent and well-respected algorithms of this kind.

1.11 ALLOCATING RESOURCES BASED ON LOAD AND IDENTIFYING USERS

Client affiliation alludes to the act of partner clients with their favored base stations (known as eNBs or gNBs, separately, in 5G and 6G), whereas stack adjusting alludes to the method of spreading workload among distinctive BSs. Later a long time has seen various ponders on client affiliation and stack adjusting in HetNets, multi-antenna frameworks and remote communication systems.

The advantage of this method is that operators tend to attach to the BS at the lowest conventional sign control, eliminating the disadvantage of conventional cellular range-expansion techniques. The work here does not maximize the sum rate, as it is done in existing literature, but rather maximizes the number of users who have satisfied their rate requirements and the number of BSs that have at least one connected user. As a result, the PSO optimizes the bias value assigned to each BS for dense HetNets, thereby enhancing load balancing. PSO-based algorithms achieve better results (in terms of resource utilization and user satisfaction) than classical PSO methods and the unified cell variety expansion bias method. In backhaul-limited networks, a multi-level multi-follower Steckberg game is proposed to solve this problem since existing methods do not consider small-cell BS and the QoS of users at the same time. The consumers are considered followers, and they compete for associations, while BSs are considered first movers and set their prices.

By implementing the PSO, the BS can calculate perfect Nash equilibrium prices. A flying BS can be used as part of a densely connected network, where BSs and users are integrated. The K-means clustering algorithm outperforms both PSO and GA to determine the optimal UAV position after they are applied. There are stimulating trade-offs among PSO and GA, where PSO-based schemes have subordinate complexity but produce better throughput, user satisfaction and active BSs. The THz (terahertz) ultra-dense HetNet exhibits high rate enhancements; however, they require novel user association mechanisms that take advantage of the channel characteristics (e.g., extreme steering broadcast and noise-limited setting). This study proposes a new way to establish user associations using the GWO that takes these specificities into account. Regarding convergence and system rate, the GWO-based algorithm performs better than the PSO-based algorithm. In edge computing systems, task offloading and user association are two applications of WOA techniques. By way of example, the PSO makes an exercise dataset for a deep neural network and enables user association. An innovative probability metric is proposed for operator overtone that reflects limited fading and meddling to evade existence stuck at local answers and to speed up a meeting.

SI strategies have found applications in cloud and edge computing, in addition to client affiliation in thick HetNets. To theoretically demonstrate the vitality utilization of shrewd manufacturing plant hardware, mist hubs are utilized, whereas a PSO is utilized to choose how the workload will be apportioned. One study [18] proposes a strategy that employs glow-worm swarm optimization (GSO) and sine-cosine calculations (SCA) to discover the perfect server combination and progress stack adjusting amid edge servers and the central cloud.

1.12   COMPUTING AT THE EDGE AND WIRELESS CACHING

5G wireless networks are different from those of previous generations. Massive connectivity is driving this growth, which means more new types of applications are being created that are computationally demanding, latency-critical, energy-intensive and data-intensive. As of 2022, the number of connected devices will have reached 28.8 billion, up from 21.5 billion in 2019. A Cisco study suggests that the number would be around 28.7 billion in 2022. There will also be a dramatic increase in traffic, for example, 12 times for augmented/virtual reality (AR/VR) and 9 times for internet gaming. In NGN, there have been several technologies introduced to meet traffic requirements (such as MIMO, millimeter-wave communication, and HetNets), but deployment and expense issues associated with wired and wireless backhaul links have forced the development of another solution. This case shows the benefits of caching at the wireless edge. To run new applications, mobile devices typically have limited computing power, storage capacity and battery life. The mobile blockchain, virtual reality and real-time online gaming are examples. The European Telecommunications Standards Institute (ETSI) Industry Specification Group (ISG) and Cisco independently introduced the concepts of MEC and fog computing in 2014. MEC and fog computing shift IT functionality, data storage, and computation away from the central server and towards the edge, thereby enabling device-level applications to take advantage of these computing standards. Applications that require high processing power and low latency benefit from this approach. Coupling offloading of computations with communication, caching, and control optimization has become a key use case of MEC frameworks from the user's point of view.

1.13   CACHING OVER WIRELESS

A cache has been developed several decades ago in many domains, including web caching and operating system memory caching. A centralized caching system cannot meet the demands of the NGN due to traffic density, user connections and increased network densification. These issues are caused by low reliability, high latency and limited backhaul capacity. Several studies have examined wireless caching concepts over the past few years. These studies typically focus on the placement and delivery of content. First, we determine where and how much content should be delivered to the requesters, then we determine how that content should be delivered to the requesters. Wireless caching systems have achieved competitive performance by utilizing SI techniques.

Wireless caching relies heavily on the concept of caching at the edge. Researchers have examined this frequently. Three phases are part of the proposed scheme, the first of which involves clustering fog nodes. A fog node may be located at any of the five BSs. A method for selecting users within each smog node's coverage to store data for all additional operators is proposed after the clustering process is complete. There is then a discrete problem of caching at the selected users, which is solved by a CACO. Several baseline schemes have a lower cache hit ratio than ACO-based methods, as evidenced by the results. As part of the D2D communications research, SI methods (PSO and bat) are also explored.

1.14   CONCLUSION

The reliability of the routing protocol in radio ad hoc nets may be improved using ant colony algorithms for dual-channel systems. With DSAR, the control and data layers were separated on a double-layer basis, reducing packet collisions and channel handoff delays and increasing network bandwidth. By transferring the blocked routing service over the network control layer to the data layer, when enough idle resources were available, the schedule of a double-layer network could be optimized and congestion reduced. Further, the reliability prediction mechanism has been put into practice, resulting in improved link reliability and fewer route restarts. Lastly, ad hoc networks can be adapted to dynamic topology changes by using ant colony algorithms.

REFERENCES

[1]   F. Akyildiz, X. Wang, W. Wang. Wireless mesh networks: a survey. *Journal of Computer Networks* 47 (4) (2005) 445–487.

[2]   N. Kumar, R. Iqbal, N. Chilamkurti, A. James. An ant-based multi constraints QoS aware service selection algorithm in wireless mesh networks. *Simulation Modelling Practice and Theory* 19 (2011) 1933–1945.

[3]   R. Ghasem Aghaei, A. Rahman, W. Gueaieb, A. E. Saddik. Ant colony based reinforcement learning algorithm for routing in wireless sensor networks. *IEEE Instrumentation and Measurement Technology Conference Proceedings*, Warsaw, 2007, 1–6.

[4]   G. Di Caro, F. Ducatelle, L. M. Gambardella. AntHocNet: an adaptive nature-inspired algorithm for routing in mobile ad hoc networks. *European Transactions on Telecommunications* 16 (2) (2005) 445–455. Special Issue: Self-Organization in Mobile Networking.

[5]   M. Dorigo, G. D. Caro. Ant net: distributed stigmergetic control for communications networks. *Journal of Artificial Intelligence Research* 9 (1998) 317–365.

[6] K. Yang, A. Galis, H.-H. Chen. QoS-aware service selection algorithms for pervasive service composition in mobile wireless environments. *Mobile Networks & Applications* 15 (2010) 488–501.

[7] M. GÄunes, U. Sorges, I. Bouazizi. ARA: the ant-colony based routing algorithm for MANETs. ICPP Workshop on Ad Hoc Networks Proceedings, Canada, 2002, pp. 79–85.

[8] M. A. Rahman, et al. M-IAR: biologically inspired routing protocol for wireless multimedia sensor networks. Instrumentation and Measurement Technology Conference Proceedings, 2008, pp. 1823–1827, Victoria, BC, Canada.

[9] B. Junlei, L. Zhiyuan, W. Ruchuan. An ant colony optimization-based load balancing routing algorithm for wireless multimedia sensor networks. 12th IEEE International Conference on Communication Technology Proceedings, 2010, pp. 584–587, Nanjing, China.

[10] B. M. a. F. Mohammed. QoS based on ant colony routing for wireless sensor networks. *International Journal of Computer Science and Telecommunications* 3 (1) (2012) 28–32.

[11] A. Zungeru, et al. Ant based routing protocol for visual sensors. In *Informatics Engineering and Information Science*, ed. A. Abd Manaf et al., Springer, Heidelberg, 2011, 250–264.

[12] I. Politis, et al. Power efficient video multipath transmission over wireless multimedia sensor networks. *Mobile Networks and Applications* 13(3-4) (2008) 274–284.

[13] A. S. Sharma. Robust ant colony based routing algorithm for mobile ad-hoc networks. Master of Science in Electrical and Computer Engineering thesis, 2019, Purdue University, Indianapolis.

[14] M. Dorigo. Optimization, learning and natural algorithms. Ph.D. thesis, Dipartimento di Elettronica, Politecnico di Milano, Italy, 1992.

[15] M. Dorigo, V. Maniezzo, A. Colorni. Positive feedback as a search strategy. Technical Report 91-016. Dipartimento di Elettronica, Politecnico Di Milano, Italy, 1991.

[16] Q.-V. Pham, T. Huynh-The, M. Alazab, J. Zhao, W.-J. Hwang. Sum-rate maximization for UAV-assisted visible light communications using NOMA: Swarm intelligence meets machine learning. *IEEE Internet of Things Journal* 7 (2020) 10375–10387.

[17] F. Jiang, K. Wang, L. Dong, C. Pan, W. Xu, K. Yang. Deep learning based joint resource scheduling algorithms for hybrid MEC networks. *IEEE Internet of Things Journal* 7 (7) (2020) 6252–6265.

[18] L. Zhong, M. Li, Y. Cao, T. Jiang. Stable user association and resource allocation based on Stackelberg game in backhaul-constrained HetNets. *IEEE Transactions on Vehicular Technology* 68 (10) (2019) 10 239–10 251.

2 Bio-Inspired Comparison Mechanism toward Intelligent Decision Support System

*Siva Shankar Ramasamy, Somsak Chanaim,
Praveenkumar Somasundaram and
Subramaneswara Rao A*

2.1 INTRODUCTION

A human process contains the basic principle of building a connection with the outside environment. Choices are made in this interaction, which leads to a discussion about whether the choices were good or terrible. Finally, people make a choice, confident that they have made the finest choice conceivable. They will almost certainly seek assistance or support from others during the decision-making process to determine whether the decision keeps reaching to end. The helpful person tries to categorize the choices as organized, unstructured or semi-structured. The optimum answer emerges from structured decision-making challenges, such as deciding to reduce the cost of travel between two sites. Unstructured choice problems are difficult to solve since the outcome is unpredictable. The intelligent decision support system (IDSS) uses Artificial Intelligence (AI) approaches to provide this unstructured decision-making process.

AI, in general, mimics the process of human decision-making, as sophisticated AI researchers have demonstrated in several real-world scenarios. Pomerol and Adam [1] define the human decision-making process, suggesting that the most significant aspects of decision-making are reasoning and recognition. This work also talks about "good" decisions; they are characterized by reasoning, which comprises weighing options and choosing the best one. Analytic approaches can be used to solve the bulk of reasoning-based decision-making problems, allowing them to be included in IDSS. On the other hand, recognition is a decision-making process that occurs without the use of clever thinking. Crisis response circumstances, like local groups of firefighters, design acknowledgment applications, finger impression and face verification, as well as situations requiring quick action, all use recognition-based decision-making. Decision-making has an emotional impact on the nervous system, and studies have proven that emotional aspects of decision-making can be represented.

DOI: 10.1201/9781003248545-2

Since the early 1970s, decision support systems (DSS) have assisted various industrial processes in making decisions. They were developed to offer a collection of tools that were well organized for the decision-making circumstances at hand to enhance the application's output. For the problem under examination, a collection of contradictory alternatives was made, and the DSS chose the optimal decision from the set.

A DSS is an organized set of tools used by one or more decision-makers to aid in decision-making by giving the situation's many components some structure and by increasing the effectiveness of the final decision. A DSS is a bit of software that enables one or more individuals to make better decisions in a particular subject by selecting the best option from a collection of often contradictory options at any given time. DSS has evolved into a model-based collection of data-processing and decision-making methodologies for a particular situation over time. Human decision-making is aided by model-based DSS [2]. Human cognitive talents were later coupled with DSS utilizing personal computers to increase the quality of decisions made. Later versions of these computer-assisted decision-making systems were created to handle multiple options, allowing the optimal answer for the task at hand to be selected. The DSS aided decision-makers in structuring data and models around a specific item to handle both structured and unstructured issues. The model, which incorporates quantitative methodologies such as simulation, optimization and machine learning, is the most crucial part of DSS. A decision model is represented using statistics.

DSS were used in the 1990s for data processing and data mining. Decision models, such as heuristic-based optimization models, are used to carry out tasks including planning, forecasting and information collecting, as well as data collection, administration and retrieval.

To assist in decision-making, humans have developed simulation models, linear programming, control algorithm models, and statistical models such as regression, among others. Afterward, the IDSS was built utilizing models in light of canny calculations. Due to their speedier critical thinking skills, consistency in choices made and higher decision quality, these dynamic models were all the more generally utilized.

PC-based dynamic frameworks utilize an unequivocal instrument in light of different hypothetical thoughts to pursue keen choices. Both subliminally and intentionally, feelings impact how the cerebrum decides. To upgrade direction, IDSS research utilizes an assortment of man-made consciousness instruments. Gigantic measures of information are expected to take care of true issues, and fake brain organizations, fluffy rationale and bio-enlivened calculations have been used to achieve this.

2.2 ROLE OF AI IN DSS

The human sensory system's learning frameworks incorporate artificial neural networks (ANN). They are generally used to surmise or gauge capabilities with a few data sources. The info, yield and hidden layers of an ANN, which are made out of three layers of connected neurons, are associated. Signals are passed among neurons and layers as indicated by initiation capabilities. Weight is put on the neural connection that is made. The weights are initially assigned at random. Figure 2.1 depicts the fundamental structure of a neural network. The input layer contains neurons that evaluate real-world data, while the output layer shows the findings to the rest of the world. Information is handled inside by the secret layer's neurons, which sit between the info and result layers. The input layer's signals are weighted before being delivered to the hidden layer, which then transmits the weighted data to the output layer. A feed-forward network is the most basic type of information-processing network. The feed-back network is a type of network that sends the output of the hidden layer back to it for further processing. After constructing the neural network's architecture, the network is ready for training, testing and prediction. Based on the learning principle, there are two types of ANN [3] algorithms: supervised learning and unsupervised learning.

The network's exhibition is physically evaluated in administered learning, and the normal result is anticipated and given to the organization. The organization is prepared to advance independently by updating its resources and endeavoring to create a result based on the input data. This occurs across a few redundancies, each directed by learning standards. The learning rate and administering factor supervise the carrying out of the learning rules. A slower learning rate prompts a more extended combination time, though a quicker learning rate prompts mistaken yield. Therefore, a quicker learning rate is required. A few learning regulations control the educational experience, including the Hopfield regulation, to give some examples. Learning regulations incorporate Hebb's standard, Delta rule, Extended Delta rule, Competitive Learning rule, Outstart Learning rule, Memory-based learning regulation and Boltzmann learning regulation. Forecast, characterization and information examination are the three significant purposes of ANN. Perceptron organizations, backpropagation organizations and coordinated irregular hunt networks are instances of forecast organizations. Learning vector quantization, counter-engendering organizations and probabilistic brain networks are utilized, while Hopfield networks

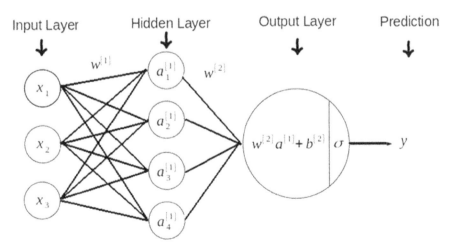

FIGURE 2.1   Structure of a neural network.

are utilized for expectation. In information affiliation situations, this type of memory incorporates the Boltzmann machine, the Hamming organization and bidirectional cooperative memory. Self-arranging maps and versatile reverberation networks have demonstrated predominant organizations for information conceptualization.

In navigation, ANNs have been urgent in accomplishing far-reaching decisions. This requires the utilization of long-haul transformative navigation. Momentary advancement is conceivable; however, it is reliant upon the progress of a task, which is affected by criticism from past periods of the errand's dynamic interaction. Long-haul development happens when a change happens over a lifetime. AI ought to have the option to change current inclination decisions in light of criticism from recently advanced choices, paying little mind to what the development requires.

2.3 ROLE OF FUZZY IN DSS

Lotfi A. Zadeh introduced fuzzy logic (FL) [4], which provides decision assistance based on how individuals think. Fuzzy logic expresses uncertainty by classifying or segmenting the input into values ranging from 0 to 1. The binary numbers 0 and 1 represent erroneous and perfectly valid statements, respectively. To attain human-like reasoning, the range of values between the extremes is frequently produced using mathematical procedures and then examined by computers. FL can help you bridge the gap between qualitative and quantitative modeling. Although an FL model's input–output mapping is quantitative, the system is fundamentally guided by qualitative linguistic rules.

The fuzzy set, which encompasses all possible solutions to a problem, contains magnificent components. The participation capability $A(x)$, where x is the number of objects in a base set, defines the universe. For different reasons, participation works such as triangular, trapezoidal, S-capability, exceptional capability and Gaussian capability are characterized. The fuzzy deduction technique uses fuzzy reasoning to choose how to plan between knowledge and outcome. The rules of mapping are used to make decisions. Fuzzy inference methods include fuzzification and defuzzification. Using expert knowledge and experience, fuzzy rules [5] are utilized to connect input variables to output variables.

The two kinds of fuzzy standards are Mamdani fuzzy principles and Takagi-Sugeno fuzzy guidelines. The fuzzifier, surmising motor, demulsifier and fuzzy rule base make up the derivation framework, likewise called a fuzzy master framework. They are fuzzified before conveying the upsides of the new contributions to the standard base module. The output variable is governed by conditional IF-THEN expressions that are utilized to build the rules. After the fuzzy values have been subjected to the rules, they are graded as fuzzy values. Fuzzy values are defuzzified and converted to corresponding crisp values before being sent into the real world. Due to its characteristics, FL has been highlighted as a good decision-making tool, which includes:

- More possibilities for defining uncertainty;
- Rule base and rule consistency and redundancy;
- Universal approximation skills can also be used to solve nonlinear problems;

- Approximate approximation can be used to get exact answers to problems;
- Simple mathematical models for an issue with a complex mathematical model.

2.4 BIO-INSPIRED ALGORITHMS

Bio-inspired algorithms [6] are a new form of algorithm that swiftly searches a search region for the best solution to a problem. Traditional search algorithms take longer to reach convergence because they use a systematic strategy to get the best answer from the search space. Traditional optimization algorithms have disadvantages.

Thus, bio-inspired algorithms examine the biological behavior of certain species to find the best solution. As a result, the collection of algorithms is referred to as nature-inspired algorithms. These methods are based on natural evolution, which occurs as a result of species interactions. Cooperative or competitive interactions between and within species are possible. Some of the capabilities of bio-inspired algorithms are:

- Adaptable to a variety of problems;
- The algorithm can be modified with fewer control parameters;
- Convergence to the ideal value is faster.

The two most noteworthy bio-driven approaches for addressing constraint-based improvement difficulties up until recently were Ant Colony Optimization (ACO) and Particle Swarm Optimization (PSO), which are inspired from underground insects and honey bees. Since then, scientists have examined microscopic organisms, fire-flies, fruit flies, bats and cuckoo birds to produce a larger category of bio-inspired calculations.

2.4.1 GENETIC ALGORITHMS

In the early 1960s, John H. Holland developed Genetic Algorithms (GAs) [7]. GA picks individuals from a population of permitted solutions and then uses genetic operators such as crossover and mutation to determine the fittest. When the convergence conditions are fulfilled, the fittest group progresses to the next generation. Each iteration ends with the former population being eliminated, and the loop starts with the new population. Multi-objective, constraint-based and other optimization problems have all been resolved using GAs. The difficulties of vehicle routing, network routing, load dispatch and job shop scheduling are a few industrial areas where GA has shown promise. Establishing the fitness function and evaluating the fitness of the solutions that emerged, mainly when the search area was broad, were two of the most challenging aspects of using GA to solve issues. The algorithmic complexity rises due to the expansion of the size of the solution space. The steps involved in a GA are:

- Initializing the population and determining the fitness;
- While the criterion for termination has been met:
  a. selection of parents;

  b. with probability p_c, there is a crossover;
  c. *pm* mutation with a high chance;
  d. decoding and calculating fitness;
  e. selection of survivors;
- discovering the most effective;
- best return.

GAs can be used to solve single- and multi-objective problems with a well-defined solution space and an easily evaluable fitness function. Scaling is required when the population size is raised for high-dimensional tasks, resulting in a reduction in algorithmic efficiency. The following are a few examples of how GA can be utilized to achieve compelling results.

- Problems with maximization and minimization;
- Sorting and searching;
- Job distribution;
- Parallel processing;
- Coordination, classification and routing.

2.4.2 PARTICLE SWARM OPTIMIZATION

Fish tutoring, bird running and bug amassing motivated the populace-based stochastic streamlining method known as PSO [8]. Drs. Kennedy and Eberhart began it in 1995. A multitude of uniform specialists cooperate in a populace and through a developmental cycle to decide the ideal arrangement. Unlike GA, PSO does not encounter change all through development. Contrarily, PSO has the benefit of being simpler to implement than GA because only a small number of variables need to be changed. PSO begins with a collection of random particles that represent the most likely answers to the issue. Following that, the algorithm updates the following generations to find the local optimum. The two best values are utilized to update each particle at the end of each loop.
  The fundamental steps for PSO are:

- Evaluates the goodness of each particle on a scale of one to ten;
- By comparing the particles, the optimal solution is found;
- New particles are created based on the best solution;

Detailed procedure for nature-inspired PSO
  1. Initialization of the population and encoding of particles: Each particle is made up of a series of binary bits.
  2. Calculation of the fitness values: Every particle has its fitness score that is expressed in real numbers (score for objective function)
  3. Modifications to the values of all positions worldwide:
      a. Every particle maintains its current optimal location (based on the objective function score).
      b. Across all particles, a global best position is also maintained.

4. Velocities are updated: Based on the data from the best and worldwide positions, calculate the new velocity.
5. Sampling new particles: new particle position creation.
6. For the following iteration, repeat steps 2–5 until the termination criteria are met.
7. Come to a halt and report the fittest particle.

PSO, on the other hand, has the advantage of being easier to implement than GA because only a few variables need to be altered. PSO starts with a set of random particles that reflect the problem's most likely solutions. Following that, the algorithm updates the following generations to find the local optimum. The two best values are utilized to update each particle at the end of each loop:

- issues with scheduling workshops and flexible learning,
- issues with reduction and augmentation,
- oscillatory and turbulent frameworks,
- thresholding and searching,
- identifying the region and managing the resources in a distributed framework.

2.4.3 ANT COLONY OPTIMIZATION

Dorigo invented ACO [9], a widely used optimization technique based on ant behavior. ACO is a probabilistic method for identifying better paths in graphs that can be used for real-world problems. The search is based on ants' trailing behavior, which constructs a path between their colony and a food source. The algorithm's agents (artificial ants) wander through a population of all potential solutions in quest of the best reply. Similar to pheromones trailing in natural ants, the agents record their positions and the quality of the meal while moving. Other agents in the population can use this recording technique to come up with better solutions.

Potential solutions to a problem are determined via probability distribution from a pool of possible options. As the agents explore the various choices, they are kept up to date locally. These impending arrangements also update the path attributes, ensuring that the superior options are chosen in subsequent advancements. The process is repeated until the ideal configuration is reached. The computation completes the pursuit action in a reasonable amount of time, according to various executions. The basic procedure for ACO is as follows:

- Initializing relevant parameters and pheromone trials; do not terminate.
- Generate ant population.
- Calculate the fitness levels of each ant.
- Use selection strategies to find the best answer.
- Update the pheromone trial.
- Stop the procedure while it's still running.

The rapidity with which ACO converges, owing to its inherent parallelism, is one of its advantages. ACO can handle NP-hard combinatorial issues as well as dynamic

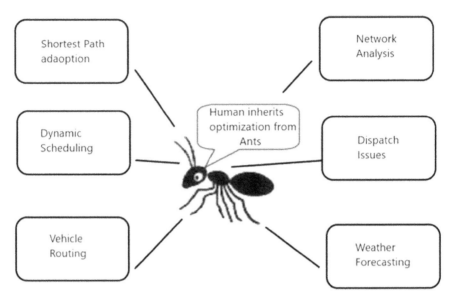

FIGURE 2.2   ACO solves some real optimization issues.

optimization and continuous optimization. Premature convergence is avoided in ACO due to the distributed computation element, resulting in faster convergence. As the issue dimension grows larger, the ACO algorithm's performance diminishes. Figure 2.2 demonstrates how the ACO has been utilized to address problems in the real world, including the following:

- The traveling salesman,
- Clustering and network analysis,
- Planning and steering,
- The task quadratic issue,
- The briefest way adaption,
- Financial dispatch issues,
- The issue of vehicle directing,
- Gaming hypothesis,
- Chart shading and set covering,
- Determining climate and money,
- Dynamic planning,
- Boundary assessment.

2.4.4   ARTIFICIAL BEE COLONY

Based on honeybee foraging behavior, the Karaboga Artificial Bee Colony (ABC) program [10] was developed. Honeybees use pheromones to communicate, delegate tasks, reproduce, forage, navigate and lay eggs. The ABC algorithm was created to mimic honeybee abilities. Three groups of bees make up the ABC: workers, observers and scouts. Half of the colony is occupied by employed bees, while observation bees occupy the other half. Each food source has one employee bee allocated to it.

The ABC algorithm has been used to discover prospective food sources since the birth of the bee colony. The validity (fitness) of the potential solution (food supply) is evaluated after it has been identified. The previous candidate solution is discarded if the hired bees discover a candidate solution with greater fitness in the subsequent step. Employed bees labor to increase the fitness of the candidate solutions that are rejected and share all of their data with observer bees. Candidate solutions are entirely wiped out of the population if the spectator bees are unable to improve their fitness. The scout substitutes a more probable candidate response from the population for the rejected response. The process will continue until more suitable candidate solutions are found. Overview of ABC are:

- Parameter choice.
- Determine how much nectar each food source produces.
- Calculate the probability using the amount of nectar.
- Determine how many observing bees will be assigned to food sources.
- Calculate each spectator bee's fitness value.
- Consider the best option.
- The phases in ABC optimization of process parameters are to update the scout bee.

Several investigations into the ABC algorithm's dance, communication, queen's behavior, mating behavior, navigation behavior and foraging activity have been conducted over the years. ABC algorithms have been combined with differential evolution to handle constraint and unconstrained optimization problems. The following are the key application areas of the ABC algorithm based on decision-making:

- Optimization of numerical functions,
- Routing and allocation on the network,
- Problems with benchmarking,
- Searching,
- Assigning and allocating,
- Distribution of probabilities.

2.4.5 Fish Swarm Optimization

Li et al. proposed Fish Swarm Optimization (FSO) in 2002 [11]. The FSO is a populace-based, shrewd bio-roused procedure that repeats in-water fish tutoring conduct. Fish usually structure swarms to look for food, safeguard themselves from hunters and keep away from impacts inside the multitude. Jumping, chasing after, amassing and looking are instances of a multitude of conduct. When employing the swarm technique to tackle optimization issues, a single fish inside the swarm is represented as a point and referred to as a potential solution. A population is formed when numerous potential solutions or points are linked.

The search space is the habitat in which the fake fish swims, and it is here that the best solution is sought. The FSO can locate the global optimization solution without first determining the local minimum, according to experiments. FSO is particularly adept at achieving global optimization while avoiding local minima. The fish's position in the multidimensional search space is used to build the population. The food satisfaction factor is used to evaluate the behavior of the fish throughout the meal search. In the hunt space, the Euclidean distance depicts the distance between two fish. The fish in the multitude travel toward the most thought food, looking for food irregularly through the hunt space. The motivation behind the advancement procedure is to limit the feast fulfillment factor, however, much could be expected. To satisfy their wholesome requests, fish structure swarms inside the populace, and all the while, they will generally draw in a new multitude of individuals. A fish will draw the consideration of people close by when it finds a food source. Inside their visual reach, some fish in the populace will want to track down more food than others. These fish will, without a doubt, follow the best one with the end goal to expand the extent of supper satisfaction. The three vital properties of FSO are visual distance, the most significant step length and the group factor. Two variables rule the calculation's exhibition: visual distance and most extreme step length. The essential way of behaving for FSO is as per the following:

- Unpredictable behavior,
- The act of looking for something,
- Changing patterns of behavior,
- Leaping behavior is a type of chasing behavior.

To conclude, FSO is a population-based multi-objective problem that can handle difficult nonlinear high-dimensional issues while simultaneously displaying all possible candidate solutions in a hyperplane. Because it just has a few parameters to tune for optimization, the method can converge faster. Furthermore, FSO converges faster than GA because it removes the crossover and mutation processes. The following are some of the most common areas where FSO is used and has been shown to perform better as an optimization solution:

- The least-squares support vector machine,
- Function optimization,
- Parameter estimation,
- Combinatorial optimization,
- Issues in geotechnical engineering.

2.4.6 FIREFLY ALGORITHM

Yang created the Firefly Algorithm (FA) [12] to solve NP-hard problems with nonconvex objective functions. The flashing nature of fireflies inspired it. The firefly method has been shown to provide acceptable optimal solutions to problems involving equality and inequality requirements. The program uses agents that look like fireflies to conduct a population-based search. The application uses a learning system that enables precise parameter adjustment, balancing exploration and exploitation. With a large number of agents communicating with one another, the algorithm iterates. Information is disseminated through the bioluminescent glowing lights.

These bright lights aid the firefly in more effectively exploring the search space than a scattered random search. The brighter firefly in the vicinity attracts each fly. The optimization approach follows the following rules, which are based on biological behavior:

• Fireflies, regardless of gender, are drawn to brighter places.
• The brilliance of a firefly and its attractiveness are inversely related.
• The value of the problem's objective function controls the brightness or light intensity of a firefly.

Due to its attraction to brightness-based behavior and ability to manage multimodality, the firefly method can handle multimodal functions and solve NP-hard optimization problems. In the following potential fields, the firefly method has been effectively applied:

• Optimization with several objectives,
• Issues with dispatch,
• Compression of digital images,
• Picking a feature,
• Unpredictable issues,
• Issues with nonlinearity,
• Multimodal design issues,
• Structural optimization,
• Predicting issues,
• Stock market,
• Optimization of antenna designs,
• Nonlinear optimization,
• Load dispatch issues,
• Scheduling problems that are NP-hard,
• Issues with a changing environment,
• Clustering and classifications,
• ANN training.

2.4.7 BACTERIA FORAGING OPTIMIZATION

In 2002, Passino published the Bacteria Foraging Optimization (BFO) method [13]. It is a stochastic global inquiry method given the way that *E. coli* searches. The tactic is based on how organic things behave. Naturally, less skilled ones are eliminated, and those with exceptional capacity survive by making rational decisions. The procedure is broken down into three stages: finding the food, dealing with the crowd and consuming the meal. This method of foraging can be employed individually or in a group setting. Through tracking food, the bacteria try to reduce the amount of energy they use per unit of time. All local bacteria use signals to communicate with one another. Foraging choices are influenced by energy use and signal transmission. The agents are bacteria, and the two behaviors that control them are swimming and tumbling. The agents in the tumble action take a random path in search of the best answer. Contrarily, while swimming, bacteria propagate throughout the population by making tiny movements in search of food. The cycle continues, with the most effective specialists remaining in the population and subpar specialists being eliminated by chemotactic relocation multiplication. The population's best agents have the best objective function and the most energy per unit of time. To account for changes in the environment induced by the removal of agents, the technique uses an elimination-dispersal operator. The approach has low convergence rates despite its simplicity and ease of implementation. The major steps involved in BFO are:

- **Chemotaxis:** Swimming and flipping motions are a big part of the chemotaxis process.
- **Swarming:** The bacteria's swarming behavior is characterized by attraction and repulsion.
- **Reproduction:** If the bacteria reach a better habitat, they will reproduce; otherwise, they will die. After the chemotaxis and swarming processes, all of the bacteria's fitness is calculated and sorted.
- **Dispersal and elimination:** Each bacterium is scattered with a probability after reproduction, but the total number of bacteria remains the same. Once a bacterium has been eradicated, it will be distributed at random to a new place.

Due to its enhanced global searching capabilities, BFO has shown its effectiveness over GA and PSO versions in various real-world problems. The failure of BFO was attributed to insufficient convergence criteria. The chosen tumbling step size has an impact on the algorithm. As a result, generalizing an explicit constraint-handling method for the algorithm is challenging. A few tweaks to the BFO algorithm's mathematical modeling and adaption techniques could improve its efficiency. The following are application areas where BFO has worked and proved to be successful:

- Load forecasting and adjustment,
- Multi-objective function optimization,
- Power system harmonic analysis,
- PID controller tuning optimization,
- Load dispatch and unit commitment,
- AI.

2.4.8 CUCKOO SEARCH OPTIMIZATION

Yang and Deb originally proposed the Cuckoo Search Optimization (CSO) [14] approach for single- and multi-objective nonlinear improvement issues in 2002. The calculation was impacted by the cuckoo bird's regular reproducing conduct, which includes they laying their eggs in bird homes. They take the host bird's eggs with the end goal of further developing the opportunity that the cuckoo eggs will incubate. This search strategy benefits the Levy flight instrument to foster people for advancement. It is a flighty step-length irregular walk given the likelihood. The three techniques utilized by cuckoos to parasitize their young are intraspecific, helpful and home takeover. At the point when cuckoos participate in intraspecific brood parasitism, they lay eggs in the home of the host bird (which is additionally of similar species). However, they could not care less about the eggs later. Coupled with the same male, two or more females deposit their eggs in the same nest and take turns taking care of the young. When a cuckoo deposits its eggs in the nest of another host bird, this is known as the nest taking over. The cuckoo search algorithm is governed by three key principles:

- One egg is laid by each cuckoo at a time, and it is deposited into a nest that is chosen at random.
- The subsequent generation will inherit the superior nests.
- The host bird in the host nest has a chance of finding a foreign egg.

The Levy flying mechanism provides a random walk with a Levy distribution-determined step length. To create new solutions, the random walk process is performed. Local searches are always faster since the movement is constantly oriented on the best option found thus far. Far-field randomization yields a small number of new answers that differ significantly from the best response currently available. The algorithm is prevented from becoming stuck in the local best by doing this. The following is provided as CSO's outline:

- Creating the first cuckoo habitat,
- Cuckoos' egg-laying style,
- Immigration of cuckoos,
- Getting rid of cuckoos in their most vulnerable habitats.

It has been exhibited that duty flights are a successful technique for settling advancement issues in CSO. The CSO strategy can merge all the more rapidly because of the Levy flight instrument's arbitrary walk part, expanding algorithmic viability. One of the disservices of the CSO technique is that it requires countless emphasis to accomplish the best response. This expanded emphasis is conceivable when both the disclosure rate and the Levy step size are unobtrusive. At the point when the disclosure rate is high and the Levy step size is short, the procedure unites quickly, but it's conceivable that the ideal arrangement isn't found. Thus, there should be a split difference between the Levy step size and the revelation rate.

The CSO calculation has shown progress in the areas recorded underneath:

- Scheduling and allocating several objectives,
- Phase equilibrium issues,
- ANN parameter optimization,
- Gradient-based optimization,
- Cluster center optimization,
- Path identification for network analysis,
- Reliability optimization,
- Economic load dispatch.

2.4.9 FRUIT FLY OPTIMIZATION METHOD

Pan [15] introduced the Fruit Fly Optimization Method (FFOM) as an evolutionary algorithm. Fruit flies' biological behavior served as inspiration for the algorithm. Fruit flies have great vision and olfactory senses, which they use to locate food. Biological scientists have proved that this type of fly can sense food even at a distance of 40 kilometers. There are two stages to the foraging behavior in the food search. The flies recognize the food with their scent in the first stage and then move close to it with their sensitive vision in the second step. The scent phase usually lasts less than the vision phase.

Levy flights have proved to be a successful approach to solving optimization problems in CSO. The Levy flight mechanism's random walk feature allows the CSO technique to converge faster, enhancing algorithmic efficiency. One of the CSO method's drawbacks is that getting the best outcome requires many iterations. When the discovery rate is low and the Levy step size is large, this increased number of iterations is achieved. The steps for implementing FFOM are:

1. Choose a random place for the fruit fly swarm;
2. Each search for food at an erratic bearing and distance from the location of the multitude after creating a new population through apheresis;
3. Assess all the newcomers;
4. Choose the fruit fly with the highest aroma focus esteem (such as the best goal), and the fruit fly group will then use vision to move to the appropriate location;
5. If the maximum number of iterations has been achieved, stop the process; otherwise, return to stage 2.

Because of the scent concentration parameter, the fruit fly algorithm can identify the global optimum faster and with greater accuracy. The approach converges without slipping into local minima due to this parameter, increasing the program's robustness. The fruit fly algorithm's update strategy is simple; however, developing a consistent update approach during the startup phase is difficult. The approach is constantly evolving and finding use in a wide range of industries. The following are some of the domains where the algorithm has found application:

- Data mining methods and operations,
- Medical industry,

- Management and finance,
- Defense.

2.4.10 BAT ALGORITHM

X. S. Yang introduced the Bat Algorithm (BA) [16] for the continuous problem domain. Mirjalili et al.[17] presented a binary version of the batting technique for the discrete problem domain in 2014. The technique is based on how bats use echolocation to find food. Bats navigate around their environment by listening for reflections of their sounds (echolocation). During the night, bats employ this method to locate their prey. A multi-objective optimization problem based on the echolocation process and the bat method was proposed to provide the optimal answer. Bats may change the frequency of their sound (pulse emission) and their flight velocity while seeking food. These traits, particularly the flying speed and pulse emission, are adjusted adaptively after the bat has discovered a potential victim. Their depth is reduced by that technique. The following principal guidelines control the BA:

- The echolocation capacity of bats determines the distance between the bat and the meal. This is then utilized to detect obstacles in the dark.
- Based on the velocity, frequency and loudness, bats' flying movement during food hunting results in random.
- Bats may also modify the frequency of sound they make.

The methodology is based on a bat population. Each bat is given an initial position at random, forming the primary population of bats. Bats have a habit of circling the population in search of the local optimum solution before moving on to the global optimum solution. Updates are made to characteristics like loudness and pulse emission during the operation. The technique is carried out again and again until the optimal option is discovered.

For nonlinear and multimodal issues, the BA has been demonstrated to be effective. It's best for high-dimensional issues when meeting convergence conditions is difficult. The BA has proven to be effective in the following scenarios:

- Optimizing the design of structures,
- Adaptive learning issues,
- Unit commitment and economic load dispatch,
- Network routing and analysis,
- Path planning and scheduling,
- Optimization with multiple objectives,
- Optimization based on constraints.

2.5 CONCLUSION

Large volumes of data and information can now be managed thanks to recent developments in computing capability. As a result, automation in various industrial applications, including banking and health care, has become increasingly difficult.

AI-based decision-making systems have risen in popularity in recent years. The capabilities of AI, bio-inspired algorithms or a combination of the two algorithms have been shown in a variety of applications.

People are excellent leaders, depending on their related involvements, ranges of abilities and information to decide. In human–machine collaboration, the objective of helping machines settle on choices given human experience returns. AI and bio-motivated calculations have helped formwise connection points. Using IDSS, the independent direction might be upgraded by gathering appropriate information, giving data to further developed execution, performing tests to approve execution, anticipating and projecting the current situation.

Future academics will be required to investigate and propose better solutions to several challenges in intelligent decision-making. Due to the following qualities, there is a large spectrum of unsolvable, complicated real-world problems:

- People find it hard to appreciate and get a handle on the connection between functional factors.
- Factors are dynamic.
- Include occasions that are trying to comprehend and notice.
- Include an enormous volume of information.

REFERENCES

[1] Pomerol JC (1997). Artificial intelligence and human decision making. *European Journal of Operational Research* 99(1):3–25.
[2] Paneerselvam S (2020). Role of AI and bio-inspired computing in decision making. *Internet of Things for Industry 4.0*: 115–36.
[3] Ergazakis E, Ergazakis K, Metaxiotis K, Bellos E, Leopoulos V (2008). An AI-based decision support system for designing knowledge-based development strategies. *International Journal of Intelligent Systems Technologies and Applications* 5(1–2):201–33.
[4] Zadeh LA, Klir GJ, Yuan B (1996). *Fuzzy Sets, fuzzy logic, and fuzzy systems: Selected papers*. World Scientific.
[5] Lahsasna A, Ainon RN, Zainuddin R, Bulgiba A (2012). Design of a fuzzy-based decision support system for coronary heart disease diagnosis. *Journal of Medical Systems* 36(5):3293–306.
[6] Olariu S, Zomaya AY, eds (2005). *Handbook of bioinspired algorithms and applications*. CRC Press.
[7] Mitchell M, Holland J, Forrest S (1993). When will a genetic algorithm outperform hill climbing. *Advances in Neural Information Processing Systems* 6:51–58.
[8] Kennedy J, Eberhart RC (1995). Particle swarm optimization. *IEEE International Conference on Neural Networks*: 1942–1948.
[9] Dorigo M, Stützle T (2003). The ant colony optimization metaheuristic: Algorithms, applications, and advances. In *Handbook of metaheuristics*, pp. 250–85. Springer.
[10] Karaboga D, Basturk B (*2007*). Artificial bee colony (ABC) optimization algorithm for solving constrained optimization problems. *International Fuzzy Systems Association World Congress,* Berlin*, pp.* 789–798.

[11] Yumin D, Li Z (2014). Quantum behaved particle swarm optimization algorithm based on artificial fish swarm. *Mathematical Problems in Engineering*, pp 1–10. DOI:10.1155/2014/592682

[12] Wang WC, Xu L, Chau KW, Xu DM (2020). Yin-Yang firefly algorithm based on dimensionally Cauchy mutation. *Expert Systems with Applications* 150:113216.

[13] Passino KM (2012). Bacterial foraging optimization. In *Innovations and Developments of Swarm Intelligence Applications*. IGI Global, pp. 219–234

[14] Yang X-S, Deb S (2013). Multiobjective cuckoo search for design optimization. *Computers & Operations Research* 40(6):1616–24.

[15] Pan WT (2012). A new fruit fly optimization algorithm: Taking the financial distress model as an example. *Knowledge Based Systems* 26:69–74. https://doi.org/10.1016/j.knosys.2011.07.001

[16] Yang XS (2010). A new metaheuristic bat-inspired algorithm. *Studies in Computational Intelligence* 284:65–74

[17] Mirjalili S, Mirjalili SM, Yang XS (2014). Binary bat algorithm. *Neural Computing and Applications* 25(3):663–81.

3 Genetic Algorithms for Graph Theoretic Problems

Xavier Chelladurai and
Joseph Varghese Kureethara

3.1 INTRODUCTION

It is widely believed that most of the inventions in science and technology have been possible only by observing nature and recreating the model. Examples range from the *Eureka... Eureka...* moments of Sir Isaac Newton to the modern works on Neural Networks, Deep Learning and Reinforced Learning. Neural networks function very similarly to human brains. By observing the fishes, boats and ships were invented. Birds flying in the sky motivated the invention of aeroplanes (see Figure 3.1). By the mimic of the echo from mountains, radio signals were invented to make revolution in the communication industry.

Genetic Algorithms [1–3] are developed very similar to the science of genetics. *Genetics* is the study of genes in living organisms. Every molecule in the living organism is represented by DNA (deoxyribonucleic acid). DNA is a combination of two chains of *polynucleotide*. Each polynucleotide is a biopolymer composed of 13 or more *organic molecules* bonded in a chain. From a common person's understanding, DNA is a chemical structure called *nucleotides* with hydrogen, oxygen, nitrogen, carbon and phosphorus. Each of the nucleotides is composed of one of four bases: adenine (A), cytosine (C), guanine (G) or thymine (T). The DNA of every living organism is unique. Every human being has unique DNA. Genetical formation combines the DNAs of the father and mother and creates the unique DNA of the child. For our understanding, we can visualize the DNA as a simple sequence of colours. The DNA of a father and a mother are shown in Figure 3.2.

The children's DNA is formed from the parents by functions such as

- Crossover;
- Mutation.

Crossover is a function in which a subset of the Father's DNA and that of the Mother are crossed. This is illustrated in Figure 3.3.

Every quality/skill is represented by a part of the DNA. During crossover, the child's DNA is formed by crossover of certain components. For example, consider a father with

DOI: 10.1201/9781003248545-3

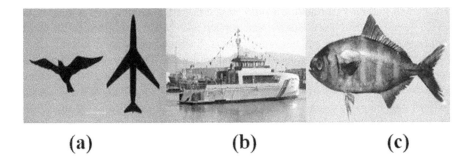

FIGURE 3.1   Aeroplane vs. bird and ships vs. fish.

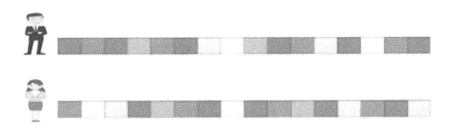

FIGURE 3.2   DNA of father and mother.

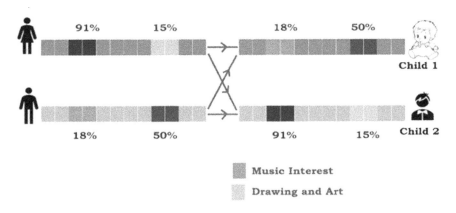

FIGURE 3.3   Crossover.

a high level (91%) of music interest and a low level (18%) of artistic interest. Suppose the mother has a low (18%) music interest and an average level of (50%) artistic interest. With cross, it is possible to have a child with low music interest and average artistic talent. It is also possible to have a child with high music talent and low artistic talent.

On a lighter note, there is a tale involving a man with a magnificent brain and a beauty queen. The beauty proposed to the brainy that they produce and give birth to a child so that the combination would yield a remarkable child with a great brain and the most beautiful body. But the man replied with regret that he feared the result would embody his beauty and her brain. This is illustrated in Figure 3.4.

An alteration of the DNA sequence is called a **mutation**. We have seen how the cross-over has supported the formation of a new DNA sequence. In the new DNA sequence, an alteration may happen to result in changing the values of some parts of the sequence. This alteration may be a result of mutants which are studied in genetics. There are various possibilities of mutation such as substitution (Figure 3.5), insertion (Figure 3.6), deletion (Figure 3.7), duplication (Figure 3.8), inversion (Figure 3.9) and translocation.

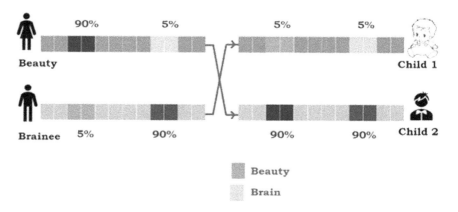

FIGURE 3.4   Two possible crossovers.

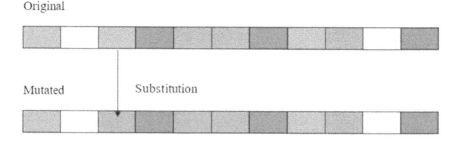

FIGURE 3.5   Substituted at one cell.

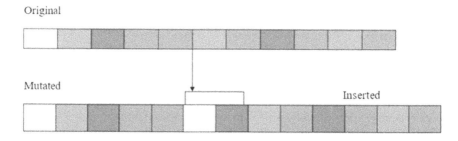

FIGURE 3.6   Insertion of one or more cells.

Original

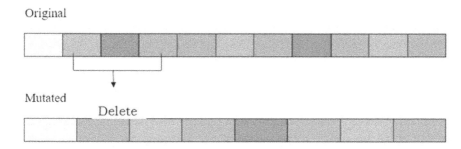

FIGURE 3.7   Deletion of one or more cells.

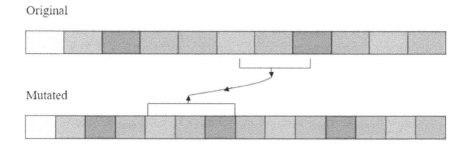

FIGURE 3.8   Duplication of one or more cells.

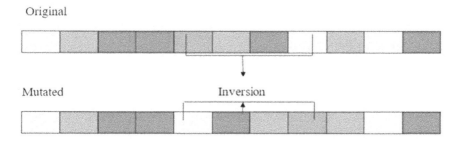

FIGURE 3.9   Inversion of a subset of cells.

3.2   GENETIC ALGORITHMS

The evolution of living organisms has happened over a long period of a few millions of years. Fundamentally, two living organisms combine to give birth to another. Given a problem, a solution can also evolve in several iterations, very similar to genetic evolution. A problem is usually represented in the form of one or more constraints and possibly an objective function to be optimized [1,4,5,6]. We search for a solution in the space of states in the two dimensions:

1. Fitness of the solution (Satisfy all the given constraints);
2. Optimality of the solution (Optimize the objective function).

For some recent algorithms related to graphs, see [2] and [3].

3.2.1 THE 8-QUEENS PROBLEM

Consider a board of 8×8 matrix. We want to place the given eight queens on the board in such a way that no pair of queens attack each other. A pair of queens attach each other if they are either in the same row, same column or diagonally in the same line. We try by placing one queen in each column and hence represent the state as a sequence of eight entries as $(s_0, s_1, s_2, s_3, s_4, s, s_6, s_7)$ In the context of the N-Queens problem, "s_j" might represent whether or not there is already a Queen placed in the jth column. It's often used in the formulation of constraints to ensure that no two Queens are placed in the same column.

For example, the state shown in Table 3.1 is represented by $(6, 2, 1, 0, 3, 4, 7, 5)$.

Let us now define the fitness function tells us how fit a given state s is. In this problem, in a given state, s, we do not want any pair of queens in attacking position. In a state, where there are eight queens, there are 28 distinct pairs of queens. The worst value of $F(s)$ is 28 and the best is 0. We can define,

$$F(s) = 28 - \text{No of pairs in attacking position}$$

For the state $s = (6, 2, 1, 0, 3, 4, 7, 5)$, there are eight pairs in attacking position. So, $F(s) = 28 - 8 = 20$. For a state x, if $F(x)$ is 28, the solution is the best fit.

3.2.2 SHORTEST PATH PROBLEM

Take into consideration the challenge of determining the shortest route between two vertices A and B in a given graph. We proceed in two steps:

TABLE 3.1
State, $s = (6, 2, 1, 0, 3, 4, 7, 5)$

	0	1	2	3	4	5	6	7
0				Q				
1			Q					
2		Q						
3					Q			
4						Q		
5								Q
6	Q							
7							Q	

---

1. Check if a given sequence of vertices is a path from A to B.
2. Among all such paths from A to B, find the shortest one.

Let $p = (p_0, p_1, p_2, \ldots p_{d-1})$ be a sequence of vertices. The fitness function F checks if the sequence p is a meaningful path. The following conditions are checked in evaluating, $F(p)$.

a. Starting point p_0 is A;
b. Endpoint p_{d-1} is B;
c. For every point $i = 0, 1, 2, \ldots d-1$, p_i is a valid vertex of the graph;
d. For every $i = 0, 1, 2, \ldots d-2$, (p_i, p_{i+1}) is a valid edge of the graph.

For a sequence of vertices, p, to be a valid solution (a valid path), we usually defined $F(p)$ in such a way that $F(p) = \begin{cases} 1 & if\ p\ is\ a\ valid\ path\ from\ A\ to\ B \\ 0 & otherwise. \end{cases}$

Among paths, p with $F(p) = 1$, our final goal is to choose the one with a minimum number of edges. We usually define an objective function/cost function. Among all such solutions, we shall find the one which minimizes the objective function.

The fundamental approach in developing the Genetic Algorithm uses the seven steps as one can see here.

1. Represent the (solution) state as consecutive natural number.
2. Define the State Space. Initially, the state may have a few members. As the algorithm progresses, more states are generated and the population steadily increases.
3. Define the fitness function. Given a state, the fitness function computes the fitness value of the state to be a final solution.
4. Define actions such as mutation and crossover. It is possible to define multiple variants of mutation and crossover.
5. Choose two states from the state space, called, father and mother. Find the fitness value of the father and mother. If any of them is already a final solution, we can abort and output the result. Otherwise continue and go to step 6.
6. Apply a sequence of actions, mutations and crossover to arrive at one or more children and add them to the state space.
7. Continue Steps 5 and 6.

A problem is often defined by five components:

- **State** (State Space, Initial State and Goal State): A *state* is a data structure that defines the problem and its status in building a solution. There can be several states and finally reach the goal state, which is the desired solution. The *initial state* refers to the given data structure before the algorithm begins. For examples, in the travelling salesman problem, the graphs showing the initial starting point are called the initial state. The goal test determines if we have reached the goal.
- **Actions:** An action is a function that changes the data structure and moves from one state to the other. When an action is executed, the state of the problem

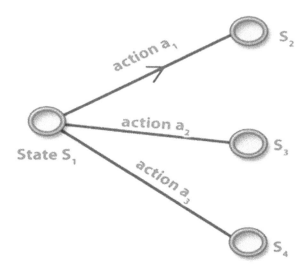

FIGURE 3.10   Representation of state and actions.

changes to another state. For example, in the eight queen's problem, from a state, we have several options to move the queens. Each move in an action results in another state. For each state, there are a set of actions applicable.

In the example given in Figure 3.10, there are three actions applicable to state s_1. From s_1, if action a_1 is executed, we reach state s_2. Similarly, action a_2 results in state s_3 and action a_3 results in state s_3.

3.2.3   Transition Model

The transition model describes the actual implementation of the action. The action and its resulting status are represented in the form of a graph. In the graph, each state is a node and the actions link the nodes. A state space refers to the set of all states.

3.2.4   Path Cost

A path cost determines the cost of the path starting from the initial state to the current state. To illustrate the above definitions and structures, consider a simple 4-queen's problem where we have a 4×4 board in which we want to place four queens in such a way that no two queens are in attacking positions. Two queens are in attacking positions if, they are in:

1.   Same row,
2.   Same column,
3.   Diagonally in the line.

Consider the 20 states, s_0 to s_{19} as described in Table 3.2.

TABLE 3.2

Action and state changes – 4 Queen's Problem

State s_0

Qn$_0$	Qn$_1$	Qn$_2$	Qn$_3$

State s_1

	Qn$_1$	Qn$_2$	Qn$_3$
Qn$_0$			

State s_2

	Qn$_1$	Qn$_2$	Qn$_3$
Qn$_0$			

State s_3

	Qn$_1$	Qn$_2$	Qn$_3$
Qn$_0$			

State s_4

		Qn$_2$	Qn$_3$
Qn$_0$	Qn$_1$		

State s_5

		Qn$_2$	Qn$_3$
Qn$_0$			
	Qn$_1$		

State s_6

		Qn$_2$	Qn$_3$
Qn$_0$			
	Qn$_1$		

State s_7

			Qn$_3$
Qn$_0$	Qn$_1$	Qn$_2$	

State s_8

			Qn$_3$
Qn$_0$	Qn$_1$		
		Qn$_2$	

State s_9

Qn$_0$	Qn$_1$		Qn$_3$
		Qn$_2$	

State s_{10}

		Qn$_2$	
Qn$_0$	Qn$_1$		Qn$_3$

State s_{11}

		Qn$_2$	
Qn$_0$	Qn$_1$		
			Qn$_3$

(*continued*)

TABLE 3.2 (Continued)

Action and state changes – 4 Queen's Problem

State s_{12}

		Qn_2	
Qn_0	Qn_1		
			Qn_3

State s_{13}

Qn_0	Qn_1	Qn_2	Qn_3

State s_{14}

Qn_0	Qn_1	Qn_2	
			Qn_3

State s_{15}

Qn_0	Qn_1	Qn_2	
			Qn_3

State s_{16}

	Qn_1		
			Qn_3
Qn_0		Qn_2	

State s_{17}

Qn_0		Qn_2	
			Qn_3
	Qn_1		

State s_{18}

	Qn_1		
Qn_0			
		Qn_2	
			Qn_3

State s_{19}

	Qn_1		
			Qn_3
Qn_0			
		Qn_2	

3.2.5 ACTION AND STATE CHANGES

In the 4-queen's problem, we can start with some initial position, say state s_0. For example, s_0 can be considered as the initial position. s_0 is not the required final state. From the initial state, we can perform some actions to arrive at a position that is better than the initial one. For example, from the initial position s_0, we can perform the following possible actions:

Action	Description	Start state	Target state
A_0	In S_0, move Qn_0 from Row 0 to Row 1	S_0	S_1
A_1	In S_0, move Qn_0 from Row 0 to Row 2)	S_0	S_2
A_2	In S_0, move Qn_0 from Row 0 to Row 3)	S_0	S_3
A_3	In S_1, move Qn_1 from Row 0 to Row 1)	S_1	S_4

Starting from S_0, we can move Qn_0 into any one of the rows, 1, 2 or 3. Similarly, we can also try moving Qn_1 to any one of the three possible rows. There are $3 \times 4 = 12$ possible actions associated with the state S_0. All such actions can be represented in the form of a graph as shown in Figure 3.11.

3.2.6 FITNESS FUNCTION

The fitness function computes a score for every state. The score indicates how close it is to the goal state. For example, in the 4-queen's problem described earlier, there are six pairs of queens: (0,1), (0,2), (0,3), (1,2), (1,3), (2,3). In the worst case, none of these six is in the non-attacking position. In the goal state e wants all six pairs to be in a non-attacking position. Let us define

$$F(s) = \text{Number of pairs in the non-attacking position}$$

Our goal is to search for a state s where $F(s) = 6$. F values of the states are shown in Table 3.3.

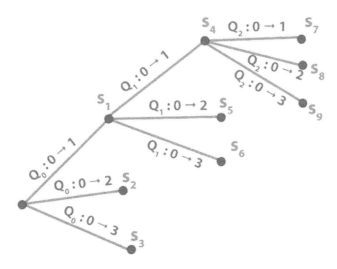

FIGURE 3.11 Graph showing actions from initial state S_0 to various states.

TABLE 3.3
States of non-attacking positions

State s	S_0	S_1	S_2	S_3	S_4	S_5	S_6	S_7	S_8	S_9
$F(s)$	0	2	2	2	2	3	5	2	4	4

State s	S_{10}	S_{11}	S_{12}	S_{13}	S_{14}	S_{15}	S_{16}	S_{17}	S_{18}	S_{19}
$F(s)$	1	4	4	0	2	3	4	5	4	6

3.2.7 OBJECTIVE FUNCTION

Consider the weighted 4-queen's problem where each cell in the board has a weight associated. This may be the rental cost for the cell. The cost may be represented by a 4×4 weight matrix. The expression "fw_ij" represents the cost of placing a Queen in the cell with coordinates (i, j).

This defines the total cost of placing the four queens in the four cells, the sum of the costs of the cells where the queen is accommodated. In the weighted 4-queen's problem, the goal state is the state where all pairs of queens area in non-attacking position and the total cost is minimum.

3.3 GRAPH COLOURING

Let G be a simple graph with n vertices and m edges. Assume that the vertices are represented by $0, 1, 2, 3, (n-1)$ and the edges are represented by the adjacency matrix a.

$$a_{ij} = \begin{cases} 1 & \text{if} (i,j) \text{is an edge} \\ 0 & \text{otherwise} \end{cases}$$

The perfect vertex colouring problem calls for assigning a colour from a colour box, to each vertex in such a way that any two adjacent vertices have different colours [4,7,8]. In this chapter, we represent the colours too with numbers 0, 1, 2, ...etc. Let us now formally define the terms used.

A k-colouring of a graph G is a function f given as,

$$f: V \rightarrow \{0,1,2,...(k-1)\}$$

3.3.1 REPRESENTATION OF A COLOURING

A k-colouring of a graph G is represented by an n-tuple $C_t = (c_0, c_1, c_2 ... c_{n-1})$, where $c_i \in C = \{0,1,2,3, ... (k-1)\}$, called the colour box or universal colour set used in this colouring C_t. Note that $\{0,1,2, 3, ... (k-1)\}$ is the set of colours used in this colouring. Note that the colour c_i is assigned to vertex i. Each colour is also represented by a number $0,1,2,3, ... (k-1)$. For example, consider the graph shown in Figure 3.12.

There are *eight* vertices and *nine* edges. The vertex set is $V = \{0,1,2,3,4,5,6,7\}$ and edge set $E = \{(0,1), (0,5), (1,2), (1,4), (3,4), (4,5), (4,6), (4,7), (5,6)\}$

The adjacency matrix is

$$\begin{pmatrix} 0 & 1 & 0 & 0 & 0 & 1 & 0 & 0 \\ 1 & 0 & 1 & 0 & 1 & 0 & 0 & 0 \\ 0 & 1 & 0 & 0 & 0 & 0 & 0 & 0 \\ 0 & 0 & 0 & 0 & 1 & 0 & 0 & 0 \\ 0 & 1 & 0 & 1 & 0 & 1 & 1 & 1 \\ 1 & 0 & 0 & 0 & 1 & 0 & 1 & 0 \\ 0 & 0 & 0 & 0 & 1 & 1 & 0 & 0 \\ 0 & 0 & 0 & 0 & 1 & 0 & 0 & 0 \end{pmatrix}$$

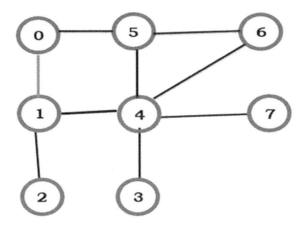

FIGURE 3.12 Graph with eight vertices and nine edges.

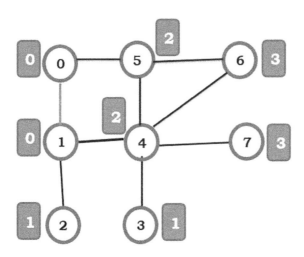

FIGURE 3.13 Colouring $C = (0,0,1,1,2,2,3,3)$.

For example, consider the 4-colouring $(0,0,1,1,2,2,3,3)$

This is a 4-colouring that assigns four colours $\{0,1,2,3\}$ to the eight vertices as follows:

Vertex	0	1	2	3	4	5	6	7
Colour	0	0	1	1	2	2	3	3

This is shown in Figure 3.13.

For example, when $k=3$, the colour box is $\{0, 1, 2\}$; the following are some 3-colourings:

$$C_0 = (0,1,0,1,0,1,2,1)$$

$$C_1 = (0,1,0,2,0,1,0,1)$$

$$C_2 = (0,1,2,0,1,1,1,0)$$

They are represented by Figures 3.14, 3.15 and 3.16. Note that the number given inside the circle is the vertex number and the number inside the rectangle with curved corners is the colour.

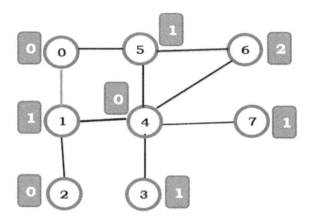

FIGURE 3.14   Colouring $C_0 = (0,0,1,1,2,2,3,3)$.

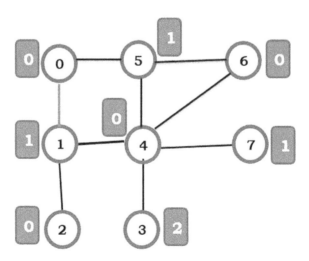

FIGURE 3.15   Colouring $C_1 = (0,1,0,2,0,1,0,1)$.

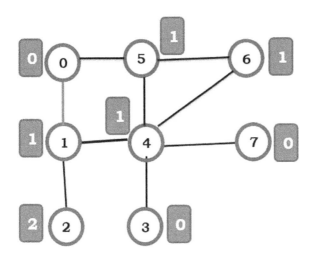

FIGURE 3.16   Colouring $C_2 = (0,1,2,0,1,1,1,0)$.

3.3.2 PERFECT COLOURING

A k-colouring is said to be *perfect* if and only if any two adjacent vertices have different colours. The direct algorithm to check if a given k-colouring $C = (c_0, c_1, c_2, \ldots c_{n-1})$ is perfect as shown below:

Algorithm: IsPerfect (C, a)

Input

1. The adjacency matrix a is an $n \times n$ matrix.

2. The given k-colouring $C = (c_0, c_1, c_2, \ldots c_{n-1})$.
   Step 1: Boolean variable *perfect* = *True*
   Step 2:

   For $i = 0$ to $n-2$ do
       For $j = i + 1$ to $n - 1$ do
           If $a_{ij} = 1$ and $c_i == c_j$ then
               perfect = false
               Break loop and go to Step 3

   Step 3: Output *perfect*

Theorem

IsPerfect(C, a) correctly determines if a given colouring is perfect in $O(n^2)$ time.

Proof

Assume that a given colouring C is perfect. As per definition, for every edge (i, j), the colours assigned to them, c_i and c_j are different. So, the condition given inside the loop in step 2, $(a_{ij} == 1$ *and* $c_i == c_j)$ is never true. So, the value perfect = True remains unaltered after completing the entire for a loop. So, *perfect = True* is the output.

Conversely, suppose C is not perfect. Hence, there exists an edge (i, j) with $c_i == c_j$. In the loop in step 2, for the specific i *and* j, the value of *perfect* is assigned *False* and the loop is broken. So, the final output is, *perfect = False*. This proves the correctness. As the two nested loops run n times each, the time complexity is $O(n^2)$.

3.3.3 VERTEX LEVEL PERFECTION

Let us investigate the perfect colouring aspect at a vertex level. Let G be a graph with the adjacency matrix a and let $C = (c_0, c_1, c_2, \dots c_{n-1})$ be a colouring of G. A vertex v is said to be perfectly coloured in a k-colouring $C = (c_0, c_1, c_2, \dots c_{n-1})$ if every neighbour of v has a different colour from v. If every vertex is perfectly coloured, then the colouring C is a k-perfect colouring for G. The *perfect colouring coefficient of a vertex v* is denoted by $PCCV(v)$. It is defined as the number of the neighbours of v, with a different colour than v. If a vertex has five neighbours and three of them have different colours than v and two have the same colour as v, $PCCV(v) = 3$. The *Imperfect Colouring Coefficient of vertex v is* denoted by $ICCV(v)$ *and is* defined as the number of neighbours of v having the same colour as v. From the very definition, for a vertex v,

$$PCCV(v) + ICCV(v) = \text{degree of } v$$

For example, consider the colouring C_0 shown in Figure 3.14. Vertex 0 has two neighbours 5 and 1 and has colours different from vertex 0. So, $PCCV(0) = 2$. $ICCV(0) = 0$. The PCCV and ICCV values of other vertices are shown in Table 3.4.

The PCCV and ICCV of colouring C_1 as shown in Figure 3.15 are shown in Table 3.5.

From the very definition of PCCV of vertex the following are true.

1. For any vertex v, $0 \leq PCCV(v) \leq degree(v)$ *and* $0 \leq ICCV(v) \leq degree(v)$.
2. $PCCV(v) + ICCV(v) = degree(v)$.
3. A vertex v is perfectly coloured if and only if $PCCV(v) = degree(v)$, *which implies that* $ICCV(v) = 0$.

The following is an algorithm to find the *PCCV* of a vertex v.

Let $G = (V, E)$ be a graph with n vertices and m edges. Let $C = (c_0, c_1, c_2, \dots c_{n-1})$ be a k-colouring of G, where $k \leq n$.

TABLE 3.4
Perfection colouring coefficient (PCCV) and ICCV of vertices for $C_0 = (0,1,0,1,0,1,2,1)$

Vertex v	degree	Colour of v	Neighbours	Colours of neighbours	PCCV	ICCV	Perfect vertex
0	2	0	{1,5}	(1,1)	2	0	✓
1	3	1	{0,2,4}	(0,0,0)	3	0	✓
2	1	0	{1}	(1)	1	0	✓
3	1	1	{4}	(0)	1	0	✓
4	5	0	{1,3,5,6,7}	(1,1,1,2,1)	5	0	✓
5	3	1	{0,4,6}	(0,0,2)	3	0	✓
6	2	2	{4,5}	(0,1)	2	0	✓
7	1	1	{4}	(0)	1	0	✓

TABLE 3.5
Perfect colouring coefficient (PCC) and ICC of G for colouring $C_1 = (0,1,0,2,0,1,0,1)$

Vertex	Degree	Colour of vertex	Neighbours	Colours of neighbours	PCC	ICC	Perfect vertex
0	2	0	{1,5}	(1,1)	2	0	✓
1	3	1	{0,2,4}	(0,0,0)	3	0	✓
2	1	0	{1}	(1)	1	0	✓
3	1	2	{4}	(0)	1	0	✓
4	5	0	{1,3,5,6,7}	(1,2,1,0,1)	4	1	✗
5	3	1	{0,4,6}	(0,0,0)	3	0	✓
6	2	0	{4,5}	(0,1)	1	1	✗
7	1	1	{4}	(0)	1	0	✓

Algorithm PCCV(v)

Input

1. Graph G with $V = \{0, 1, 2, 3, \dots n{-}1\}$.
2. Adjacency matrix a which is an $n \times n$ Boolean matrix.
3. A k-colouring $C = (c_0, c_1, c_2, \dots c_{n-1})$ where each $c_i \in \{0, 1, 2, \dots k{-}1\}$, the colour box.

1. $pcc = 0$
2. For $i = 0$ to $n - 1$ and $i \neq v$ do
    if $(a_{vi} == 1$ and $c_v \neq c_i)$
        $pcc = pcc + 1$
3. Output pcc

Theorem

Algorithm pcc (v) determines the perfect colouring coefficient of v in $O(n)$ time. If $pcc(v)$ is the degree of v, v is said to be *perfectly coloured* by C. Perfect colouring coefficient of a given k-colouring C, is the number of vertices perfectly coloured by C.

3.3.4 PERFECT COLOURING COEFFICIENT OF A GRAPH FOR A COLOURING C, PCCG(C)

In an (n, m) graph (n vertices, m edges), if a k-colouring C perfectly colours all the n vertices, then C is a perfect colouring. In this case we say that the graph is perfectly coloured by C. Let $C = (c_0, c_1, c_2, \dots c_{n-1})$ be a k-colouring of C. Let $PCCV(C) = (p_0, p_1, p_2 \dots p_{n-1})$. This means, for a vertex k, the $PCCV(k) = p_k$. Let $ICCV(C) = (i_0, i_1, i_2, \dots i_{n-1})$ be the ICCV of the vertices. This means that $i_k = ICCV(k)$ where k is a vertex. $k=0,1, 2, \dots n-1$.

The following are obvious results from the definition.

1. $i_k + p_k = degree\ of\ vertex\ k.$

2. $\displaystyle\sum_{k=0}^{n-1} p_k + \sum_{k=0}^{n-1} i_k = Sum\ of\ degrees =.\ 2m$

The *perfect colouring coefficient of graph G* for the k-colouring C, PCCG(C), is the number of edges (i, j) where the colours c_i and c_j are different. When C is a perfect colouring, PCCG(C) = m. The following is an obvious result that follows from the definition.

Theorem

For any k-colouring C of graph G with n vertices and m edges,

$$\sum_{k=0}^{n-1} PCCV(i) = 2PCCG(C)$$

Further, if C is a perfect colouring, the above value is 2m.

We now present a direct algorithm to find the PCCG(C) for any graph G for a k-colouring C.

Algorithm PCCG(C, a)

Input: 1. A graph G is represented by its adjacency matrix a, a is an $n \times n$ matrix.

2. A k-colouring $C = (c_0, c_1, c_2, \dots c_{n-1})$.

Step 1. $pcc = 0$ # pcc denotes the perfection colouring coefficient.
Step 2. For $i = 0$ to $n - 2$ do
        For $j = i + 1$ to $(n - 1)$ do
                if $a_{ij} == 1$ and $c_i \neq c_j$ then
                    $pcc = pcc + 1$
Step 3. Output pcc.

Theorem

Algorithm PCCG(C, a) correctly determines the perfect colouring coefficient of the colouring C in graph G.

Proof

In step 1, we initialize the pcc as zero. At this stage of the algorithm, we have not seen any edge having a perfect (different) colouring. In step 2, the loop runs across all possible edges. The condition, $a_{ij} == 1$ and $c_i \neq c_j$ identifies the edges which have the two vertices coloured differently. When this condition is true, the counter pcc is incremented. So, by the definition of PCCG, the counter pcc correctly counts all the edges with perfect colours. This proves the correctness. As step 2 has a nested loop, the loop runs $O(n^2)$ times. This shows that the algorithm PCCG(C, a) correctly computes PCCG in $O(n^2)$ time.

3.3.5 PERFECTION BOOSTER COLOURS FOR A VERTEX

Let $C = (c_0, c_1, c_2, \ldots c_{n-1})$ be a k-colouring. Let the colour universe $U = \{0,1, 2, \ldots k-1\}$ be the set of all colours used in the colouring C. $|U| = k$. In the colouring C, we try to replace the colour of a vertex v with another colour, without disturbing the colours of other vertices. For vertex v, the set U is partitioned into three sets as follows:

$C_U^0 = $ Set of colours, when assigned to v does not change $PCCV(v)$. This set contains the present colour of v in C.
$C_U^{-1} = $ Set of colours other than c_v, when assigned to v, decreases the $PCCV(v)$.
$C_U^+ = $ Set of colours other than c_v, when assigned to v increases the $PCC(v)$.

C_U^+ is called the Perfection Booster Set of v. The number of elements in C_U^+ is called the Perfection Booster Opportunity of v in C. Every element of C_U^+ is called a perfection booster of v.

Let the open neighbourhood, $N(v)$, denote set of neighbours of v other than v. Now, $N[v] = N(v)$ *together with* v ... $N[v]$ is called the closed neighbourhood of v. $N(v)$ is partitioned into two sets, viz., *perfect neighbours* and *imperfect neighbours*.

The *perfect neighbours' set* is the set of neighbours of v having distinct colour than v. Let it be $N_{perf}(v)$. The *imperfect neighbours set* is the set of neighbours of v having the identical colour as that of v and is denoted by $N_{imp}(v)$. Therefore,

$$N_{imp}(v) = N(v) - N_{perf}(v)$$

Theorem

Suppose $N_{imp}(v)$ is non-empty. Let c' be a colour which is not assigned to any vertex of $N[v]$ [9]. If we assign c' to v and do not change the colours of $N(v)$, then v becomes perfectly coloured. Since $N_{imp}(v)$ was originally non-empty, $c' \in C_U^+$,

Proof

Colour c' is chosen as a colour not assigned to any vertex in $N[v]$. When such a colour c' replaces the colour of v, in the new colouring C', the colour of v is different from that of each of its neighbour. So, the vertex v becomes a perfectly coloured vertex in C'.

Theorem

Consider a k-colouring C of G. Assume $N_{imp}(v)$ is non-empty. Consider a colour c' originally assigned to one or more vertices of $N_{perf}(v)$. Assume that c' is assigned to t vertices of $N_{per}(v)$. Let C' be the colouring got by changing colour of v to c'. $t < (N_{imp}(v))$ if and only if $pcc_{c'}(v) > pcc_c(v)$, where the suffix c and c' represent the colouring assigned to vertex v. In other words, $c' \in C_U^+$ if and only if $t < |N_{imp}(v)|$.

Proof

When the colour of v is changed to colour c', the following changes take place in the system.

1. All the vertices in $N_{imp}(v)$ more to $N_{perf}(v)$ in the revised colouring. So, the number of vertices in $N_{perf}(v)$ increases by $N_{imp}(v)$.
2. The vertices which originally had the colour c', (t vertices) of $N_{perf}(v)$ now move to $N_{imp}(v)$. This decreases the count of $N_{perf}(v)$ by t.

Since originally, $t < |N_{imp}(v)|$, The net count of $N_{perf}(v)$ *increases*. This proves, $c' \in C_U^+$.

Assume that $c' \in C_U^+$. This means by definition, when we assign the colour c' to v,

$$|pcc_{c'}(v)| > pcc_c(v)|$$

When the colour v is changed from c_v to c', the vertices of $N_{imp}(v)$ moves to $N_{perf}(v)$. Also, the t vertices which has colour c' moves from $N_{perf}(v)$ to $N_{imp}(v)$. This is the only change happening. Because of this change if the $pcc(v)$ has improved this means that

$$t < |N_{imp}(v)|$$

Hence the proof is complete.

3.4   MUTATION WITH SUBSTITUTION

Consider an (n, m) graph G. Let C_f (Father) and C_m (Mother) be two k-colourings on G. Let the vertex v be chosen such that $PCCV(v) = p_f$ in the colouring C_f and $PCCV(v) = p_m$ in C_m. Consider the two child colourings got as follows:

1. C_1 is got from C_f by substituting the colour of v with c', where c' is a colour which is not assigned to any vertex of $N[v]$.
2. C_2 is got from C_m by substituting the colour of v with c', where c' is a colour which is not assigned to any vertex of $N[v]$.

This operation is called *mutation by substitution*. By theorem mutation by substitution makes children C_1 and C_2 having v as a perfectly coloured vertex.

3.4.1   MUTATION BY INVERSION

Consider the (n, m) graph G. Let C_f (Father) and C_m (Mother) be two k-colourings on G. Let u and v be a vertex such that $PCCV(u) = p_{fu}$ and $PCCV(v) = p_{fv}$ in the colouring C_f and $PCCV(u) = p_{mu}$ and $PCCV(v) = p_{mv}$ in the colouring C_m. Consider the two child colourings got as follows:

1. C_1 is got from C_f by substituting the colour of v with c', where c' is a colour which is not assigned to any vertex of $N[v]$.
2. C_2 is got from C_m by substituting the colour of v with c', where c' is a colour which is not assigned to any vertex of $N[v]$.

Theorem (Mutation by Swap)

Let u, v be two vertices and c_u and c_v be their colours in a k-colouring $C = (c_0, c_1, c_2, c_3 \ldots c_{n-1})$. Given that c_u is not the colour of any of the vertices in $N[v]$ and c_v is not the colour of any of the vertices in $N[u]$. By swapping the colours of u and v, we get a colouring in which both u and v are perfectly coloured and for any other vertex x, $PCCV(x)$ either remains unchanged or increases by 1.

Proof

The colour c_u is not a colour of any of the vertices of $N[v]$. When c_u is assigned to v, in the new colouring, v is perfectly coloured. By the similar argument, when colour c_v is assigned to u, u becomes perfectly coloured.

Consider a vertex x which does not belong to $N[u] \cup N[v]$ (see Figure 3.17). By the swapping of colours c_u and c_v, the colouring coefficient of x is not impacted. Let $x \in N(u)$. If x was originally having colour c_v, $PCCV(x)$ increases by 1 in the new colouring. If x was not having the colour c_v originally, the value of $PCCV(x)$ is not impacted by the new colouring. By a similar argument if $x \in N(u)$, the value of $PCCV(x)$ increases by 1 and remains unchanged otherwise.

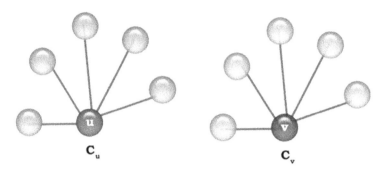

FIGURE 3.17   N[u] and N[v].

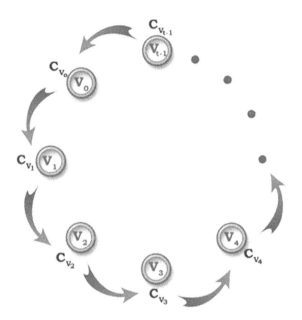

FIGURE 3.18   Mutation by rotation of colours.

3.4.2   MUTATION BY ROTATION

Let $v_0, v_1, v_2, \ldots v_t$ be vertices having colours ($c_{v_0}, c_{v_1}, c_{v_2}, \ldots c_{v_{t-1}}$) in a k-colouring C = ($c_0, c_1, c_2, \ldots c_{n-1}$). Given that c_{v_i} is not the colour of any of the vertices in $N[v_{i+1}]$, where $i = 0, 1, 2 \ldots t{-}1$. Here when $i = t{-}1$, the last node v_{i+1} becomes $v_t = v_0$. We change the assignation of colours in C as follows:

Assign colour c_{v_i} to v_{i+1} where $i = 0,1,2\ldots . (t{-}1)$. When $i = t{-}1$, the colour $c_{v_{t-1}}$ is assigned to v_0. This is shown in Figure 3.18.

This operation is called *mutation by rotation* of colours.

Theorem

In *mutation by rotation*, every vertex v_i in the cycle become perfectly coloured. For all other vertices, x, $PCCV(x)$ either remains unchanged or increases by one.

Proof

As per hypothesis, the colour c_{v_i} is not a colour of any of the vertices of $N[v_{i+1}]$. When we assign c_{v_i} to v_{i+1}, the new colour of v_{i+1} is different from the colour of every vertex of $N[v_{i+1}]$. So, v_{i+1} becomes perfectly coloured. When $i = t{-}1$, $i{+}1$ become 0 as per notation. This proves that the cyclic rotation makes all the vertices in the cycle (v_0, v_1, v_2,... . v_{t-1}) perfectly coloured. Let $x \in N(v_i)$. If x was originally having the colour c_{v_i}, by changing colour to $c_{v_{i-1}}$ the $PCCV(x)$ increases by 1. If x was not originally having the colour c_{v_i} the value $PCCV(x)$ is not impacted. This shows that for each vertex x not in the set $\{v_0, v_1, v_2 ... . vt_{-1}\}$, the $PCCV(x)$ either remains unchanged or increases by 1.

3.5   CROSSOVER AT VERTEX LEVEL

Let C_f and C_m be two k-colourings of a graph G with n vertices and m edges. Let u_f, v_f be two vertices with the minimum and maximum $PCCV$ values respectively in colouring C_f. This means that

$PCCV(u_f) \leq PCCV(v)$ for all v belonging to colouring C_f
$PCCV(v_f) \geq PCCV(v)$ for every vertex v of G in colouring C_f.

Similarly, Let u_m, v_m be two vertices with minimum and maximum $PCCV$ values respectively. This means that

$PCCV(U_m) \leq PCCV(v)$ for every vertex v of G in colouring C_m
$PCCV(V_m) \geq PCCV(v)$ for each vertex v of G in colouring C_m

We can interpret this as follows: The father has a *poor* skill level in the attribute u_f and *rich* skill level at attribute v_f. The mother *is poor* in another attribute u_m and *rich* in a fourth attribute v_m. We are talking about four different attributes, u_f, v_f, u_m, v_m. Table 3.6 shows the four attribute skill levels of father and mother.

TABLE 3.6
Four attributes and their values

Attributes	u_f	v_f	u_m	v_m
Father	Poor	Rich	Not Known	Not Known
Mother	Not known	Not Known	Poor	Rich

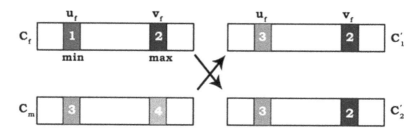

FIGURE 3.19   Crossover step 1.

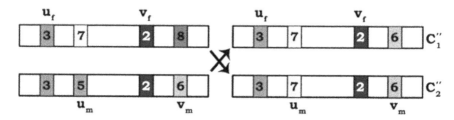

FIGURE 3.20   Crossover step 2.

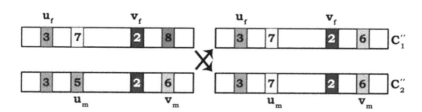

FIGURE 3.21   Colourings Cf and Cm PCCV values of the four vertices.

The child gets the skill level rich or poor or medium (Not Known) in each of the four attributes from that of either father or mother. There are 81 or more possibilities of the child formation. These are called the crossover actions. The crossover shown in Figures 3.19 and 3.20 are done to get the children with the rich skills in all four attributes.

We have four vertices u_f, v_f, u_m and v_m. The *PCCV* values of these four vertices can be understood better by Figure 3.21.

3.5.1   COLOURINGS C_F AND C_M PCCV VALUES OF THE FOUR VERTICES

The crossover is defined by replacing the minimum value colours by the colours from the spouse. This can be done in any one of the 81 different possible ways. The following examples are one of them. This is done in two steps.

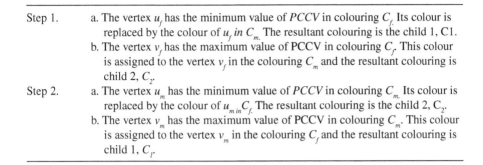

Step 1.
a. The vertex u_f has the minimum value of $PCCV$ in colouring C_f. Its colour is replaced by the colour of u_f in C_m. The resultant colouring is the child 1, C1.
b. The vertex v_f has the maximum value of PCCV in colouring C_f. This colour is assigned to the vertex v_f in the colouring C_m and the resultant colouring is child 2, C_2.

Step 2.
a. The vertex u_m has the minimum value of $PCCV$ in colouring C_m. Its colour is replaced by the colour of $u_{m \, in}C_f$. The resultant colouring is the child 2, C_2.
b. The vertex v_m has the maximum value of PCCV in colouring C_m. This colour is assigned to the vertex v_m in the colouring C_f and the resultant colouring is child 1, C_1.

3.5.2 Crossover for Perfect Subgraph

Any induced subgraph S of G is a *perfectly coloured subgraph* if for every edge (u, v) in S, vertices u and v have different colours. An induced subgraph S is said to be *fully imperfectly coloured* if for every edge (u, v) in S, u and v have the same colour. If the induced graph S is connected and fully imperfectly coloured, all the vertices of S have the same colour. Consider the following induced subgraphs of G:

- P_f is perfectly coloured in C_f.
- I_f is fully imperfectly coloured in C_f.
- P_m is perfectly coloured in C_m.
- I_m is imperfectly coloured in C_m.

These four subgraphs have $PCCG$ values full (means $PCCG(P)$ = no of edges in P), null (zero) or unknown as shown in Table 3.7.

In formation of children from these four subgraphs, each with three possible values each, there are at least 81 (3^4=81) different possibilities. Each of these children is the outcome of a crossover. The best and worst possibilities of the cross-over are shown in Figure 3.22 and the random crossovers are shown in Figures 3.23 and 3.24.

TABLE 3.7
PCCG values

	P_f	P_f	P_f	P_f
Father C_f	Full	Null	Unknown	Unknown
Mother C_m	Unknow	Unknow	full	Null

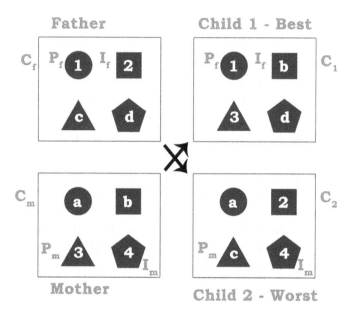

FIGURE 3.22 Crossover: Best and worst possibility.

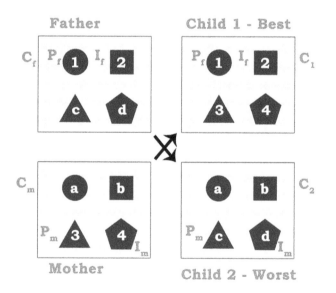

FIGURE 3.23 Random crossover 1.

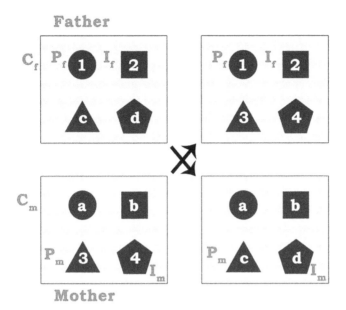

FIGURE 3.24   Random crossover 1.

3.6   GENETIC ALGORITHM TO FIND THE CHROMATIC NUMBER OF THE GRAPH

Input: A graph G with n vertices and m edges represented by the adjacency matric, a.

Output: The chromatic number k and a perfect k-colouring

Step 1: $k = n$

Step 2: Continue the following steps until it breaks out. Beyond some specific time when *Function Infinity() is TRUE*, go to step 3.

Step 2.1: State Space = set of randomly generated 10 n-tuples of integers 0 to $k-1$.

Step 2.2:

Step 2.2.0 Let C_f and C_m be two states from the State Space.

Step 2.2.1: Compute PCCG(G) for C_f and C_m.

Step 2.2.2: If PCCG(G) = m in C_f or in C_m then the particular state, C_f or C_m is a perfect k-colouring. Abort the loop and go to Step 2.3. Otherwise continue to step 2.2.3.

Step 2.2.3: Compute two children C_1 and C_2 using a sequence of mutations and crossover.

Step 2.2.4: Add C_1 and C_2 to the State space.

Step 2.2.5: If PCCG(G) = m in C_1, or in C_2 then the corresponding state C_1 or C_2 is a perfect k-colouring. Abort the loop and go to Step 2.3. Otherwise continue to loop from Step 2.2.0.

Step 2.3: When we reach here, for the given value of k, there is a perfect k-colouring. Now, make $k = k-1$ and proceed to the loop Step 2.1

Step 3: When we reach here, for the given value of k, there is no perfect k-colouring. So, conclude that the Chromatic Number is $k+1$.

Theorem

The above algorithm most likely finds the chromatic number of the graph.

Proof

The chromatic number lies between 1 and n. Step 1 begins with $k = n$ and checks if there is a perfect k-colouring. If so, we decrement the value of n and check. In the graph G, when we assign vertex i with colour i, this is obviously a perfect n-colouring. So, this algorithm begins with n and decrements whenever there is a k-colouring. When $\underline{k} = 1$, all the vertices are assigned the same colour. As the number of edges is at least 1, this is not a perfect colouring. This guarantees that we reach step 3 for some value of k.

The state space we begin in step 2.1 continuously grows as the iterations continue. We select a father and a mother state. Actually, it is possible to improve the performance of the algorithm by selecting the father and mother in such a way that PCCG(G) value is high for the colourings C_f and C_m. The mutation actions and crossover actions defined in this chapter gives a high level of confidence that the PCCG(G) value increases for the children. It is also possible to include a control to make sure only the children with higher PCCG values are added to the population. This makes sure that the value of PCCG moves towards m and reaches perfection in a few steps. This proves that the algorithm can be used to find the chromatic number with a high level of confidence.

3.7   CONCLUSION AND FUTURE WORK

In this chapter, we described an evolutionary approach to determining a graph's chromatic number. The algorithm uses the metrics such as PCCV and PCCG. The perfect colouring coefficient of vertex determines the perfectness around the vertex. We can also define the second order perfection coefficient of a vertex as follows: Let $N_2[v]=$ $\{u: u$ is at a maximum distance of 2 from $v\}$. Consider the induced subgraph of $N_2[v]$. The second order perfection coefficient of v denoted by $PCCV_2(v)$ in a k-colouring C is the number of edges (x, y) perfectly coloured (x and y have different colours). It is possible to extend it to $PCCV_i(v)$ for any $i = 1, 2, 3$ and so on. It is interesting to study the relationship among these values.

REFERENCES

[1] Chelladurai, X., Iyengar, S. S. (1998) *Introduction to Parallel Algorithms*, John Wiley & Sons.

[2] Chelladurai, X., Kureethara, J. V. (2021) Algorithms for the metric dimension of a simple graph, *Lecture Notes in Networks and Systems*, 132, pp. 91–105.

[3] Chelladurai, X., Kureethara, J. V. (2021) Parallel algorithm to find integer k where a given well-distributed graph is k-metric dimensional, *Advances in Intelligent Systems and Computing*, 1333, pp. 145–153.

[4] Duffy, K., O'connell, N., Sapozhnikov, A. (2008) Complexity analysis of a decentralized graph colouring algorithm information processing, *Letters,* 107(2), pp. 60–63.

[5] Garey, M. R., Johnson, D. S. (1979) *Computers and Intractability: A Guide to the Theory of NP-Completeness*, W. H. Freeman.

[6] Lewis, R. M. R. (2015) *A Guide to Graph Colouring: Algorithms and Applications*, Springer.

[7] Fawcett, B. W. (1978) On infinite full colourings of graphs, *Canadian Journal of Mathematics*, 30(3), pp. 455–457.

[8] Zuckerman, D. (2007) Linear degree extractors and the inapproximability of Max Clique and chromatic number, *Theory of Computing*, 3, pp. 103–128.

[9] Khot, S. (2001) Improved inapproximability results for MaxClique, chromatic number and approximate graph colouring, 42nd Annual Symposium on Foundations of Computer Science, pp. 600–609.

4 A Survey of Prevalent PCA/LDA Methods Based on Bio-Inspired Facial Recognition Algorithms

Palaniappan N

4.1 INTRODUCTION

Facial recognition systems based on biological traits are appealing because they are simple to use. The human face is made up of a variety of structures and features. As a result, facial images have given their potential in a variety of applications and disciplines like surveillance, home security, border control, etc. It is one of the most often used biometric authentication systems in recent years. Consumers are already being offered facial recognition as an ID (identification) system outside of phones, such as at airport check-ins, sports stadiums and concerts. Furthermore, because this technology does not require any human intervention to work, it is possible to identify persons only based on photographs captured by the camera. The ability of a human to recognize faces is amazing. One may instantly identify hundreds of faces they have learned over their life, even after spending years away. This fitness is quite strong, despite significant variations in the appearance brought on by review conditions, temperament, aging and interruptions like scenes or modifications to the hairstyle or beard growth. Since they can advance both fictitious knowledge and practical applications, registering models for facial recognition is particularly intriguing. Robotized facial recognition approaches will be helpful for a wide range of concerns, such as criminal recognizability, security frameworks, image processing and human–PC interaction.

4.2 FACIAL IMAGE PROCESSING

The images used for facial recognition are named facial images. The facial image represents the face area of a human (top of the head to chin). They are used for identification, verification and watch list purposes. Identification is to identify the image by comparing it with the images available in the database. The verification process is to match the identity of the person with his enrolled images. A watch list is to verify the person's identity with the images in the watch list. As illustrated in Figure 4.1, facial images used for facial recognition go through several stages. Image capture, face detection, feature extraction, normalization and compression are the steps involved.

 DOI: 10.1201/9781003248545-4

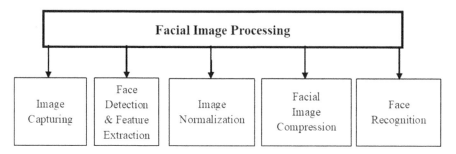

FIGURE 4.1   Phases of facial image processing.

4.3 FACIAL RECOGNITION

Facial recognition (FR) is a special case of object recognition that is very difficult to automate. Because there are so many distinct types of items that a computer would need to be able to recognize, automating object recognition is challenging. Since faces can change so significantly from person to person, they are even more challenging to identify. The differences between the faces are relatively minor, even though they appear to be quite similar in their most frequent form (the frontal aspect). This means that it is highly challenging to distinguish between different frontal face photos using conventional pattern recognition techniques. The three basic categories of facial recognition methods are intensity pictures, video sequences and methods requiring additional sensory input like 3D data or infrared photography. The main goal of feature-based approaches is to extract visual features, which are subsequently utilized to calculate a picture's intensity. On the other hand, holistic approaches concentrate on the overall composition of the image to determine intensity. There are two primary methods: feature-based and holistic.

The eyes, mouth, nose and other fiducial features are some of the specific face points that are identified and extracted using feature-based techniques. Then measurements are made using these markings. In essence, this implies that the points on a person's face are being converted into a series of numbers that indicate how far apart those points are. The software examines a person's face and takes measurements of their nose width and eye-to-eye distance. It then searches for a match by comparing these measurements to a database of other people's faces. When recognizing faces, a person is identified holistically, which implies that the entire image is used rather than just certain traits. There are two types of systems for solving problems: those that use statistics and those that use AI. To detect faces, AI systems use tools like neural networks and machine learning algorithms.

4.4 STATISTICAL MODELS

The least complex variant of universal ways of reasoning views the facial image as a 2D presentation of force values, and verification is accomplished by directly associating the information face with any further countenances in the educational assortment. Even though this approach has been shown to work well in clear-cut situations, it is computationally costly and executes into the usual challenges associated with direct association-based methods, for example, aversion to confronting direction, size, variable lighting conditions, foundation mess and commotion. The direct matching strategies' acknowledgment viability is hampered by the way that they try to group in a space with generally high dimensionality. A few elective methodologies have been created to neutralize the scourge of dimensionality.

4.4.1 Principal Component Analysis

Principal Components Analysis (PCA) was initially used to financially portray facial pictures by Sirovich and Kirby [1]. They exhibited the way that any face can be capably tended to along the eigenface coordinate space and that any face can be approximated by using only a couple of eigenfaces and they are looking at projections along each eigenface.

Turk and Pentland [2] discovered that projections along eigenfaces might be used as strategy characteristics to perceive faces in light of Sirovich and Kirby's revelations. They had the option to create an insistence structure that creates eigenfaces, which interface with the eigenvectors allied through the mind-boggling eigenvalues of the recognized face (plans) covariance cross-section. They did this by contrasting their scenarios with the eigenfaces and those of realized people's face pictures. This allowed them to see unmistakable faces after some time. Face affirmation takes place in the component space that the eigenfaces structure, which dramatically decreases the dimensionality of the primary space. At last, the weight vector is made by projecting the two test pictures into this eigenspace, and the Euclidean distance between two face key vectors is determined. If this worth is under a specific limit, two given pictures are said to coordinate, suggesting that they have a place with a similar individual. At the point when just a solitary picture of each individual is given, PCA seems to perform really, however when numerous pictures per individual are free, it holds unwanted differences because of lighting and looks. PCA FR precision is over 90% by and large and components such as overlighting, fluctuations and various foundations affect the acknowledgment. Figure 4.2 shows the different courses of FR utilizing PCA.

The basic steps are:

- Compile x_i from an n-layered data collection x, with i=1, 2,…, m.
- Normalize each and every image.
- Compute mean mx and deduct it from all relevant data using $x_i - m_x$.
- Create the covariance matrix using these formula: $C = (x_i - m_x)(xi - mx)^T$.
- Choose the network C's eigenvalues and eigenvectors.
- Compare the eigenvectors and order the eigenvalues in decreasing order.
- Choose the key d <= n eigenvectors and build the informational database for the new depiction.
- A comparability measure is used to compare each predicted preparation picture with the projected test picture. The picture of the preparation, which is the most similar to the test picture, is the result.

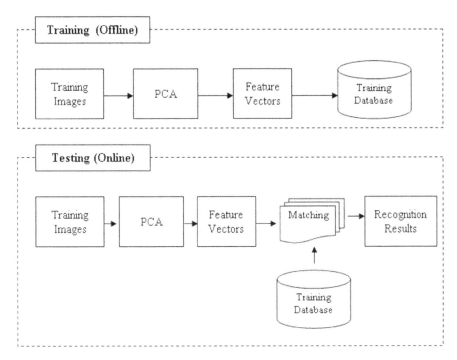

FIGURE 4.2 Various processes of facial recognition using PCA.

4.4.2 LINEAR DISCRIMINANT ANALYSIS

For characterization problems like the PCA computation, Linear Discriminant Analysis (LDA) is a dimensionality reduction strategy. Fisher's Discriminant Examination is another term for LDA, which looks for vectors in the fundamental space that, in contrast to PCA, best distinguish between classes.

LDA directly joins autonomous highlights to produce the most notable mean disparities between the objective classes. Finding a straight change that enables highlight groups to be isolated the greatest after the change, which may be accomplished through dissipate grid inquiry, is the fundamental LDA rule. LDA's goal is to increase the dissipate framework across classes while reducing the dissipate network inside classes.

The fundamental procedure is defined as:

- Compute the within-class scatter matrix S_w:

$$S_w = \sum_{j=1}^{C} \Box \sum_{i=1}^{N} \left(x_i^j - \mu_j \right)\left(x_i^j - \mu_j \right)^T$$

where x_i^j is the ith model of jth class,
    μ_j is the mean of class
    C is the total classes
    N_j is the count of samples in jth class

- Compute between-class scatter matrix S_b,

$$S_b = \sum_{i=1}^{N} \left(\mu_j - \mu\right)\left(\mu_j - \mu\right)^T$$

where μ signifies the mean of entire classes

- Compute the eigenvectors of the projection matrix

$$W = \text{eig}\,(S_w^{-1}\,S_b)$$

- Use a proximity metric to compare the projection lattice of the test image to the projection framework of each training image. The image of the preparation, which is the most similar to the test image, is the result.

4.5 FURTHER DEVELOPMENTS OF PCA AND LDA METHODS

Researchers extended eigenfaces and other PCA, LDA-based methods to fulfill their needs and improved the FR rate. A few of the recent works are listed in Table 4.1. Most of these methods result in better recognition methods than the baseline techniques. Table 4.1 shows the various improved PCA and LDA algorithms year-wise.

TABLE 4.1
Improved PCA and LDA algorithms

Year of publication	Improved algorithms based on PCA and LDA
2010	2D Kernel PCA [3]
2010	Laplacian Bidirectional PCA [4]
2013	Deep PCA [5]
2016	Modular Two-Dimensional PCA [6]
2018	Histogram Equalized Deep PCA [7]
2020	Incremental Weighted LDA [8]
2022	Hybrid LDA [9]

4.6 BIO-INSPIRED FACIAL RECOGNITION METHODS

Another form of clever registration strategy has recently been developed in order to overcome the limitations of traditional man-made reasoning advances. One of the essential characteristics of these ingenious figure improvements is that they operate more like a single biological entity or a group of easily perceivable organic things. In most cases, these technologies are more efficient than standard AI methods. To distinguish them from typical AI approaches, these intelligent computing methods are referred to as bio-inspired algorithms (BIA) – computing inspired by nature. BIA has made significant advances in the field of facial recognition research .

There are numerous publications available on bio-driven methods for improving the FR problem, and the majority of them have shown the effectiveness of these strategies, especially when combined with conventional methods. These methods are categorized into four major types based on the BIA methods involved. They are Evolution, Collective Behavior in Animals, Central Nervous System and Human Immune System. Evolution methods involve Evolutionary algorithms which are further classified into Genetic Programming, Genetic Algorithm, Differential Evolution and Memetic algorithms. Various branches of collective behavior in animals, i.e., Swam Intelligence, are Particle Swam Optimization, Bacterial Foraging Optimization, Ant Colony Optimization and Artificial Bee Colony. Artificial neural networks is the base of Central Nervous Systems and the popular methods involved are Self Organizing Maps, Recurrent Neural Network, Radial Basis Function Network, Feed Forward Neural Network, etc., Artificial Immune System covers the area Human Immune System. The basic BIA methods in FR and their various categories are shown in Figure 4.3.

The prevalent methods mostly used along with the BIA are PCA, LDA, 2DPCA, MLPCA, GNP-PCA, Naïve Bayes, GNP-MAS, Fisher Method, Fisher LDA PCA-Ma, Gabor Filter, PCA-IN, DCT, DWT, KPCA and Support Vector Machine (SVM). When these approaches are analyzed, it becomes evident that PCA and LDA are used in about 90% of BIAs. So, BIAs combine PCA and LDA and are discussed below one by one. Evolutionary algorithms, along with the aforementioned algorithms, make up the majority of BIA methods. Only evolutionary approaches are taken into account in this survey out of the four main categories of currently available BIA Face Recognition systems due to the abundance of published research works.

4.7 EVOLUTIONARY ALGORITHMS

Evolutionary Algorithms (EAs) are a general name for evolutionary algorithms, development methods, genetic computations and hereditary writing computer programs. They have been successfully applied in a variety of search, streamlining and AI fields. EAs are used to locate direct solutions for problems that people are unable to handle. When freed from human prejudices or biases, the flexible concept of EAs can provide outcomes that are on par with and frequently even superior to the best human endeavors. It has been demonstrated that adding problem-specific heuristics to EAs can produce highly efficient methods in the area of combinatorial optimization. These

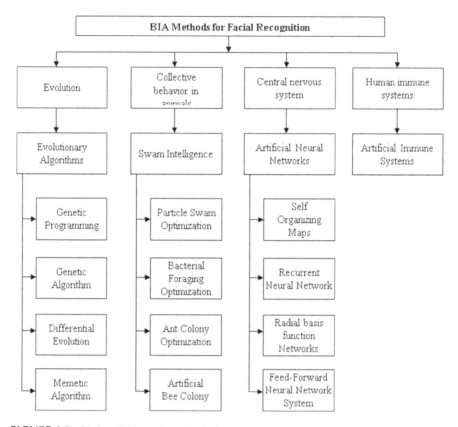

FIGURE 4.3   Various BIA methods for facial recognition.

hybrid EAs incorporate domain expertise and population-based search techniques to combine the benefits of effective heuristics.

4.8   GENETIC PROGRAMMING AND GENETIC ALGORITHM

Genetic Programming (GP) is a subset of evolutionary algorithms, which includes machine learning (EA). GP employs an algorithm inspired by biological evolution and its mechanisms to accomplish a unique purpose. This algorithm uses random mutations, crossings, fitness functions and many generations of evolution. By classifying data (classification), finding a functional relationship between data properties (symbolic regression) and assisting in the design of electrical circuits, antennas and quantum algorithms, GP can help with these tasks.

Genetic algorithms (GAs) with evolutionary inspiration incorporate mutation, natural selection, inheritance and crossover concepts. In a GA, an initial dataset is "run" through hundreds or thousands of "generations" to evaluate the output and give each character a specific weight. Optimization, categorization and prediction problems are all addressed by GAs. A hybrid FR method was created by Bozorgtabar et al.

[46] employing GP and PCA. The features are extracted using PCA, and the picture groups are then classified using GP.

For experiments, the AT&T face image database is used. Due to its low FR rate (67.5%), this study shows that GP alone is not suited for FR, and to enhance the outcomes, GP is subjected to a leveraging algorithm.

Abegaz et al. [10] present an algorithm that improves the PCA-based FR by using features optimization and applying weights via Genetic Algorithms. FRGC dataset is used for testing the algorithm and proves that the feature selection/weighting method enhances the overall performance of the PCA-based methods.

An effective FR model which is based on PCA, GA and SVM is established by Hu Ahi and Sanyang Liu [11]. In this strategy PCA is utilized to lessen feature dimension, GA to optimize search strategy, and SVM is used to realize classification. The CAS-PEAL database is used for verifying the performance of this algorithm.

Adil Boughida et al. [12] introduce a Facial Expression Recognition method that involves PCA, Gabor Filters, SVM and GP. JAFFE, CK and CK+ are the facial image datasets used for evaluation. Since the JAFFE database consists of 53,050 features per image, PCA is utilized to reduce the number of features. PCA reduces the number of features to 212 from the available 53,050 features. GP calculation is utilized to improve the SVM hyperparameters and results in 96.30%, 94.20% and 94.26% FR rates for JAFFE, CK and CK+ data sets separately.

Firoz et al. [13] present a PCA-based Genetic Algorithm for Human Face Recognition. In this work, PCA is employed to reduce the computational time and improve the processing speed of FR. GA has used an optimization technique for getting optimal solutions from the large search space. JAFFE face database is used and achieved an approximate FR rate of 96%.

Al-Arashi et al. [14] propose a strategy that allies GA with PCA and the exhibition beats PCA regarding precision and order. For testing ORL and Yale information bases are utilized. Further, the exhibition of the framework is more successful when the quantity of pictures per class is expanded.

This paper [15] presents a new theorem to deduce that PCA can be used to select the eigenvectors to be used in the LDA method using GA (GA-PCA). The advantages of this method are best possible bases for dimensional reduction are achieved using GA-PCA and LDA computational efficiency is increased by adding a whitening procedure. The FERET and CMU PIE databases are used for experimenting. This GA-Fisher gives an improvement of 2% to 3% to the Fisher method.

4.9 DIFFERENTIAL EVOLUTION

The transformative calculation incorporates Differential Evolution (DE). It is a populace-based stochastic streamlining technique that was created by Storn and Cost. Genuine boundaries and genuine esteemed capabilities are improved along these lines. The DE calculation, as opposed to the GA strategy, centers around transformations and utilizations the change administrator as a pursuit system and choice administrator to direct the hunt toward great spots in the hunt space. The GA technique depends on hybrid activities. Designing, insights and money all utilize this enhancement procedure. In the event that an issue is nondifferentiable, nonconsistent, nonstraight, uproarious, level, multilayered or has various nearby minima, imperatives or stochasticity, DE can be utilized to distinguish approximations to arrangements. It is utilized in the formation of computerized channels also. A practical approach for FR was created by Malipeddi and Lee [16] using PCA and DE. Finding a feature subset from the high-dimensional feature collection is particularly challenging, despite PCA being the widely used subspace projection approach in FR. The best subset of PCA features that the DE algorithm could extract for FR is here. Experimental facial databases include Yale A, Yale B, AR and ENT. It was found from the studies that choosing the right eigenvectors for FR required a trial-and-error study. Some features are irrelevant even after the dimensional data has been reduced using a PCA and LDA technique combo. Zorarpaci [17] suggests a technique dubbed DBDERF+ PCA, a hybrid dimensionality reduction approach made up of supervised and unsupervised methods, to solve this issue. An ensemble random forest classifier is adopted for robust envelope feature selection, a dichotomous binary differential evolution (DBDE) and a new variation of binary differential evolution. This strategy is more effective than the traditional PCA and PCA+LDA approach.

Yoo et al. [18] depict the plan of a face acknowledgment calculation that utilizes polynomial-based outspread premise capability brain organizations and component extraction from 2D-LDA. The complete face acknowledgment framework utilizes the proposed polynomial-based outspread premise capability brain networks as its acknowledgment part, while information pretreatment is achieved utilizing the 2D-LDA gave information preprocessing approach. DE is utilized to advance the key plan boundaries. The experimental findings for the Yale and ORL databases' benchmark face datasets show how successful and efficient the 2D-LDA technique with DE is when compared to other methods like PCA and PCA-LDA fusion.

4.10   MEMETIC ALGORITHM

A memetic algorithm (MA) is a developmental calculation that utilizes a particular nearby inquiry technique to work on the wellness of people. A populace put together metaheuristic search procedure attracts respect to the thoughts of organic development and Richard Dawkins' image idea. It is spurred by Darwin's standards of regular development (characterized as a unit of copy social development that is fit for nearby refinements). All chromosomes and descendants are allowed to acquire some insight through a nearby hunt before being integrated into the developmental interaction, which is a particular element of MAs. MAs consolidate worldwide and neighborhood search to think up a powerful algorithmic procedure for transformative figuring A memetic calculation (Mama) is a developmental calculation that improves the wellness of people by utilizing a specific nearby inquiry system. Contrasted with customary hunt strategies, MAs are more useful and lead to predominant solutions. It utilizes a populace-based metaheuristic exploration approach and incorporates the natural development and image speculations of Richard Dawkins.

Darwin's speculations of regular development act as its essential wellspring of motivation (characterized as a unit of copy social development fit for neighborhood

TABLE 4.2
Consolidation of evolutionary algorithm methods

Author	Evolutionary algorithm	Prevalent method	Prevalent method used	Testing database	FR rate
Bozorgtabar et al.	Genetic Programming	PCA	Hybrid	AT & T	Improved
Abegaz et al.	Genetic Algorithm	PCA	Features optimization	FRGC	Improved
Hu Ahi & Sanyang Liu	Genetic Algorithm	PCA and SVM	PCA –dimension reduction; SVM – realize classification	CAS-PEAL	Improved
Adil Boughida et al.	Genetic Programming	PCA	Dimension reduction	JAFFE, CK, and CK+	Excellent
Firoz et al.	Genetic Algorithm	PCA	Reduction of computational Time	JAFFE	Improved
Al-Arashi et al.	Genetic Algorithm	PCA	Hybrid	ORL and Yale A	Improved
Zheng et al.	Genetic Algorithm	PCA and LDA	PCA – dimension reduction; LDA – increasing computational efficiency	FERET and CMU PIE	Improved
Malipeddi and Lee	Differential Evolution	PCA	Dimension reduction	Yale A, Yale B, AR and ORL	Eigenvectors selection needs a trial-and-error search
Zorarpaci	Differential Evolution	PCA and LDA	Dimension reduction	ORL	Better
Yoo et al	Differential Evolution	2D-LDA	Feature extraction	Yale and ORL	Efficient
Kumar et al.	Memetic Algorithm	PCA	Feature extraction and dimension reduction	ORL and Yale B	Improved
Kumar et al.	Memetic Algorithm	PCA	Feature extraction and dimension reduction	ORL	Superior to the baseline eigenface method

refinement). All chromosomes and descendants are permitted to acquire insight through neighborhood concentration before starting the developmental interaction, which is a trait of AMs. A strong algorithmic procedure for scaled registering is delivered by MAs, which coordinate worldwide and neighborhood search with an EA for investigation and a nearby quest technique for double-dealing. An EA does the investigation, while the neighborhood search strategy handles double-dealing. Contrasted with customary pursuit strategies, MAs are more useful and lead to prevalent solutions. This work presents a PCA-Memetic Calculation (Mama) strategy [19] for highlight determination. The utilization of MAs has permitted PCA to be extended, with the previous being utilized for include extraction and dimensionality decrease and the last option being used for highlight determination. On the ORL and YaleB face data sets, reproductions were run with the Euclidean standard as the classifier. It was found that PCA-Mama outperforms the eigenface method as far as acknowledgment rate. The viability of PCA is reached out with hereditary calculation (PCA-GA) and the recommended PCA-Mama approach is looked at. The PCA-Mama approach's prevalence over the PCA-GA technique was adequately exhibited by the outcomes.

Kumar et al. [20] introduce a novel method for face recognition feature selection based on MA. PCA has been utilized in this work to reduce the dimensionality and extract features and I have been used to choose the features for a face recognition application. The studies have been carried out using the ORL face database. The findings show that, in terms of the face recognition system's recognition rate, the suggested method is superior to and beats the baseline eigenface method. The above-discussed evolutionary algorithm methods are consolidated in Table 4.2.

4.11 CONCLUSION

A challenging topic in the study of digital processing is facial recognition which has recently gained much interest because of its extensive applicability in numerous sectors. Current facial recognition systems have advanced to some extent when working in limited environments. However, they fall far short of the ideal of operating well in all the various scenarios that applications using these techniques frequently meet. More bio-inspired facial recognition systems have developed throughout the years as a result of their intelligent problem-solving capabilities, adaptability, scalability and adaptable nature. Future advancements in facial biometrics with bio-inspired techniques may be advantageous.

REFERENCES

[1] L. Sirovich and M. Kirby. "Low-dimensional Procedure for the Characterization of Human Faces." *Journal of the Optical Society of America A: Optics, Image Science, and Vision*, 4, pp. 519–524, 1987.

[2] M. Turk and A. Pentland. "Eigenfaces for Recognition." *Journal of Cognitive Neuroscience*, 3, pp. 71–86, 1991.

[3] A. Eftekhari, et al. "Block-wise 2D Kernel PCA/LDA for Face Recognition." *Information Processing Letters*, 110, pp. 761–766, 2010.

[4] W. Yang, et al. "Laplacian Bidirectional PCA for Face Recognition." *Neurocomputing*, 74, pp. 487–493, 2010.

[5] V. E. Liong, J. Lu, and G. Wang. *"Face Recognition Using Deep PCA."* 9th International Conference on Information, Communications, & Signal Processing, IEEE, 2013.

[6] S. Venkatramaphanikumar and K. V. Krishna Kishore. "Face Recognition with Modular Two Dimensional PCA under Uncontrolled Illumination Variations." *International Journal of Electrical and Computer Engineering*, 6, p. 1610, 2016

[7] K. Rujirakul and C. So-In. "Histogram Equalized Deep PCA with ELM Classification for Expressive Face Recognition." 2018 International Workshop on Advanced Image Technology, IEEE, 2018.

[8] N. Kumar and S. Madhavan. "Incremental Weighted Linear Discriminant Analysis for Face Recognition." In *Advances in Communication and Computational Technology*, Springer, 2021, 677–687.

[9] V. R. Thushitha and Priya. "Comparative Analysis to Improve the Image Accuracy in Face Recognition System Using Hybrid LDA Compared with PCA." International Conference on Business Analytics for Technology and Security, IEEE, 2022.

[10] T. Abegaz, et al. "Hybrid GAs for Eigen-Based Facial Recognition." IEEE Workshop on Computational Intelligence in Biometrics and Identity Management, IEEE, 2011.

[11] H. Zhi and S. Liu. "Face Recognition Based on Genetic Algorithm." *Journal of Visual Communication and Image Representation*, 58, pp. 495–502, 2019.

[12] A. Boughida, M. N. Kouahla, and Y. Lafifi. "A Novel Approach for Facial Expression Recognition Based on Gabor Filters and Genetic Algorithm." *Evolving Systems*, 13, pp. 331–345, 2022

[13] F. Mahmud, et al. "Human Face Recognition Using PCA Based Genetic Algorithm." International Conference on Electrical Engineering and Information & Communication Technology, IEEE, 2014.

[14] W. H. Al-Arashi, H. Ibrahim, and S. A. Suandi. "Optimizing Principal Component Analysis Performance for Face Recognition Using Genetic Algorithm." *Neurocomputing*, 128, pp. 415–420, 2014.

[15] W.-S. Zheng, J.-H. Lai, and P. C. Yuen. "GA-Fisher: A New LDA-Based Face Recognition Algorithm with Selection of Principal Components." *IEEE Transactions on Systems, Man, and Cybernetics, Part B (Cybernetics)*, 35, pp. 1065–1078, 2005

[16] R. Mallipeddi and M. Lee. "Ensemble Based Face Recognition Using Discriminant PCA Features." IEEE Congress on Evolutionary Computation, IEEE, 2012.

[17] E. Zorarpacı. *"A Hybrid Dimension Reduction Based Linear Discriminant Analysis for Classification of High-Dimensional Data."* IEEE Congress on Evolutionary Computation, IEEE, 2021.

[18] S.-H. Yoo, S.-K. Oh, and W. Pedrycz. *"Design of Face Recognition Algorithm Realized with Feature Extraction from 2D-LDA and Optimized Polynomial-Based RBF NNs."* Joint IFSA World Congress and NAFIPS Annual Meeting, IEEE, 2013.

[19] D. Kumar, S. Kumar, and C. S. Rai. "Feature Selection for Face Recognition: A Memetic Algorithmic Approach." *Journal of Zhejiang University: Science A*, 10, pp. 1140–1152, 2009

[20] D. Kumar, S. Kumar, and C. S. Rai. "Memetic Algorithms for Feature Selection in Face Recognition." Eighth International Conference on Hybrid Intelligent Systems, IEEE, 2008.

5 Augmented Reality-Enabled IoT Devices for Wireless Communication

*Siva Shankar Ramasamy, Chokkanathan K,
Aniwat Phaphuangwittayakul and
Vijayalakshmi S*

5.1 INTRODUCTION

The Internet of Things' (IoT) [1] full potential can only be realized with the help of augmented reality (AR), a promising new technology. The numerous forms of statistics generated by IoT devices and additives are used by AR packages to increase staff productivity and capability. Organizations must develop a collaborative IoT-AR strategy rather than tackling these technologies separately to swiftly start a positive cycle of cost savings, revenue growth and greater profitability that may result in a double-digit increase in top and bottom lines. This chapter includes a free IoT-AR app that illustrates how businesses might exploit such advantages.

Gartner estimated that the number of IoT-related devices will rise from approximately 6 billion in 2016 to 11 billion through 2018 and 20 billion by 2020. An informative "Big Bang" has been brought on by this growth. Cisco Systems and IDC estimated that in 2016 the volume of IoT-generated records would reach 22 zettabytes (or 22 trillion gigabytes). That quantity more than tripled to 52 zettabytes by the end of 2019, and it was predicted to reach 85 zettabytes by the end of 2021. However, because the number of records is growing so quickly, many businesses are unable to make use of all the gathered information. Huge quantities cause processing times to be slow, which causes the records to get caught in records lakes. Additionally, the databases have too many sources to synthesize, and the statistical sets lack a logical order. As a result, many businesses are having trouble producing data-based insights that staff members can use at the right time and in the right place. Traditional visualization techniques, which aren't always effective at displaying data from various sources, are a separate, frequently disregarded effort to effectively use massive volumes of data. However, statistics must be presented simply in order for the general audience to readily understand them.

DOI: 10.1201/9781003248545-5

AR is useful in this situation. IoT [2] devices gather data from the actual world so that it can be analyzed, whereas AR devices render the digital record back into the real world so that users can view and interact with it.

5.2 THE SWEET SPOTS FOR IOT: AR SOLUTIONS

Unlike virtual reality software, which forces the user to enter a simulated environment, AR apps overlay digital data on top of the user's real-world environment. To give the appearance that digital information is a part of the outside world, AR software might, for example, integrate digital content to live camera feeds. Such functionality would allow users to interact with records more naturally.

Numerous businesses have created AR applications that leverage artificial intelligence to condense vast volumes of data in various forms, including IoT information, into certain crucial actions. Those movements and facts are then offered to personnel at the right time and vicinity to be able to make knowledgeable choices and better execute their duties. Agencies that aren't experimenting with joint IoT-AR techniques run the risk of being left behind by rivals in several industries.

5.3 RAPID USAGE OF IOT AND AR

Multiplied reality (AR) and the IoT are currently receiving a lot of attention as major empowering advancements for creating locations more dazzling and intuitive. Figure 5.1 shows IoT and AR usage.

AR [3–5] comes under an intuitive medium that gives an angle in this gift reality extended via spatially enrolling helpful PC-produced information. It assists individuals with understanding the arena and enhances their understanding of taking care of troubles and doing actual undertakings. IoT alludes to a corporation of actual gadgets and ordinary articles inserted with negligible processing components for detecting, gathering, conveying and, in any event, participating with the actual gadgets. Such a basis will deliver the basis to extremely good situations through a combination of

FIGURE 5.1 IoT and AR usage.

widespread statistics investigation and placing-based total administrations (e.g., non-stop examination and computerization).

Although AR and IoT may share a variety of aspirations and seemingly incorrect thoughts, they may be mutually beneficial. Customers can photograph IoT devices and their associated statistics in the immediate area with great ease thanks to AR. In general, a spatially enlisted and outward-extended interface provides a quick and semi-sizeable interface and is, along these lines, simple to realize and extremely helpful, especially for routine or probably anywhere utilization. The AR user can interact with an (IoT) object in split seconds while wearing a flexible or head-protective device. They can also manipulate data and related AR datasets for the given particular administration, recognize the state of cutting-edge information from the IoT object and connect with the actual object using straight control through regular collaboration, as an example.

Note that the semi-big method is the interface that may be imagined and labored in an ongoing way making use of the expanded digital substance to companion IoT objects in truth. Alternately, for AR, IoT as a framework for "all over" management gives a talented manner of making AR "versatile" further by looking after the essential records of the executives (e.g., following statistics and content material) in a dispersed and object-driven way. Along those traces, any IoT item can be gotten to on the spot domestically in a steady manner and the adaptable interface taking into consideration vicinity-based topographical and accelerated truth administrations using AR clients. Moreover, putting mindful AR administrations is made doable with the aid of making use of and taking gain of the greater subtle weather facts made handy by using the IoT framework.

Moreover, to involve AR as a point of interaction with IoT, we look past investigations that showed the way AR can give a characteristic and normal method for speaking with IoT objects, in contrast to exclusive techniques without a visible, context-oriented or spatial enlistment. We concentrate on these three areas since they are essential for the creation of a strong IoT-AR framework: information on the board, object-directed following and interface configuration. We initially summarized earlier investigations to determine the status and direction of the momentum studies.

The usage of AR in business is growing in importance as more businesses extend the technology's application beyond its first testing grounds in advertising and sales. Other competencies, mostly in manufacturing, operations, providers and training, make up this expansion. Instead of the creation of specialized devices, the growth of AR has been facilitated by the spread of smartphones and other portable devices that support it.

5.4 AR, IOT AND WIRELESS COMMUNICATIONS

5.4.1 Augmented Reality

To identify the most profitable trends, BCG and PTC performed a quantitative analysis with more than 200 executives from businesses utilizing IoT or AR technology, or both. We also interviewed several senior executives. Surprisingly, a lot of people think that IoT and AR work best together. Over 76% of those building AR-only solutions think that integrating IoT into their programs may be advantageous, while 81% of the organizations questioned are using IoT and contemplating the use of AR.

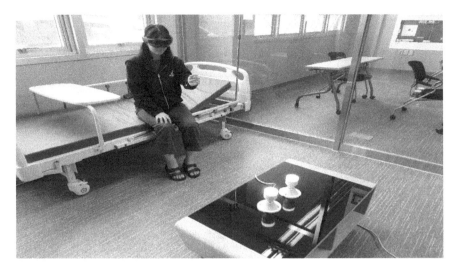

FIGURE 5.2 Viewer's natural senses.

The IoT's true potential is being unlocked by a generation with enormous promise called AR. To help employees be more successful and efficient, AR programs use the various types of data that are produced by IoT devices and additives.

IoT is an arrangement of interconnected PCs, electronic and virtual contraptions, family things, creatures and individuals who can be in every way doled-out one-of-a-kind identifiers and have the capacity of sending information over an organization without the requirement for direct human or PC-to-human correspondence. Figure 5.2 clearly shows the viewer's natural senses.

Using a spatial show (digital projector) to enhance a real-world object (a wall) for a presentation is a straightforward example of AR. IoT represents the Web of Things, which is an organization of actual gadgets and ordinary things that are embedded with essential processing parts for recognizing, assembling, imparting and, in any event, communicating with the actual items.

5.4.2 WORKING PRINCIPLE

1. Define tracking information of AR objects in the offline process.
2. Filter long-range distance objects out of viewing volume.
3. AR data distribution with peer-to-peer communication.
4. Feature or 3D model matching to track a thing.
5. Augment the virtual object and control the physical object.

- The future approach for AR frameworks, which is entirely based on physical items and takes scalability into account, is depicted in Figure 5.3.
- The association between the physical and digital item IDs must be established in advance before an AR user can collect fake markers (or natural qualities) from surrounding items.

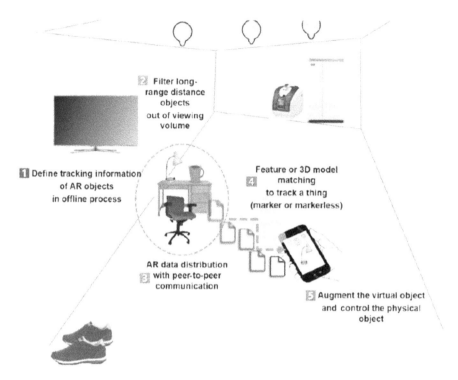

FIGURE 5.3 Digital projector.

- The user can then view the filtered AR items while holding onto their mobile device in various locations. These items are neighboring IoT-successful things according to their relative distance or path from the user.
- The "content" and "characteristics" reports for each item with the associated sensor are then sent straight to the consumer AR device.
- The client of AR can then consolidate the virtual thing while at the same time wearing a video-transparent head-mounted show (HMD) or utilizing a versatile cell phone with an associated camera module.

Figure 5.4 portrays a framework that consolidates expanded reality (AR) with the Web of Things (IoT), alongside an evaluation of Human–PC Connection (HCI) styles that incorporate universal PCs and increased communications.

Applications are where the majority of IoT items are used. Using the web to enable interactions with actual items is a promising strategy, as shown by Google's physical web. Here, items can show their own dynamic, cross-platform contents that are represented by URLs and well-known languages like HTML and JavaScript. The "webization" of components, or the availability of many IoT solutions, including AR, under a common web framework, is what allows us to envision the future.

Additionally, we must consider the features of AR content that are compatible with IoT devices because of the wide variety of IoT device kinds. This is comparable to the

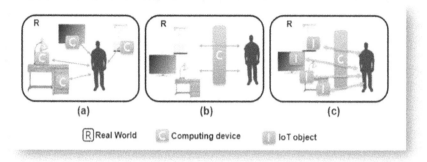

FIGURE 5.4 Human–computer interaction.

idea that settings for website elements differ across desktop and mobile computing platforms, it should be emphasized.

5.4.3 INTERNET OF THINGS

The Internet of Things is a term that portrays actual parts that are equipped with sensors, registering power, programming and other innovation – interface with different gadgets and frameworks through the web or different correspondence organizations and trade information with them.

Any ordinary or artificial object that can be assigned an IP address and transmit data over a network, including a person with a heart monitor implant, animals with a biochip transponder, a vehicle equipped with sensors to alert the driver when tire pressure is low, and beyond, can be collectively termed IoT devices. IoT-enabled devices and data centers are shown in Figure 5.5.

1. The IoT is a sensor network made up of billions of clever devices that connect people, systems and other initiatives to gather and share information.
2. The Web of Things (IoT) concept involves connecting any device with an on/off switch to the internet. This category includes nearly anything you can think of, such as cells, coffee makers, laundry washers, headphones, lighting, wearable technology and pretty much everything else. This also holds for machine additives, such as the drill on an oil rig or the jet engine of a plane.
3. The IoT is a sizable network of connected "matters" (which additionally consists of humans). The relationships between people, objects, and object-object connections could be related to dating.
4. The smart TV is the international market-leading consumer IoT tool. According to a Deloitte study, 25–35% of consumers worldwide have a TV that can connect to the internet. However, the IoT business is expanding quickly in other areas.

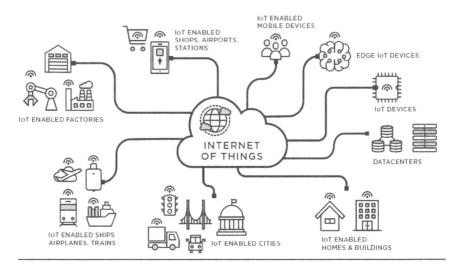

FIGURE 5.5   Overview of IoT.

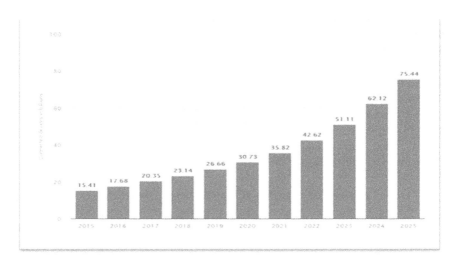

FIGURE 5.6   Growing demand for IoT.

Please refer Figure 5.6 to realize the growing demand for these gadgets in the near destiny. Some of the applications of IoT are shown in Figure 5.7.

5.5   TOP 10 KEY IOT ADVANCES AND PATTERNS: GARTNER

- **Pattern No. 1:** Man-made consciousness (artificial intelligence): "Information is the fuel that drives the IoT, and an organization's ability to derive meaning from it will shape their long-term success."

- **Pattern No. 2:** Social, lawful and moral IoT: These incorporate responsibility for and the consequences of the inferences made utilizing it, algorithmic inclination, security [6] and consistency with principles like the General Data Affirmation Rule. "Effective sending of an IoT arrangement requests that it's at this point not simply strong yet furthermore socially appropriate."
- **Pattern No. 3:** Infonomics and information broking: The possibility of Infonomics takes the adaptation of data comparatively by involving considering it to be an essential business endeavor resource for being recorded inside the corporate obligations. By 2023, the looking for and advancing of IoT measurements transforms into an essential piece of numerous IoT frameworks.
- **Pattern No. 4:** The shift from insightful edge to astute cross-section: The shift from incorporated and cloud to part models is pleasantly in progress inside the IoT space. These lattice models will allow extra adaptable, shrewd and responsive IoT frameworks – albeit habitually at the expense of extra intricacies.
- **Pattern No. 5:** IoT governance: As the IoT keeps on broadening, the requirement for an administrative structure that guarantees suitable direction in the presentation, carport, use and erasure of records connected with IoT [7] undertakings turns out to be increasingly fundamental.
- **Pattern No. 6:** Sensor advancement: The sensor market was expected to develop constantly through 2023. New sensors will allow a more extensive scope of circumstances and exercises to be recognized which could give a lot more extensive thought process.
- **Pattern No. 7:** Confided in equipment and working framework: By the year 2023, we anticipate examining the integration of hardware and software combinations that collectively create more reliable and secure IoT systems.
- **Pattern No. 8:** Novel IoT client encounters: Client appreciation pushed is through four elements: new sensors, new calculations, new revel in models and settings and socially cognizant surveys.

FIGURE 5.7 Applications of IoT.

- **Pattern No. 9:** Silicon chip advancement: By 2023, it's normal that new exceptional intention chips will reduce the strength utilization expected to run IoT gadgets.
- **Pattern No. 10:** New remote systems administration innovations for IoT: IoT organizing incorporates adjusting a bunch of contending necessities. In exact, they need to find 5G, the approaching close-to period of low earth circle satellites and backscatter networks.

5.6 OPTICAL WIRELESS COMMUNICATION

Wireless communications [8] are a kind of data communique this is done and added wirelessly. This is a wide term that includes all techniques and sorts of connecting and speaking among extra gadgets through wireless conversation technologies and gadgets. Figure 5.8 depicts three layers of the wireless network. In recent years, optical wireless communication (OWC) advances have drawn impressive exploration interest due to some of their magnificent capabilities. A remote network founded on the optical range is designated "OWC." OWC has wound up a decent integral innovation to radiofrequency (RF)-based remote advancements for future correspondence organizations, which incorporate fifth and sixth innovation (5G and 6G, individually) discussion frameworks. OWC innovations have various noticeable abilities comprehensive of the enormous range, unreasonable records cost, low dormancy, inordinate well-being, low worth and low power utilization, tending to the very upsetting necessities of 5G and then some 5GB correspondences.

The launch of the 6G verbal trade machine is expected to be somewhere in the range of 2027 and 2030. The 6G particularly has not yet been precisely analyzed; however, numerous scientists are dealing with it. Among the various investigations, issues are ability improvement, development inside the number of associations, idleness decrease, security improvement, energy execution advancement, individual QoE level upgrade and unwavering quality turn of events, which permits you to be tended to by utilizing each 5G and 6G correspondence structures. The 6G correspondence device is expected to be an overall correspondence office, with the transporter degree being various overlaps better when contrasted with 5G.

5.6.1 Benefits of Wireless Communication

- Remote organizations are less expensive to place in and keep.
- Information is communicated faster and at a high speed.
- Scaled-down security and establishment costs in contrast with other states of organizations.
- Remote organization can be gotten to from any place, without fail.

5.6.2 Applications of Wireless Communication

- Security structures.
- Television far-flung control, cell telephones.
- Wi-Fi and wireless [9] strength switch.
- Computer interface devices and various Wi-Fi communication-based total projects.

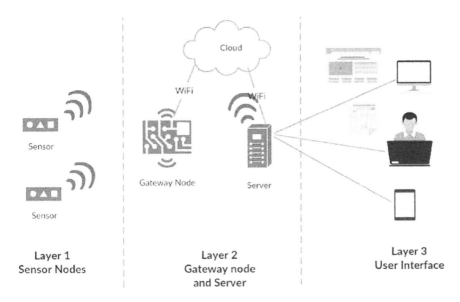

FIGURE 5.8 Layers of wireless network.

Going with the approach of remote systems administration and the Web of Things (IoT), regularly increased truth (AR) frameworks to envision virtual three-dimensional styles of this present reality are advancing into shrewd and intuitive AR connected with the set of variables for actual things. We propose the integration of AR and IoT [9] reciprocally, enabling AR to cover objects seamlessly with a satisfactory level of performance and interacting with IoT in a more cohesive manner. Identify three key elements for organizing this type of collaborative integration.

- Conveyed and object-driven realities control (comprehensive of AR administrations);
- IoT-directed observing;
- Consistent transaction and content interoperability.

As of late, increased truth (AR) and the Web of Things (IoT) have gotten immense interest as key permitting innovations for making spaces more intelligent and more prominent intuitive. AR is an interactive medium that provides a view of the real world augmented through spatially registering relevant computer-generated information. It permits people to figure out the world and intensifies their insight for fixing issues and breaking down genuine obligations. IoT alludes to an organization of real devices and customary things implanted with the least registering components for detecting, gathering, imparting or, in any event, connecting with the actual things. Such a foundation will give the premise to brilliant conditions through aggregate gigantic data examination and setting-based contributions.

5.7   WORKING PRINCIPLE OF VAR-IOT

The principal focus of the Visualization Augmented Reality System for IoT (VAR-IoT) is to supply a specific viewpoint depiction. This model is utilized in various AR-based applications in IoT affiliations, broad for normal IoT objects. The clients can have facilitated endeavors with automated genuine variables subordinating absolutely to authentic IoT objects. The proposed structure depends upon incorporated modules, intensive IoT and AR. The architecture of Var-IoT is shown in Figure 5.9.

The fundamental module depends absolutely upon sensor progressions for sorting out the IoT social class contraptions. The second AR module provides a three-layered visual representation of the extensive global surroundings. The proposed VAR-IoT structure has three modules: close-by IoT affiliation and encounters management, a parking spot module and an AR show and exchange module. The IoT network module is based on related gadgets with a 5G-based completely proposed neighborhood with side and coursed handling on the web associations. The clients use multi-cameras to picture any area of the floor or dispute envisions from fascinating spots. The cameras are right now in cells and contraptions in IoT affiliations. The actual functionalities of the parking spot module rely entirely on isolated experiences management, online data processing, and image processing levels. The isolated part checks as far as possible and readies the positions and course of the IoT gadget's mechanized camera. The separated module also gives the appraisal of the camera limits, which integrates superfluous and normal, after which finds out the overall ability and bearing between

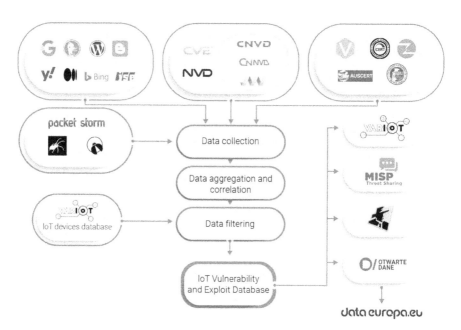

FIGURE 5.9   Var-IoT.

| Electric Control Sensors | Temperature Control Sensors | Security Cameras | Smart Locks Sensors | Glass Breakage Sensors |

FIGURE 5.10 Various sensors for IoT.

cameras. The web dealing with stage chooses the bits of knowledge of contraptions and their headings. The image dealing with module methods and the real factors converts them into three-layered virtual things and gives the AR yield. This module framework the body got from the electronic camera powers it into virtual things by using directions.

The IoT organization and realities handling module manage the cost of the associated gadgets, region and distributed computing on the web contributions. Users utilize multi-cameras to visualize any area of the floor or object within the vicinity from different perspectives. The correspondence strategy among IoT contraptions includes sensor focuses, PDAs, actuators and other control gadgets and the foundation. The IoT contraptions are mentioned into boss sorts: wonderful gadgets annexed with AR errands and sensor focuses to uncover and encounter the gifted home's regular components, for example, gas spillage, water spillage, gas strain and utility meter taking note. Figure 5.10 illustrates various sensor nodes, where several cameras are positioned within the vicinity, allowing individuals to visualize objects within their home from different locations. The headings of things are seen to offer an unmistakable depiction.

$$\text{Camera} = \begin{bmatrix} \text{Rotation} \\ \text{Translation} \end{bmatrix} \text{Projective Transformation}$$

There are three key components: distributed AR data on the board; object-oriented tracking; and location-based augmented reality (AR) integration, highlighting the subsequent benefits of combining IoT and AR. The potential integration of such elements serves as a catalyst for intelligent and intuitive AR services. The AR management patron cooperates straightforwardly with the IoT item of hobby within the set-off vicinity and, upon the association, quickly gets putting huge AR datasets (for following or redid administration content). Depending on the specific context, relevant and available services, such as basic product information displays, equipment management, or instructional guides, are presented in their authentic form. This can be achieved through various means, including a portable graphical user interface (GUI), AR glasses, mobile AR, voice commands, spatially registered AR, or simple overlays, facilitating interaction.

5.8   DRIVING KINDS OF IOT REMOTE TECH AND THEIR BEST USE CASES

5.8.1   LOW-POWER WIDE AREA NETWORKS

Low-Power Wide Area Networks (LPWANs) are fresh out of the new peculiarity in IoT. By offering long-range correspondence on little, more affordable batteries that are extreme for quite a long time, this own group of innovations is reason-developed to help huge-scope IoT networks rambling over significant modern and business grounds. LPWANs can in a real sense join all types of IoT sensors – working with a few bundles from resource following, ecological observing and office of the executives to inhabitance identification and consumables checking. A few bundles incorporate consumables following, natural checking, inhabitance location and resource following.

- Additionally, it's basic to see that LPWANs envelop extraordinary innovations and contending norms. Instances of LPWAN advancements in the confirmed range are LTE-M and NB-IoT, and working in the unlicensed range incorporates Sigfox, MY THINGS and LoRa.
- Different LPWAN advancements have unmistakable scopes of by and large execution in unique circumstances. For instance, adaptability and nature of administration can be huge issues with unlicensed innovation and power admission for ensured LPWANs. Make certain to consider the normalization of the LPWANs to guarantee your IoT people's security, unwavering quality and interoperability.

Working Principle

A low-strength immense locale local area (LPWAN) or low-strength wide-district (LPWA) organization or low-energy organization (LPN) is a sort of remote telecom broad area network intended to allow extended territory interchanges at a low digit rate among things (associated devices), comprising of sensors working on a battery. The low power, low piece charge and expected use recognize this type of organization from a remote WAN that is intended to join clients or organizations and bring additional insights, the utilization of more prominent strength. The LPWAN realities cost goes from 0.3 Kbit/s to 50 Kbit/s reliably with the channel. An LPWAN might be utilized to make a confidential remote sensor organization, yet will likewise be a transporter or foundation provided by utilizing the third festival, allowing the owners of sensors to convey them in the discipline without making an interest in passage data transfer capacity.

LPWANs are commonly employed in various applications, including smart metering, smart lighting, asset tracking and monitoring, smart cities, precision agriculture, energy management, manufacturing, and other industrial IoT solutions.

Advantages
- Low power usage;
- Low costs/long-lasting batteries;

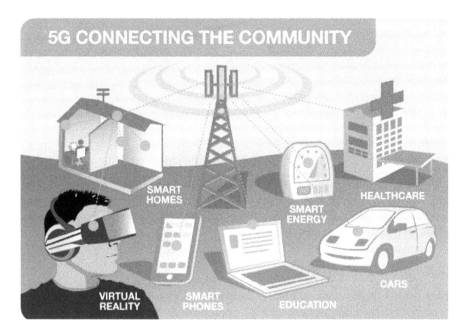

FIGURE 5.11 5G connecting the community.

- Long-distance communications;
- Low number of gateways and free radio spectrum.

5.8.2 3G/4G/5G

An overview of the 5G network is shown in Figure 5.11. Well established within the customer cellular marketplace, the mobile [10] community gives dependable broadband and dispatches supporting different voice calls and video web-based programs. On the drawback, they force particularly high utilitarian expenses and energy necessities. While cell networks are not reachable for most of the people of IoT packs energized by battery-worked sensor associations, they coordinate fittingly in careful use cases alongside associated vehicles or fleet control in transportation and systems. For instance, in-auto infotainment, site visitors coordinating, unparalleled primary catalyst help structures (ADAS), close-by fleet telematics and noticing commitments can all rely on unavoidable and high exchange speed versatile accessibility.

5.8.3 Zigbee and Other Cross-section Convention

Zigbee is a short-range, low-power, wireless technology commonly deployed in mesh topology to extend coverage by relaying sensor data across multiple sensor nodes. Compared to LPWAN, Zigbee offers better data rates, but at the same time, it exhibits significantly lower power efficiency due to its mesh nature. In view of their real fast reach (<100 m), Zigbee and relative grid shows (e.g., Z-wave, string, etc.) are the best

FIGURE 5.12   Bluetooth communication between devices.

for medium-range IoT applications with an even scattering of center points in proximity. Ordinarily, Zigbee is an amazing enhancement to Wi-Fi for various home computerization use events like smart lighting establishments, focal air controls, security and energy control and so on.

5.8.4   BLUETOOTH AND BLE

Characterized in the class of Remote Individual Region Organizations, Bluetooth has a speedy reach correspondence time appropriately positioned inside the buyer commercial center. Bluetooth Classic was initially designed for point-to-point or point-to-multipoint (up to seven slave nodes) data exchange among user devices. Communication between Bluetooth devices is shown in Figure 5.12. Optimized for power consumption, Bluetooth Low Energy (BLE) was later introduced to address short-range consumer IoT applications. These days, BLE is generally combined into well-being and clinical wearables in addition to Shrewd Household gadgets.

The Bluetooth popular, similar to Wi-Fi, utilizes the FHSS strategy (Recurrence Jumping Spread Range), which incorporates parting the recurrence band of 2.402–2.480 GHz into 79 channels (alluded to bounces), each 1 MHz broad. Then, at that point, it communicates the sign utilizing a grouping of channels perceived to each sending and getting station. The Bluetooth stylish is basically founded on an expert/slave functional mode. The time span piconet is utilized to allude to the organization shaped by one gadget and all contraptions saw inside its reach. Up to 10 piconets can coincide inside a solitary inclusion area.

An expert can at the same time associate with as many as seven fiery slave gadgets (255 while in stopped mode). Gadgets in a piconet have a consistent location of three pieces, for a limit of eight contraptions. Gadgets in stopped mode are synchronized yet do not on their own substantially manage inside the piconet. As a general rule, at a given second, the grip device can be connected to a solitary slave immediately. Accordingly, it speedy switches among slaves so one can cause it to appear as though it's far simultaneously associated with all the slave devices. Bluetooth grants piconets to be connected to one another so you can frame a lot more extensive organization, alluded to as a scatternet, the use of positive devices which go about as a scaffold among the two piconets.

Benefits
- It evades obstruction from other remote gadgets.

- It has lower power utilization and is effectively upgradable.
- It has better range compared to infrared correspondence.
- It is utilized for voice and information movement.

Applications
- In PCs, scratch pad and remote PCPC, cell phones and PDAs (individual advanced collaborator);
- In printers, remote headsets, personal area networks (PANs), and even LANs (neighborhood) to move information records, recordings and pictures.

5.8.5 Wi-Fi

The approach of Wi-Fi is clearly shown in Figure 5.13. There is a compelling need to give a clarification for Wi-Fi [11], given its fundamental situation in offering high-throughput measurements switch for both organization and homegrown conditions. Notwithstanding, in the IoT region, its fundamental snags in inclusion, versatility and power consumption make the innovation an extraordinary arrangement significantly less ordinary. Forcing extreme energy necessities, Wi-Fi is consistently as of now not a reasonable answer for colossal organizations of battery-worked IoT sensors, particularly in modern IoT and sharp structure situations. All things considered, it more relates to associating contraptions that might be helpfully connected to an energy outlet like shrewd home gadgets and home hardware, computerized marks or security cameras.

FIGURE 5.13   Wi-Fi strategy.

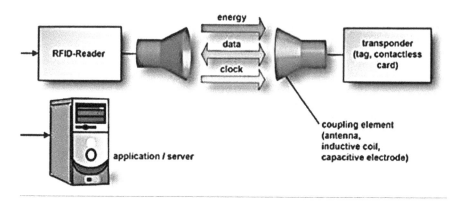

FIGURE 5.14 Working model of RFID.

5.8.6 Radio Frequency Identification

Radio Frequency Identification (RFID) utilizes radio waves to send modest quantities of data from a RFID tag to a peruser inside an exceptionally brief distance. The working Model of RFID is depicted in Figure 5.14. Till now, it has worked with an essential transformation in retail and coordinated operations. By attaching RFID tags to various items and systems, companies can track their inventory and assets in real-time, resulting in improved inventory management, production planning, and streamlined supply chain control.

The RFID IoT unrest empowers new IoT programs, along with shrewd mirrors, savvy cupboards and self-checkout, in the retail district. For medical care, RFID enables IoT applications such as patient tracking in healthcare facilities, automated inventory management, and tracking and management of expensive hospital equipment.

RFID has a spot with a party of improvement intimated as Programmed ID and Information Catch (AIDC). AIDC strategies definitely become mindful of devices, collect information about them and enter the data straightforwardly into PC structures with close to no human intervention. RFID strategies use radio waves to play out this. At a crucial degree, RFID structures incorporate three segments: an RFID tag or sagacious name, an RFID peruser and a radio wire. RFID names contain a planned circuit and a receiving wire, which may be utilized to confer genuine elements to the RFID peruse. The peruser then changes the radio waves over absolutely to an additional usable sort of records. Data collected from the imprints is then transmitted through a communication interface to a number of devices, such as computers, where the data can be stored in a database and analyzed later on.

RFID Tags and Smart Labels

The defensive material relies upon the application. RFID labels arrive in different shapes and sizes and are either uninvolved or dynamic. Inactive labels are the most generally utilized, as they are more modest and more affordable to execute. Inactive labels should be "controlled up" by the RFID peruser before they can communicate information. Dissimilar to inactive labels, dynamic RFID labels have an installed power supply (e.g., a battery), in this manner empowering them to communicate information consistently with RFID.

Advantages
- Following resources and overseeing stock and setting-aside time and cash through computerization;
- Further developing information exactness and accessibility and upgrading well-being and security;
- Better control of creation and upgraded quality and detectability and expanded incomes.

Applications
Inventory management, asset tracking, personnel tracking, controlling access to restricted areas, ID badging, supply chain management, and counterfeit prevention (e.g., in the pharmaceutical industry) are all common applications of RFID technology.

5.9 AR, INSTALLATION AND MAINTENANCE

AR is the actual-time use of facts, consisting of textual content, pics, audio and digital improvements integrated with real global gadgets, to be displayed on a head-established display. When a maintenance technician acquires new skills for maintenance and assembly, they can be very complex and challenging. AR can assist the technician by providing instant access to remote experts when necessary. AR can also manually carry out maintenance responsibilities on system elements that want to be processed. It needs to gain knowledge in various skills, which is vital for acquisition and renovation. AR is appropriate for this kind of aspect. It enables trustworthy communique between technicians running on a vessel anywhere in the world of engineers.

5.10 FUTURE OF IOT IN INDIA

The IoT [12] can bring the following business revolution, rework society and set up a new atmosphere to serve no longer just humans but humanity. In an IoT-enabled globe, people will get hold of uniquely personalized services on demand, even as societies will gain from optimized useful resource use with minimal effect on the surroundings.

- **Speed:** 5G may be ten times quicker in comparison to modern LTE networks. The commercial achievement of IoT relies upon its performance. 5G data transfer will grow its speed. It will allow communication faster than ever with different IoT gadgets, smartphones and capsules, software within the form of its app or internet site and so on.
- **Connectivity**: A steady and regular network will bring greater productivity to the IoT gadget. 5G networks can be more reliable to establish extra stable

connections. Connected gadgets will get real-time updates especially electronic locks, protection cameras and other tracking structures. IoT surroundings ready with 5G internet carriers will ruin the stereotype. It will enhance the infrastructure and bridge the gap between rural and urban areas.

- **Agriculture**: AI-powered IoT mechanisms will enhance agricultural [8] control. The environmental sensors and facts will help farmers predict what is coming their way. 5G-connected farming devices will maximize crop yields with minimum use of water, pesticides and fertilizers.
- **Healthcare**: Healthcare can be extra useful with 5G network connectivity. Health wearables can be more effective in supporting alarm fitness troubles at hazard. It will enhance the great of telemedicine offerings. Similarly, stay transmission of excessive-definition surgery videos can be remotely monitored. 5G will bring meaningful capability to patients and their medical doctors.
- **Automotive**: 5G will notably improve the automobile enterprise, for instance, driverless motors or connected automobiles. This works with the aid of the augmented fact (AR) and digital reality (VR) era. Certainly it will decorate community-facilitated communication for self-sustaining driving and enhance vehicular communication services as nicely. As an end result, there will be blessings that include vehicle convenience and protection, averting injuries, coordinated use and real-time nearby updates.
- **Communications**: The verbal exchange carriers will put up wireless broadband as opposed to fiber networks. Therefore, it's going to substantially lessen fees. AR and VR generation will alternate the consumer revel in gaming, e-trade and other consumer-centric programs. Consumer revel may be revolutionized as low latency and high facts prices might be achieved.
- **Security**: 5G will transform the college security systems. 24x7 live monitoring may be completed with no buffering. It will equip the steady records switch. As a result, it will tighten up safety. It will be very beneficial to government administration and protection companies.
- **Smart Cities**: The cities will become smart and techno-advanced. For instance, sensors and huge facts will offer more green visitor management. The waste control device turns extra obvious. When a certain threshold is reached, the waste container receives a degree sensor. So the control platform of a truck driving force receives a notification on the phone. It avoids half-empty drains. The wireless technology will assist motors to talk with one another and civic infrastructure.

5.11 CONCLUSION

This chapter gives the perception of the terms augmented reality, IoT and wireless communications. Likewise uncovers the applications and the benefits of those arising advancements. Reconciliation of these three innovations supports the significant applications, for example, LPWANs, Wi-Fi, developing 4G/5G/6G organizations,

RFID, Bluetooth and so on. Increased reality-empowered Web of Things for remote specialized gadgets have been the primary setting and upheld with significant applications like LPWANs, Wi-Fi, advancing 4G/5G/6G organizations, RFID, Bluetooth and BLE and ZigBee and other cross-section conventions alongside their working, applications and benefits. Expanded reality (AR) and the Web of Things (IoT) are moving advancements and could upset the resulting innovation of business items. Different scientists and business associations expand applications and devices for the shrewd homes and savvy urban communities. AR tracking for everyday items and direct control-based AR interaction for substantial issues are categorized based on the three key components. Additionally, we explored current AR bundles and exhorted future possibilities related with IoT contraptions. All in all, when utilized correctly, Augmented Reality-enabled IoT could be the cornerstone of managing various sectors, ultimately leading to the digitization of the entire world.

REFERENCES

[1] Jo, D.; Kim. G. J. Local context-based recognition + Internet of Things: Complementary infrastructures for future generic mixed reality space. In Proceedings of the 21st ACM Symposium on Virtual Reality Software and Technology, Beijing, 2015.

[2] White, G.; Cabrara, C.; Palade, A.; Clarke, S. Augmented reality in IoT. In Proceedings of the 8th International Workshop on Context-Aware and IoT Services, Zhejiang, 2018.

[3] Phupattanasilp, P.; Tong, S. Augmented reality in the integrative Internet of Things (IoT): Application for precision farming. MDPI Sustainability, 2019, 11(9), 1–17.

[4] Gimenez, R.; Pous, M. Augmented reality as an enabling factor for the Internet of Things. In W3C Workshop: Augmented Reality on the Web, Barcelona, 2010.

[5] Radkowski, R. Augmented reality to supplement work instructions. In Model-Based Enterprise Summit, Gaithersburg, 2013.

[6] Chokkanathan, K.; Shanmugaraja, P.; Ramasamy, S. S.; Ouncharoen, R.; Chakpitak, N. A survey on role of blockchain in smart cities. International Journal of Computer Science and Network Security, 2021, 21(7), 1–7. https://doi.org/10.22937/IJC SNS.2021.21.7.1.

[7] Shanmugaraja, P.; Chokkanathan, K.; Ramasamy, S. S.; Nandakumar, S. D. A smart robotic based garbage/sewage management system using IoT. Turkish Journal of Physiotherapy and Rehabilitation, 2021, 32(3), 3510–3514.

[8] Ramasamy, S. S. Sustainable development in agriculture through information and communication technology (ICT) for smarter India: Sustainable agricultural development through ICT in India. International Journal of Social Ecology and Sustainable Development, 2021, 12(3), 79–87. https://doi.org/10.4018/IJSESD.2021070106.

[9] Ramasamy, S. S.; Suyaroj, N.; Chakpitak, N. Forest protection by fire detection, alarming, messaging through IoT, blockchain and digital technologies in Thailand Chiang Mai Forest Range. In International Conference on Data Science, Computation and Security, Lavasa, 2022.

[10] Muller, L.; Aslan, I.; Krußen, L. GuideMe: A mobile augmented reality system to display user manuals for home appliances. In Proceedings of the 10th International Conference on Advances in Computer Entertainment, Twente, 2013.

[11] Park, Y.; Yun, S.; Kim, K. When IoT met augmented reality: Visualizing the source of the wireless signal in AR view. In Proceedings of the 17th Annual International Conference on Mobile System, Applications, and Services, Seoul, 2019.

[12] Lee, S.; Lee, G.; Choi, G.; Roh, B.; Kang, J. Integration of OneM2M-based IoT service platform and mixed reality device. In Proceedings of IEEE International Conference on Consumer Electronics, Las Vegas, 2019.

6 Organic Computing in Cyber-Physical Systems

Ezhilarasan K and Jeevarekha A

6.1 INTRODUCTION

Nature is always fascinating and we the humans are always obsessed with the elegant and linearly organized process of nature. But the real world is greatly complex and nonlinear beyond our thoughts. To understand the dynamics of a natural process, it has to be modelled into dynamical equations. The more the number of interconnected variables in the equation, the more the complexity. Solving such a system with a high degree of complexity is quite a herculean task even by computational methods. However, this does not limit us in the exploration of complex systems. The advent of high-speed computers and development in Information and Communication Technology (ICT) facilitates the understanding of natural processes and harnesses the pragmatic applicability of the same for the betterment of society. The design of several controlling systems is indeed inspired by natural processes. The upgraded versions of controlling systems make our day-to-day life easier and more comfortable.

Computers though started as mere calculation devices now rule over the world. The discovery of microcontrollers/processors was another milestone in the history of humans. Broadly, computers can be categorized based on their performance and applications.

They are information processors and embedded systems as illustrated in Figure 6.1. Information processors process the data and deliver the output. Our laptops, desktops and supercomputers are examples of information-processing systems. Such information processors are designed to perform multiple tasks, whereas embedded systems are hardware systems instructed to perform specific tasks at a fixed time routine.

6.1.1 EMBEDDED SYSTEMS

Based on the performance, embedded systems can be categorized into four types, as shown in Figure 6.2 [1].

DOI: 10.1201/9781003248545-6

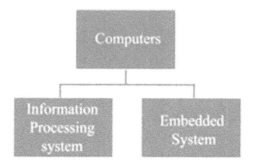

FIGURE 6.1   General classification of computation devices.

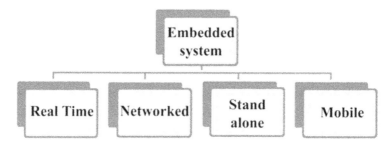

FIGURE 6.2   Functional classification of the embedded system.

a. Real-Time Embedded System

These systems are designed to provide the output within the specified time limit. A well-known example of Real-Time Embedded System (RTES) is the traffic control system. The sign and colour of the traffic signal have to change or remain for a particular duration according to the volume of vehicles crossing the particular road. In those cases, embedded systems have to react to the situation without much time delay; otherwise it might lead to accidents.

b. Standalone Embedded System

Embedded systems that are capable of working independently are called standalone systems. This kind of embedded systems does not require the approval of the host system to operate. Some of the notable examples of this standalone embedded system are automated washing machines, calculators and so on.

c. Networked Embedded System

Embedded systems that are capable of communicating via the network are called networked embedded systems. In this type, embedded systems are connected to a central hub. Therefore, the connected nodes can either communicate with each other or with the server. For example, in an ATM, after withdrawing a certain amount of money, the information about the balance amount will be updated via the network to all other ATMs.

d. Mobile Embedded System

Mobile embedded systems are simple, portable and easy to use. Some examples of mobile embedded systems are MP3 players, mobile phones and so on.

6.1.2 CHARACTERISTICS OF EMBEDDED SYSTEM

Irrespective of the classification, all embedded systems should possess the following important characteristics. Some of the salient features are highlighted in Figure 6.3.

- It is well known that embedded systems are hardware systems designed using microcontrollers/microprocessors to perform the assigned task. Instructions that are coded within embedded systems cannot be altered by the user. Hence, embedded systems perform a particular task repeatedly over a period.
- Peripherals are used to connect input and output devices in the embedded system.
- Embedded systems should possess the ability to sense the changes in the environment and communicate them to the peripherals, thereby real-time decisions can be made by the system.
- Embedded systems should consume less power and operate with high efficiency.

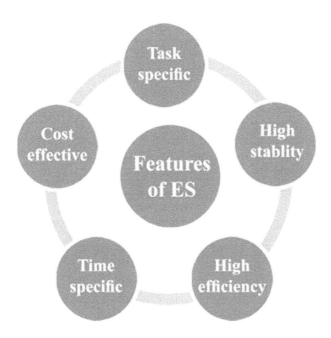

FIGURE 6.3   Salient features of embedded system.

- Embedded systems are designed to do their jobs within a short period/ prespecified time. Decisions should be made faster; otherwise it might lead to unwanted events. The importance of faster response can be realized in the traffic control system. The late response might lead to brutal accidents.
- Most of the embedded systems require fewer user interactions, that is, the machine will be highly automated so that no or fewer user interfaces was required.
- Few embedded systems are designed to work based on external impacts as in Global Positioning System (GPS).
- Reduction in user interaction makes the embedded systems more reliable and stable. Hence most embedded systems work for a long time without any failure; in other words, the lifespan of embedded systems gets increased.

6.1.3 APPLICATIONS OF EMBEDDED SYSTEM

Embedded systems can be found almost in every field and it has many diverse applications starting from household application to medical/healthcare and defence application [2,3]. Among all other applications, the industrial application is quite phenomenal as it even leads to the Industrial Revolution (IR) 4.0. Figure 6.4 explains various versions of the Industrial Revolution and the role of embedded systems in IR.

As realized in Figure 6.4, the introduction of embedded systems created a buzz in the industrial sector as it increased productivity, safety and energy efficiency and considerably reduced the time duration and power. We are now in the realm of Industrial Revolution 4.0 [4] and this chapter is devoted to discussing Cyber-Physical Systems (CPS) which are responsible for IR4.0.

6.2 CYBER-PHYSICAL SYSTEM

The upgraded version of the network-embedded system is the CPS. The CPS integrates communication-enabled computation on devices with the physical components [5]. Here, physical components refer to interactive systems that are capable of sensing and reacting to the external environment. In other terms, CPS are networked embedded systems with sensors and actuators controlled by cyber components. Since CPS are still in the developing zone, there is no strict layout for the design of CPS [6]. Figure 6.5 explains the basic components of a CPS.

IR1.0	IR2.0	IR3.0	IR4.0
Machines operated using stream power	Machine powered with electricity and oil	Introduction of automated embedded systems	Fully automated Cyber Physical Systems

FIGURE 6.4　Versions of the Industrial Revolution.

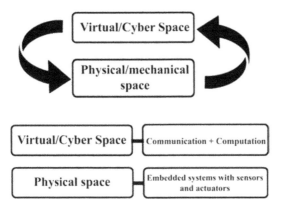

FIGURE 6.5 Basic structure of the cyber-Physical System.

In the structure, virtual space/cyber components refer to devices that are capable of computing, storing and communicating the data/information, whereas physical components comprise embedded systems that are capable of sensing the variation in the environment.

The image depicts a diagram illustrating the relationship between virtual/cyber space and physical/mechanical space. It highlights the interplay between the two realms and their influence on each other. The image effectively conveys the interconnectedness of virtual/cyber space and physical space. It underscores that the physical world is not isolated from the digital realm, but rather intertwined through the presence of embedded systems and the exchange of data and information.

6.2.1 Cyberspace

Computation and communication are important aspects of cyber components. Different network protocols such as 3G/4G technology, Wi-Fi and GPS can be accessed by cyber components in cyberspace for communication. Such a network system should be highly secure and fast. In addition to communication, cps systems should be able to store the data collected from physical components. The data thus collected from the components of a physical system are stored either in cloud storage or in local servers. The data storage setup should be equipped with vast database management features, faster recovery of files after disaster and safety. For monitoring and controlling the dynamics of physical processors, SQL queries and data manipulation technologies are used [5].

6.2.2 Physical Space

An embedded system with sensors and actuators forms the physical components. The data collected by sensors or tracking devices are transmitted to local storage systems. Actuators that are part of the physical system change the output state as dictated by the microcontrollers [7].

6.2.3 Characteristics of CPS

There is no particular CPS architecture and research is still in progress to find the optimal design for CPS. However, while modelling CPS, the following important points have to be considered.

- The integration of physical and cyber components enables self-learning and self-adaptation of CPS.
- The instruction given in the controller can be reconfigured concerning the response of the environment, through feedback loops.
- Every physical component should be empowered with communication capabilities.
- Time and space location of different physical components has to be synchronized with the information systems properly as it is crucial for real-time operation.

6.2.4 Applications of CPS

There are ample applications of CPS and some of the important applications are in agriculture, transportation, aerospace and so on as given in Figure 6.6

a. Transportation

With the growth in the human population, the number of the vehicle gets also increased. Hence parameters like air pollution, traffic issues and safety details have to be taken care of for sophisticated and safe rides. With the support of CPS aided

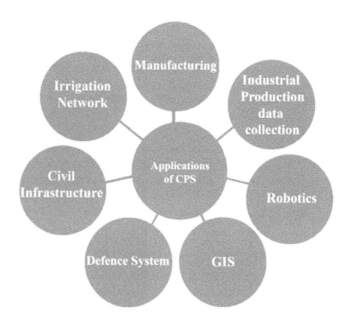

FIGURE 6.6 Applications of the Cyber-Physical System.

with intervehicle sensing and computing techniques, secured travel can be assured. As CPS is best at finding the route, traffic congestion can be avoided and thus it saves time for users. CPS is very much useful in air traffic management as well.

b. Agriculture

CPS enables constant monitoring of soil health, moisture and temperature of the agricultural land. Thus, it helps in monitoring the condition/nature of soil from the sowing of seeds to harvesting. This reduces crop wastage and ensures high yields to meet the growing demand of human populations.

c. Medical Science

Instead of standalone devices in the medical field, communication-enabled physical devices can monitor and get a full picture of a patient's health conditions from multiple sensors and be able to get a whole picture of the health issue accurately. Since CPS are capable of making decisions from the data collected from the current health state and symptoms of the patients, long-term health conditions can be predicted and many diseases can be identified earlier. Thus, in the medical field, CPS is used in the following aspects:

- to improve the functioning of medical devices, and
- to acquire an accurate and sensible health picture of patients.

d. Smart Grid

To meet the growing need for electricity, the smart grid provides better solutions. The self-deciding networked systems manage and monitor the electricity need and provide supply accordingly thereby saving electricity for future generations.

e. Geo-Information System

In the Geo-Information System (GIS), CPS is used in various ways to improve urban area development. IoT and GIS are integrated with CPS for the development and management of urban areas.

6.2.5 CHALLENGES IN CPS

Providing a unified framework that amalgamates the theory of network and physical resources is much more tedious and still is in the development process. Some factors like noise measurement, stability and perturbation in the environment have to be considered for the calculation/computation process. However, transforming these physical requirements for computation purposes is not an easy task for computer scientists and engineers.

- The First challenge faced by the researchers is to establish spatial and temporal synchronization between the computation process and the physical process. Once synchronization is achieved, physical processes can easily be controlled by networked embedded systems that are real-time decisions that can be taken by CPS.

- The Second challenge is to increase the robustness, efficiency and quality of sensors to make them cover a large range of areas.
- CPS are easily prone to cyber threats and malicious attacks as it has lots of access points. Closed loop operations in CPS reduce minor faults and errors. That is while using open loop software, the entire system may get failed because of a small mistake and therefore feedback system has to adopt.
- Another challenge is to ensure the maximum level of safety while thinking of safety-critical applications like autonomous vehicle drivers with fewer cars.
- Ongoing research focuses on the way of protecting the information/data from the sensors and also on the identity of the owner. CPS has to restrict unauthorized usage of the same.
- CPS system has to guarantee that there exist clear taxonomies, protocols and reasons to protect the particular devices from cyber threats or from central productive devices trying to be a part of the network.
- Once all their challenges are addressed the full potential of CPS will be identified and a lot more applications can be harnessed.

Organic Computing (OC) provides a better and more efficient solution to fare all the abovementioned challenges.

Scientists trust that OC provides an efficient solution to the problems addressed in the previous section. OC does not imply the usage of organic material in the designing of electronic instruments instead it denotes high automated computing system. OC enables systems to be highly adaptive, efficient, reliable and secure.

6.3   ORGANIC COMPUTING

The term Organic Computing was initially coined by the members of the "Computer Architecture" group in the German Science Society in the year 2002 in a workshop. Later on, it was used in club fields like neuroscience, molecular biology and software engineering. But as previously mentioned, OC has no connection with living things rather it refers to systems that are capable of organizing themselves in response to the environment.

6.3.1   CHARACTERISTICS OF OC

OC refers to systems that possess the following characteristics:

- Systems should configure themselves so that is should be able to modify the parameters. This property is referred to as self-adaptation.
- The system should be able to change its relations with other subsystems thereby changing the system's structure. Briefly, it should possess self-organization property.

- OC should be able to diagnose and heal failures by communicating with other systems and sensors. This property is termed a self-healing property.
- System should be able to detect cyber threats thereby protecting the systems from hackers.
- OC should be able to stabilize even after the continuous influence of subsystems. This property is called a self-stabilizing property.

In addition to the abovementioned property, OC should exhibit some other properties such as self-integration, self-management, self-optimization and self-explaining behaviours. However, the central problem in designing reconfigurable hardware is to predict a good reconfiguration strategy. The self-organized decision-making skills of termites, ants and honeybees are a great inspiration for designers. Though behaviours of individuals are simple, their self-organizing behaviour while functioning as a colony for colony-building, and trail-laying behaviour while food searching, is highly complex. Several clustering algorithms and optimization techniques were inspired by the biological model's emergent behaviour.

6.4   OC FOR CPS

The principle of OC is mainly used to solve complex tasks safely and securely. CPS systems have to be self-optimized to protect systems against security threats. Some of the research trends that incorporate OC techniques to CPS are as follows.

- The research work [8] focuses on protecting CPS that are easily prone to different ways of threats in sensor networks, control layers of CPS and human interface layers. Several ideas were proposed to strengthen various layers in the architecture of the CPS creation layer, cognition layer and social layers. Each layer is optimized to improve the functionality of the system at a major level.
- Raphael Maas [9] adopted Organic Robot control architectures (ORCA) to CPS to make them highly automated. In ORCA each subsystem is assigned a certain task and by combining these tasks, complex functionality of the system can be obtained. Each subsystem is monitored and modified by another subsystem to enhance and optimize the performance of the system in a decentralized manner.
- Empowering each system with communication and self-optimization capabilities makes the entire system self-organized and automated thus making these systems suitable for solving complex problems. This form of self-optimization was inspired by the behaviour of social insects like ants, bees, termites etc.
- OC can be used for faster image processing. Marching Pixel (MP) approach is used to unravel emergent algorithms from parallel array arrangement of pixel processor elements.
- Self-organized intervehicle communication which is a form of OC has been proposed in traffic management to identify traffic jams.
- Researchers work on Organic Traffic control (OTC) to develop self-learning and self-optimization capabilities in the controller architecture. This is vital because traffic light controllers need to respond quickly according to the changes in the traffic pattern [10].

- Another predominant application of OC is in the field of mobile robotics. Inspired by the functioning of the human nervous system and immune systems, robots were designed with the ability to react faster to external stimulation.

6.5 CONCLUSION

CPS that integrate cyberspace and physical space started to revalorize the world because of their immense capabilities. However, combining two heterogeneous systems is not an easy task and there are plenty of technical difficulties that have to be addressed by the researchers for the successful designing of a CPS. Some of the important properties of OC systems like self-optimization, self-adaptation and self-organization techniques should be seeded in the CPS to make them highly automated, reliable and safe. However, finding the optimal algorithm at various stages of architecture is quite difficult and researchers are constantly working on those challenges to fill out the gaps in OC.

REFERENCES

[1] Jabeen, Q., et al. 2016. A Survey: Embedded Systems Supporting by Different Operating Systems. arXiv:1610.07899.
[2] Marwedel, P. 2011. *Embedded Systems Foundations of Cyber-Physical Systems. 2nd* edition. Springer Science.
[3] Kopetz, H. 2019. *Simplicity Is a Complex Foundation of Cyber-Physical Systems Design*. Springer.
[4] Manavalan, E., Jayakrishna, K. 2019. A Review of Internet of Things (IoT) Embedded Sustainable Supply Chain for Industry 4.0 Requirements. *Computers & Industrial Engineering*. 127:925–953.
[5] Al-Ali, A. R., et al. 2018. Cyber-Physical Systems' Role in Manufacturing Technologies. AIP Conference Proceedings. 1957:050007. https://doi.org/10.1063/1.5034337.
[6] Balas, V. E., et al. 2020. *A Handbook of Internet of Things in Biomedical and Cyber Physical System*, vol. 165. Springer Intelligent Systems Reference Library.
[7] Yang Liu, Y., et al. 2017. Review on Cyber-Physical Systems. IEEE/CAA Journal of Automatica Sinica. 4(1):27–40. https://doi.org/10.1109/JAS.2017.7510349.
[8] Hahner, J., et al. 2013. A Concept for Securing Cyber-Physical Systems with Organic Computing Techniques. 26th International Conference on Architecture of Computing Systems. 2013:1–13.
[9] Maas, R., et al. 2012. *Applying the Organic Robot Control Architecture (ORCA) to Cyber-Physical Systems*. 38th Euromicro Conference on Software Engineering and Advanced Applications. 250–257. https://doi.org/10.1109/SEAA.2012.74.
[10] Zeadally, S., Jabeur, N. 2016. *Cyber-Physical System Design with Sensors Networking Technologies*. Control, Robotics and Sensors Series 96. The Institution of Engineering Technology.

7 Granular Computing for Bio-Inspired IoT Networks

Kalaichelvi N, Mageshwari V,
Charanya Nagammal T and Gayathri SP

7.1 INTRODUCTION

Network technologies are blooming globally to meet the increasing needs in building communication, industries, businesses and government. The Internet of things (IoT) is an emerging technology that participates more in recent communication, mobility and monitoring needs [1]. It enables connection not only between human beings but also between nonliving organisms. For example, the water level of a dam can be intimated to a system connected via the internet. Thus, IoT is widely in use for smart systems that connect a huge number of devices and applications via the internet [2]. IoT can be involved in varieties of applications like monitoring the movements of a rare kind of animal from a remote city, using sensors, actuators, processors, applications and smart devices like mobile phones connected via an IoT gateway as shown in Figure 7.1 [3–5].

IoT technology was introduced with the idea of making information available online. But in recent days it has evolved to keep things connected online and provide services online. It includes devices like biological creatures, home appliances and even a street light like any object with a monitoring system. It can be applied to various applications like agriculture, home appliances, security systems, monitoring systems, smart city development, healthcare systems, manufacturing industries, energy sectors and education [6,7]. The wide usage of this technology is because of its quality to automate things with web-enabled sensors and smart devices. The data created by the sensors are uploaded and maintained in the cloud that can be accessed by the devices connected to the IoT network via the internet. Thus, the generated large data can be processed using big data analytics or AI. Even though it is automatic, humans can intervene to set or reset the devices manually based on the application involved.

7.2 GRANULAR COMPUTING

Granular computing (GC) is an innovative technology that integrates multiple views and components from different fields. It has been viewed as multidisciplinary innovation as it facilitates solving real-world problems by providing a systematic and

DOI: 10.1201/9781003248545-7

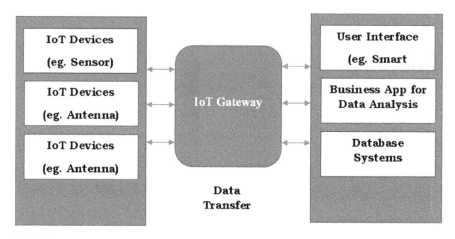

FIGURE 7.1   An IoT system.

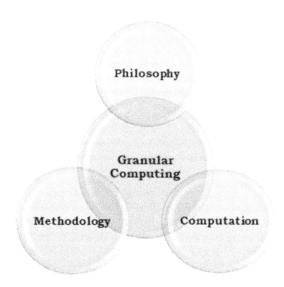

FIGURE 7.2   Perspectives of GC.

natural way of analyzing and understanding. GC changes the way of thinking and problem-solving to more practical and philosophical levels [8].

It provides the model for information processing, in which the information is divided into information granules. Different authors gave their views on GC. Yao views the triarchic theory of GC as a structured process of thinking within the philosophical perception, problem-solving from methodological perception and data processing from computational perception, as shown in Figure 7.2 [9].

GC can also be considered a supporting platform from conceptual and algorithmic perception for the study and design of human-centric intelligent systems, claim Bargiela and Pedrycz.

Fuzzy sets initiate information processing as human-centered. This paves the way to develop GC in different aspects. Among the research trends of GC, the shift from machine-centered approaches to human-centered approaches plays the main role. The rough set can also be incorporated into GC as per the view of Skowron and Stepaniuk. The syntax, semantics and operations of information granules can be modeled through rough approximations.

The most important issue for solving a problem in GC is granulation. Zadeh defines two major operations in GC; they are granulation and organization. According to him, "Granulation is the process of decomposing the whole into separate granules and Organization is the process of integrating the granules as a whole." This definition was taken as an argument to conclude that granulation itself can be defined as the process of both construction and decay. The construction process involves building a larger and higher level of granules, which is a bottom-up approach. Similarly, the process of segmenting greater granules into minor and lower-level granules is supposed to be decomposition, which is a top-down approach. There are applications in which both construction and decomposition go hand in hand. In such applications, if decomposition is concentrated more without considering the construction process, it may end up with inefficient granulation.

7.2.1 How GC Works

GC [10] facilitates solving the complex problem by dividing the task into several small modules, then analyzing for the correlation between them. This process makes the analytical work easier as it permits several applications to execute simultaneously on various problem areas.

For instance, consider a satellite image, where at a lower resolution, the clouds can be seen. But, by applying the granulation, that is at a higher resolution fine more details could be seen. Therefore, GC allows users to access and process the details at the granule level.

Example: GC can be applied to identify the value of N in a mathematical problem such as "N = (6 x 5) / (3 + 2)." By applying the BODMAS rule, which specifies the order in which operations are carried out, i.e., multiplication, division, addition, subtraction and parentheses are used to group the "granules." It helps the user solve the problem easier. If the problem were to follow GC, 6 is multiplied by 5 first to get 30, and then 3 and 2 are added to get 5. The final solution is obtained by dividing 30 by 5. By dividing the equation into smaller chunks, it becomes easier to solve as depicted in Figure 7.3.

GC forces us to do the data analysis from various perspectives and acquire the knowledge available in information at different levels. It also makes the user identify various methods to solve the problem, depending upon the knowledge that we acquire.

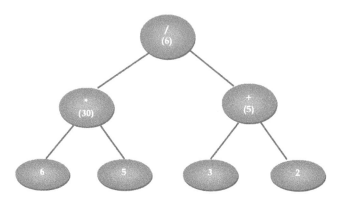

FIGURE 7.3   Computational example for GC.

7.2.2   BASIC ISSUES OF GC

The main problems in GC are granulation and computation, which are related to each other. Construction and interpretation are dealt with granulation. Computation deals with computing and reasoning with granules and their structure.

GC can be viewed from two perspectives, they are, algorithmic and semantic. The sequence of a process for granules construction and its related computations are the main concerns of algorithmic study and the quality of use of an algorithm and its interpretation are the concerns of semantic study. Both aspects are essential and significant, as the semantic study develops the knowledge of avoiding the misuse of the model, and algorithmic study results in identifying the efficient and resourceful tools and methods of GC. The semantic study provides proper clarifications and justification for a particular GC model [11].

7.3   BIO-INSPIRED COMPUTING

Biologically Inspired Algorithms (BIA) focus more on solving complex optimization problems. In recent times, this algorithm has been explored to solve the problem, in a better way compared to the conventional method of optimization. Bio-inspired computing imitates the behavioral pattern of an organism to crack those problems. Through this methodology, several attributes can be addressed to face the challenges in future network scenarios. The future network will demand an architecture that supports scalability and adaptive robust designs to address the real-time changes and possible failures caused by high and large heterogeneous networks [12].

BIA is classified as an evolutionary algorithm and swarm intelligence algorithm. The former is based on natural biological evolution, and the latter is based on the behavioral model of organisms that live in colonies such as ants, bees, birds, fireflies, etc. Some of the common algorithms are the Genetic Algorithm, Ant Colony Optimization, Artificial Bee Colony, Particle Swarm Optimization and Artificial Immune Algorithm. With the rapid development of various bio-inspired algorithms for various reasons, the working principle of Ant Colony Optimization is being considered to illustrate BIA.

7.4 IOT NETWORKS

7.4.1 IoT Technology

The IoT involves different technologies categorized into software, hardware, communications and layers of platforms. This section describes a few such technologies.

- **Software:** The component that makes IoT applications smarter is software. Software is responsible for connection establishment among hardware devices and cloud, data collection, data analysis and decision over the collected data, data visualization, etc.
- **Hardware:** physical components that participate in the IoT network are called hardware devices. These devices enable communication between the components in the network. Based on the complexity, the size, shape and level of technology involved in building the network varies. Few of the hardware devices are sensors, actuators, processors and other network components [13].
- **Communication:** This is the layer that enables smartness in the IoT network. This provides a gateway that allows communication and data transfer between IoT devices all over the world. But the main aspect is choosing the right technology for communication. This is done based on the needs of the IoT network. Few of the IoT network solutions are short-range radio solutions and medium- and long-range WAN solutions.

Under short-range solutions, Bluetooth and radio-frequency identification (RFID) are some of the technologies in use. Similarly, under medium-range solutions, WIFI, ZIGBEE and thread are used. Narrowband IoT (NB-IoT), low-power-range wide-area networking (LoRaWAN), and Sigfox are used for the long-range medium solutions.

- **Bluetooth:** The widely used technology in wearable electronic devices like earphones is Bluetooth. It is given more priority because of its low cost and less power consumption. The major drawback of such technology is its reduced efficiency for transferring more amount of data.
- **WIFI:** The technology comes under IEEE 802.11, called wireless fidelity in short WIFI is the most widely used medium for wireless communication. It's a short-range communication medium that connects smaller devices like smartphones, tabs, home appliances like CCTV cameras, etc. The limitation of this technology is its capability to allow only low-power consuming devices to get connected.
- **RFID:** An electronic chip tagged with the object under the monitor allows for storing data about the object. It uses radio-frequency technology with an identity for each object, thus called radio-frequency identification. The components of RFID are a built-in antenna, a transceiver and a transponder. The transceiver and antenna combined are called an RFID reader or interrogator. It has the advantage of low cost and efficient performance in tracking remote objects, their status and location. RFID can work either in a fixed mode

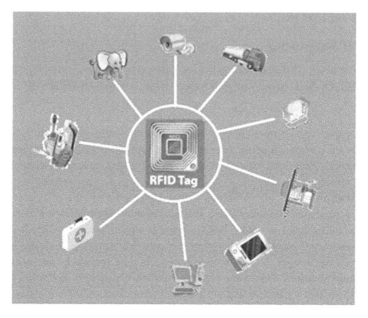

FIGURE 7.4   Structure of RFID.

or mobile. The RFID tag contains a microchip, memory storage with an electronic product code (EPC), an antenna and universal identification (UID). The
radio signal from the object activates the RFID tag which in turn sends a signal
back to the antenna read as data by the reader. The structure of RFID is shown
in Figure 7.4 [14].

- **Wireless Sensor Networks (WSN):** The information world is connected with
  the physical world by the wireless sensor network. WSN is used to monitor the
  changes that occur in environmental conditions and report them to the readers
  as responses. A wireless radio network is used for communication between the
  independent nodes of this network. The nodes have their sensor, microcon-
  troller, memory, radio transceiver and a battery. The collected data is received
  in the destination node through the sink node. Thus, the coordination between
  the nodes establishes proper communication [15].

7.5   BIO-INSPIRED IOT NETWORKS

The existing bio-inspired communication protocols, networks and procedures are
built using natural biological phenomena as a foundation for comfort. Imitating the
laws and ways of commanding such systems are offered along with open exploration challenges for bio-inspired networking. We provide an overview of the current
state-of-the-art bio-inspired networking based on examples from several networking
paradigms.

Swarm Intelligence

Swarm Intelligence (SI) is a fairly new branch of AI that is used to simulate the communal conduct of natural warms in the environment. Some of such communal warms are ant colonies, fireflies, dragonflies, honey bees, immune system's white blood cells (WBC), bacterial infections and bird flocks. Even though these colonies (insects or swarm individuals) have their restrictions with limited capabilities, they interact with each other with certain common behavioral patterns to cooperatively achieve everyday jobs essential for their survival.

Ant Colony Optimization

Ant Colony Optimization (ACO) is a part of superior research terminologies such as ant algorithms or swarm intelligence those deal with algorithmic approaches inspired by the behavior of natural biological phenomena of ant colonies to solve real-world problems.

The basic idea behind this ACO is analyzed from the food searching behavior of real ants. There are two types of actions taken the real ants. One is the ant which goes first is called FANT that is a forward and that creates the route from source to the destination despite searching for its food. The other action is taken from the ants which follow the same route of FANTs called BANT which is backward and which gathered the useful information of FANT during its entire travel from source to destination.

Having this scenario as a basic model we found the three phases of algorithms.

1. Discovery of Route Phase
2. Maintenance of the Route Phase
3. Handling the failure Phase

The discovery of the routing phase is used to identify the route from source to destination. If there are different routes are there then FANT found out the shortest route and that will be followed by the BANTs. Once the shortest path is found, the FANT establishes the tract to the destination. A routing table is created to store the destination address and next step. A node is used to receive this information in the routing table. The node which represents the source address of FANT represents also the destination address of the previous node, which in turn, represents the address of the next step. Then the nodes forward to its neighbor BANT. This can be followed in the first phase. During the second phase, the BANT established the destination path. When all nodes reach the destination, all should be maintained in this phase. During the third phase, when missing the nodes that are sent by the FANT, BANT chooses a different path. Under this condition, it finds another way to its destination. If an alternate path is there, then nodes can be forwarded to their neighbor to communicate their destination. This can be depicted in Figure 7.5.

FIGURE 7.5   Ant Colony Optimization (https://figshare.com/articles/figure/_Ant_Colony_ Optimization_Algorithm_processes_/1418788).

PARTICLE SWARM OPTIMIZATION

Particle Swarm Optimization (PSO) is an optimization method inspired by natural biological processes, to organize the dependent entities such as clusters. It optimizes the latency of different personal and global types of clusters and their nodes. PSO is a global minimization method that yields a solution to the problem in terms of a dot or a plane in an n-domain space. An elementary velocity is connected to each particle in this space as a means of communication among the particles in a swarm. In this context, a computer resource is an edge node. These nodes are moved through the space, and based on the time interval, the result can be calculated based on merit. Meanwhile, the nodes have increased the speed of time toward a higher capacity in the same communication, the location of the node can be updated by using the following equation:

$$Li(t) = w * li(t-1) + c1 * rand1 * (Pi.best - Xi(t-1) + c2 * rand2$$

$$\_ (Pg.best - Xi(t-1)) (1)$$

$$Xi = xi (t-1) + Li(t) (2)$$

where

  w is coefficient of inertial weight (navigating in its way) indicates the impact of the preceding round's velocity vector ($Li(T)$) on the velocity vector of the current round ($Li(T+1)$).

  $c1$ is a training coefficient constant (along the best value path for the node being examined).

  $c2$ is the training coefficient constant (along the path of the best node among the entire population).

  $rand1$ & $rand2$ are random numbers with uniform dispersal between 1 and 2.

  $Vi(T-1)$ is $(T-1)^{th}$ iteration's velocity vector.

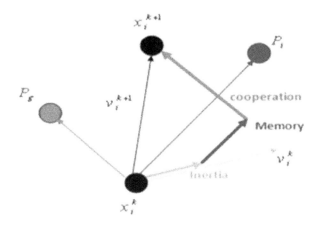

FIGURE 7.6 Particle Swarm Optimization (www.sciencedirect.com/science/article/pii/S0377042710004796).

$Xi(t-1)$ is $(T-1)^{th}$ iteration's position vector.

Figure 7.6 shows a diagrammatic representation of PSO [16].

FIREFLY ALGORITHM

This algorithm evolved in 2008 and came out with the imitation of the natural and blinking behaviors of fireflies. The algorithm comes under the concept of a metaheuristic algorithm, which is stimulated by the nature and randomness of almost all swarm intelligence methods. As we are facing a lot of changes in the wireless sensor networks, we are having a certain limited number of energy sources.

The clustering-based routing method is the main method used to limit the consumption of power in wireless sensor networks which in turn aims to increase the reliability and lifetime of the network. The Firefly Algorithm gathered information about the location and energy range of cluster head nodes as a repository for the base station. In turn, the base station computed how many times the cluster head can stay as a head. The network assumptions of this algorithm consist of nodes that are randomly distributed. It consists of the following specification.

- The sensor nodes are homogeneous with limited energy consumption.
- The sink nodes don't have energy limitations and they are fixed in the network once then the stable network is built.
- The power consumed for sensing the signal as well as processing the data is not taken into consideration.
- Sensors of the network do know their locations.
- Sensors continuously sense signals around themselves and transfer those data at a stable speed to the cluster head.

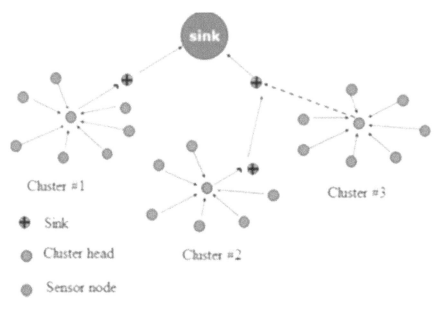

FIGURE 7.7   Clustering-based Firefly Algorithm (www.hindawi.com/journals/tswj/2015/780879/).

- Information regarding the cluster is collected by the cluster head and moved to the sink. The sinks then transmit those data to the base station directly or through a communication network.
- The duration of data collection from sensors and transfer of aggregated data to the sink is called one period.

The concept of the Firefly Algorithm is shown in Figure 7.7.

ARTIFICIAL IMMUNE SYSTEM

A multilayered system in the human body protects us from foreign particles. This system is composed of skin, respiratory system, destructive enzymes, stomach acids, natural immunity and specific immunity. Natural immunity is present at birth. Specific immunity is the one categorized under adaptive immunity. It focuses on learning, adaptability and memory. There are various theories in the artificial immune system, among which the immune network uses idiotypic network theory, negative selection mechanism, 'clonal selection' and 'somatic hypermutation' theories. Figure 7.8 shows the models of the immune system.

It also includes adaptation, protecting the body from autoimmune attacks and memory of immune system models.

IMMUNE NETWORK THEORY

This network theory is being proposed in 1974 by Niels Jerne and Geoffrey W. Hoffman. According to this theory, the immune system preserves an idiotypic

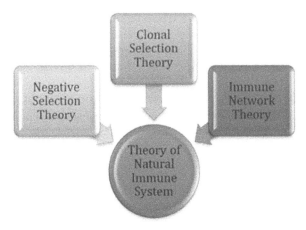

FIGURE 7.8 Models of immune system.

network, which consists of interconnected B cells to recognize antigens. To stabilize the network, both cells stimulate and suppress each other in some way or another. Two cells are said to be connected if they both share their affinities exceeding their threshold. The connection strength is directly relational to the affinities shared.

NEGATIVE SELECTION MECHANISM

The immune system contains the ability to identify unknown antibodies that enter the body under the negative selection mechanism. It also provides tolerance for self-cells. While the T-cells are generated, the receptors are made over the process of pseudo-random genetic rearrangement. Followed by an editing process in the thymus, which process is called negative selection. In this negative selection, those T-cells that don't bind with self-protein are allowed to come out of the thymus, and the other T-cells that react against self-proteins are destroyed. These matured T-cells are then allowed to perform an immunological function by circulating throughout the body and hence protect the body from foreign antiagents.

CLONAL SELECTION PRINCIPLE

The clonal selection principle focuses on the way the adaptive immune system responds to an antigenic stimulus. The clonal selection includes two major concepts, they are cloning and affinity maturation. Cloning is the concept of the proliferation of the cells which recognize the antigen. Affinity maturation is the concept of identifying the closer match between the antibody and its antigen. The closer the match is stronger the bond. The essential features of clonal selection principles are a clone and somatic hypermutation.

7.6 APPLICATIONS OF GC IN BIO-INSPIRED IOT NETWORKS

GC offers services to applications that work with granules of information with plenty of tiny tasks. This facilitates information engineering, uncertainty management and artificial intelligence engineering. Thus, GC can be better implemented in bio-inspired applications where the biological elements are considered granules.

The IoT networks consist of billions of interconnected devices with various technologies involved to deliver smart and personalized services and applications. Intelligent networking techniques where bio-inspired concepts are involved can be well implemented in reducing energy usage. In such situations, GC deals with the granules which are the individual entities of the IoT network. The granules are capable of working on individual data in parallel with each other which minimizes the energy and time for the IoT network to process.

7.7   LITERATURE SURVEY

Saleem et al. [17] have analyzed to provide secure IoT applications in data exchanging over 5G or beyond networks. The biological systems have the habit of adapting nature to the environment. They reconstruct themselves from damages caused by nature. This property is needed to be imitated by the defense algorithms in cybersecurity. Kozik et al. [18] tried to implement the concept of GC in cyber security with a novel method that detects the cyberattack in information granules. The method frames information granules from the network data.

Aftab et al. [19] proposed a clustering algorithm for bio-inspired network devices using the dragonfly algorithm to cluster drones' networks in IoT. The head election clustering is done based on the connection with the base station. The fitness function works on the residual energy and position of the drones to ensure efficient communication. Gómez et al. aimed to reach a maximum signal-to-interference ratio and used devices in action. They analyzed the problem by applying bio-inspired PSO, GA and Artificial Bee Colony Algorithm which are compared with traditional Monte Carlo simulation algorithm.

Sackey et al. [20] proposed an intelligent routing algorithm that extends the lifetime of IoT networks with the help of bio-inspired natural phenomena. This phenomenon considers the human ideology in knowledge discovery. This keeps more active nodes and transfers data packets with reserved energy.

7.8   CONCLUSION

This chapter summarizes the concepts of GC, IoT networks, bio-inspired computing and bio-inspired networks with a discussion on the advancement of GC in bio-Inspired IoT networks. GC is a recent trend in the data processing field that deals with granules of data. These granules are grouped with similar properties to each other. The near future is going to be ruled by IoT networks which will compose billions and billions of network devices which are needed to be processed in parallel with distinct or same data. GC is involved to improve efficiency and reduce the energy and time consumption of processing of the IoT networks.

REFERENCES

[1] R. Alonso-Sanz. Cellular automata and other discrete dynamical systems with memory. International Conference on High Performance Computing & Simulation, 2012, p. 215.

[2] M. A. Razzaque, M. Milojevic-Jevric, A. Palade, and S. Clarke. Middleware for Internet of Things: A survey. *IEEE Internet Things J.,* vol. 3, no. 1, pp. 70–95, 2017.

[3] H. Kagermann, J. Helbig, A. Hellinger, and W. Wahlster. Recommendations for Implementing the Strategic Initiative Industries 4.0: Securing the Future of German Manufacturing Industry – Final Report of the Industries 4.0 Working Group. Forschungsunion, 2013.

[4] C. Witchalls and J. Chambers. *The Internet of Things Business Index: A Quiet Revolution Gathers Pace.* The Economist Intelligence Unit, 2013, pp. 58–67.

[5] S. K. Datta and C. Bonnet. MEC and IoT based automatic agent reconfiguration in Industry 4.0. International Conference on Advanced Networks and Telecommunications Systems, 2018, pp. 1–5.

[6] F. Shrouf, J. Ordieres, and G. Miragliotta. Smart factories in Industry 4.0: A review of the concept and of energy management approached in production based on the Internet of Things paradigm. International Conference on Industrial Engineering and Engineering Management, 2014, pp. 697–701.

[7] K. K. Patel, et al. Internet of things IOT: Definition, characteristics, architecture, enabling technologies, application future challenges. *International Journal of Engineering Science and Computing*, vol.6, no. 5, pp. 6122–6131, 2017.

[8] N. Senthilkumaran and C. Kirubakaran. Granular computing: A theoretical study. International Journal of Computer Science Trends and Technology, vol. 2, no. 1, pp. 119–124, 2014.

[9] J. T. Yao, A. V. Vasilakos, and W. Pedrycz. Granular computing: Perspectives and challenges. IEEE Transactions on Cybernetics, vol. 43, no. 6, pp. 1977–1989, 2013.

[10] www.techslang.com/definition/what-is-granular-computing.

[11] Y.Y. Yao. Granular computing. 4th Chinese National Conference on Rough Sets and Soft Computing, 2004, pp. 1–5.

[12] C. Zheng and D. C. Sicker. A survey on biologically inspired algorithms for computer networking. *IEEE Communications Surveys & Tutorials*, vol. 15, no. 3, pp. 1160–1191, 2013.

[13] www.avsystem.com/blog/iot-technology.

[14] https://behrtech.com/blog/6-leading-types-of-iot-wireless-tech-and-theirbest-use-cases.

[15] D. Jain, P. Krishna, and V. Saritha (2012). A study on Internet of Things based applications. arXiv:1206.3891.

[16] V. Nagaraju, R. Gayathri, K. Hemalatha, B. Heartyannis Janani. Bio-inspired optimization algorithms in wireless sensor networks. Journal of Critical Reviews, vol. 7, no. 8, pp. 3081–3085, 2020.

[17] W. Mazurczyk, S. Moore, E. W. Fulp, H. Wada, and K. Leibnitz. Bio-inspired cyber security for communications and networking. *IEEE Communications Magazine*, vol. 54, no. 6, pp. 58–59, 2016.

[18] R. Kozik, M. Pawlicki, M. Choraś, and W. Pedrycz. Practical employment of granular computing to complex application layer cyberattack detection. Complexity, pp. 1-9, 2019.

[19] F. Aftab, A. Khan, and Z. Zhang. Bio-inspired clustering scheme for internet of drones application in industrial wireless sensor network. *International Journal of Distributed Sensor Networks*, vol. 15, no. 11, 1550147719889900, 2019.

[20] S. H. Sackey, J. Chen, J. A. Ansere, G. K. Gapko, and M. Kamal. A bio-inspired technique based on knowledge discovery for routing in IoT networks. 23rd International Multitopic Conference, 2020, pp. 1–6.

8 Artificial Intelligence for Bio-Inspired Security

Preethi Nanjundan and Karpagam C

8.1 INTRODUCTION

Several new methods for overcoming the limitations of AI have been developed recently. They feature mechanisms that are intuitive to both individuals and groups of organisms in addition to their lifelike functions. They are also generally more efficient than traditional AI. In order to distinguish them from traditional AI methods, these methods are referred to as bio-inspired intelligent algorithms (BIAs). BIAs have increased our understandings of neuroscience and biological systems and have been applied to numerous fields [1].

Nature can be divided into two aspects. The process of creating new inventions begins by copying the structure of creatures. Human beings applied the principles of bird flight to invent the manned glider and the echolocation sonar, for instance. Various inventions were influenced by the bird flight principles. Another is to come up with algorithms (technologies) using principles of nature. Ant Colony Optimization (ACO), which uses ant foraging as an example, and Genetic Algorithm (GA), which employs inheritance, mutation, selection and crossover, were both developed in these areas. In the future, science and technology will pose ever more challenges for human beings. A traditional AI algorithm is often too simple in its structure or function to meet the development needs. A variety of AI algorithms have been developed during the 20th century, including bio-inspired neural networks, artificial immune algorithms and membrane computation algorithms. Other intelligent algorithms (such as ACO and GA) also exhibit this property. These algorithms work in a more biological manner than other methods [1].

8.1.1 SECURITY OF INFORMATION IN MILITARY OPERATIONS

By applying high-level protection measures to the army's information systems (IS), military engineers can offer a critical tactical and operational advantage in the event of a crisis. It is imperative that information control and management systems (C4I) and secure military IS remain secret to maintain stability between opposite forces and to preserve honor. Taking the opposite path can lead to serious problems that are hard to quantify, whether in terms of material or moral costs. Network security systems must therefore adhere to military specifications and requirements. There would be

DOI: 10.1201/9781003248545-8

a possibility of combining smart tactics to block attacks of a zero-day nature [2]. Security and confidentiality algorithms and methods have been developed in a variety of domains, which enable integrity, confidentiality, availability, nonrepudiation and authentication [3].

8.1.2 CLOUD SECURITY IS CRUCIAL

Cloud computing, made possible by a third party through the internet, consists of being able to access hard- and storage-based computing resources, networks and interfaces. These resources provide users with on-demand access to infrastructure, computing power, applications and services. The users can access information and data when and where they want based on their preferences. In addition to being agile, scalable, cost-efficient and independent of devices and locations [4], cloud security has a number of advantages (Figure 8.1) over conventional computing.

In cloud environments, security remains a major challenge due to their characteristics: complexity, heterogeneity, widespread access via the internet and virtualized resource sharing. Traditional approaches to security like static and boundary-based arrangements clearly do not work as the sole countermeasure. An intelligent countermeasure is required to meet the challenges of cloud computing and an evolving threat domain by being autonomy, self-managing and self-organized. In nature, complex patterns can be found emerging from the interactions among agents, even if they are not often used in cloud security countermeasures. Coordinating and sharing information allows changes to occur without being controlled centrally, allowing for self-organization. By adapting to learning, surviving and adapting to many different environments and interactions, biological systems have learned and evolved [5].

FIGURE 8.1 Advantages of cloud security.

Cloud computing security regularly does not use bio-inspired approaches, but they have been studied less frequently than the general area of cloud computing research. Though bio-inspired algorithms are overwhelmingly beneficial, cloud computing has used them less than many other areas like network, pattern recognition, data mining, wireless sensor networks, robotics, etc. Nevertheless, algorithms stimulated by nature may provide the best solution by virtue of their adaptive nature. However, when this technology faces persistent adversaries, zero-day attacks and cloud infrastructure, it fails, since it does not adapt and escalate its security strategies to slow down or even stop an adversary's intensity and sheer aggression. Even though GAs are some-times more efficient and specific in the selection of unique features for detection. These systems, which are often complex and reserved for specific scenarios rather than general use, typically address trust assurance, authentication, authorization and access control, as well as intrusion detection. Nevertheless, bio-inspired solutions for cloud security, for instance, have been designed and applied as pure solutions, such as encryption, data in storage security, intrusion detection, trust, etc. The prop-erties of biology allow it to adapt and survive by evolving and becoming aware of its environment. In essence, nature creates a superior intelligence. Despite limited ini-tial information, weakly informed systems can find the best solution in large search spaces, making them the best choice when prediction is difficult. Literature shows that current reactive methods for protecting cloud environments have diminishing returns due to persistent threats, as well as sophisticated attacks, so heuristic opti-mization is the way to go [5].

8.1.3   Bio-/Nature-inspired Algorithms for Detecting Malicious Activity

Cyberattacks can often be detected via AI and learning algorithms. The use of machine learning is making it easier than ever before to detect malicious behavior quickly and accurately. Nature-inspired as well as bio-inspired algorithms are part of a branch of machine learning algorithms. In their design, algorithms act in a similar manner to the natural patterns found in nature, biology, social systems and life science. The examples include generic algorithms, swarm intelligence, artificial immune systems, evolutionary algorithms, artificial neural networks (ANNs), fractal geometry and chaos theory. As opposed to traditional machine learning algorithms, bio-inspired algorithms emphasize optimization. Nature serves as a means to produce something that is as perfect as possible, like selecting the best possible samples from a popula-tion. They apply these principles in practice by optimization and find the best solu-tion to any given problem. Anomaly detection algorithms detect malicious behavior by detecting its most appropriate mechanism, as their primary purpose is to identify abnormal behavior. Nature-/bio-inspired algorithms can also optimize the potential features that may be used in attack detection. It is designed to reduce the complexity and computational cost of malware detection while also selecting an optimal set of features. Nature-/bio-inspired algorithms can accommodate a range of variable quan-tity in the form of type and endurance. The opportunity is thus given to expand the types of variables available to such algorithms, thus expanding its features [6].

Current network security systems are progressively demonstrating a limited ability to detect new threats, with an estimate of 50–70% of new threats being able to be detected. The development of cybersecurity must therefore take on a new orientation [7].

In the Bio-inspired Security Research Group (BSRG), we strongly believe that future cybersecurity solutions should be designed, developed and deployed in a way that will allow us to fully utilize nature's experience [7]. A broad division of current research in this field can be made according to how a concept is derived:

- Inspired by the characteristics or defense mechanisms of a given organism (internal or external). Internal mechanisms include, for instance, an immune system, whereas external features include, for instance, camouflage or mimicry techniques.
- In addition to finding inspiration in the behavior of various organisms, one can seek inspiration from the association between prey and predators and cooperative behavior [7].

8.2   SECURITY NEEDS TO BE BIO-INSPIRED

Increasing reliance on data for the global economy has made computer security increasingly important. The complexity of the systems that must be kept secure calls for models that abstract the overlapping interdependencies between heterogeneous components that work together to provide the desired service [8].

Cloud computing and the Internet of Things require enhanced security and trust. Embedded devices and sensors play an important role in the adoption of these technologies. The Internet of Things allows a vast amount of data to be collected and made accessible through objects connected to them. Businesses that generate high value and profits use and benefit from web-based technologies. As RFID, sensors and communication technologies all grow in importance, IoT is undergoing a rapid expansion. They help to generate intellectual property (IP), but the quality of IP protection is not as high as it could be. In this regard, cloud-based systems are essential as they provide universal accessibility and reliable utility computing. As cloud computing expands, organizations need more secure software and hardware solutions to protect their networks and firewalls from IP-rich data being transferred overseas. Increasingly, methods of enhancing security based on bio-inspired principles have attracted significant attention [9].

Computer security can be maintained with a number of different methods, such as backup, encryption, approved users, passwords, firewalls, intrusion detection and application safeguards. In keeping a network secure, it is important to authenticate each user, usually by using a username and password. After users have authenticated themselves, By enforcing access policies, a stateful firewall can determine what services an individual can use. It does successfully prevent unauthorized access, however, this component is ineffective in screening for potentially harmful content, such as worms. A good intrusion prevention system (IPS) can be useful in detecting and preventing this kind of malware. An IPS monitors network traffic for suspicious contents, volumes and anomalies to guard against spells such as denial of service.

Communications between hosts using the network may also be encrypted for privacy reasons.

Systems of similar complexity and greater complexity are equipped with self-healing processes crucial to their continued existence. Those who want upcoming computer systems to succeed in complex and hostile environments must emulate these systems [10].

The study of cryptography involves designing cryptographic algorithms that provide security of data during transmission and even while data is at rest. Biological phenomena have been useful for solving many computational problems in recent times. A related field of research is named Biologically Inspired Computing (BIC). Additionally, there has been research into biologically inspired algorithms applied to cryptography as well as standard cryptographic algorithms. In engineering and technology, biology can solve a wide range of problems because of its ability to process complex information and provide many solutions. Biological systems and processes are the basis for many modern artificial systems; these include neural networks, immune systems, genetic mechanisms, etc. BIC paradigms that are used in cryptography are GA, Artificial Immune System, Cellular Automata, ANNs and ACO [11].

8.2.1 THE ROLE OF BIO-INSPIRED SECURITY

For more than 40 years, computer scientists and engineers have studied natural evolution and developed algorithms to generate solutions to problems that were too difficult to solve using traditional analytical methods [12,13].

The purpose of nature study is to observe, analyze and understand our environment. An organism that grows breathes, requires energy and evolves is a living organism. There is increasing evidence to suggest that nature's systems are hierarchical, adaptive and synchronized. As plants, bees, birds and beetles, for example, the Sun rises and sets in a predictable pattern. Many problems faced by artificial systems can be solved by learning from nature and using it as a source of inspiration. By comparing biological applications to computer systems in a similar way, we demonstrate how computer systems and biology are related.

Despite its recent emergence, bio-inspired research has been extensively studied and applied in numerous fields [14] with diverse bio-inspired techniques.

Since cyber security systems have been deployed for decades, many inherent limitations in the existing infrastructure make care of the present-day network safety devices unscalable and give a rival an advantage. Among these limitations are:

1. interactions between devices on the network are nonexistent, making it difficult to obtain global knowledge;
2. a lack of awareness of oneself;
3. there is a lack of self-correcting mechanisms for network devices. For example, it requires error-prone and time-consuming manual configuration, which is not effective in mitigating real-time attacks.

Security infrastructure is managed by multiple parties due to the multiparty nature of the management it is difficult to diagnose misconfigurations and resolve conflicts. On the other hand, biological systems have intrinsic appeal because they were created through billions of years of evolution. In addition to their general adaptability to different environmental conditions, these systems should also be resilient to failures and damages, successful and enduring. Working together with a limited set of rules while utilizing global intelligence (which extends beyond individual superposition) [14].

8.2.2 Aspects of Bio-inspired Systems

Nature exploration, analysis and understanding involve learning about and investigating the world around us. Living things are in the study of life science because they grow, breathe, need energy and evolve into new forms for survival. Nature is structured to be hierarchical, adaptive and synchronized in both space and time, according to an extensive study of the topic. Among other examples, bees search for nectar so plants can produce food and birds fly together in perfect coordination in order to make food. A specific time is set for sunrise and sunset. Many of the problems in man-made systems can be solved by inspiration and ideas provided by nature. An engineering system is considered biologically inspired if it has similar characteristics to a biological system, such as following the same procedure as the former or having a similar process as the former does. For now, it might be useful to answer a very basic question: Why should we consider biology to be a source of inspiration? Several characteristics of these systems provide an answer to this question, including:

- In order to survive against harsh conditions, organic systems are adaptive to their environments.
- Despite disappointments caused by numerous issues, they have the ability to recover quickly and remain strong.
- Using only a few simplified rules, they can accomplish seemingly impossible tasks.

The animal can learn, resolve and regenerate itself efficiently in a changing environment [13].

Although bio-inspired cybersecurity offers many elegant solutions, the vast majority of those efforts are simply ad hoc analogies between biological systems and human-designed systems. According to them, researchers should apply a functional abstraction approach, in which they should determine what features of natural algorithms could be used to build purposeful, tailored (even optimized) solutions based on those abstracted features [15].

8.3   WHY AI HAS IMPROVED SECURITY?

Increasing enterprise complexity and an expanding attack surface will exacerbate the threat landscape as enterprises evolve. The amount of time-varying indicators that need to be examined by your company depends on its size [16]. The AI and ML technologies have emerged as critical technologies in information security, as they can analyze millions of data points and identify a wide range of fears – from malware that exploits zero-day weaknesses to phishing attacks that exploit risky behavior. Through a continuing process of learning, these technologies recognize new types of attacks today based on previous insights. Identifying and responding to deviations from established norms is enabled by the building of profiles of users, assets and networks based on the history of their behavior [16].

8.3.1 An Introduction to AI

Technology that uses acquired and derived information to understand, learn and act is known as AI. There are three key principles of AI today:

- **Assisted Intelligence,** a commonly existing technology today, enables people and governments to accomplish more.
- **Augmented Intelligence**, currently gaining momentum, Providing opportunities that were previously unattainable to people and organizations.
- **Artificial Intelligence**, being advanced for the upcoming, structures machines that act on their own. One of the most widely used examples will be self-driving vehicles.

In essence, AI has some characteristics of human acumen: a store of domain-specific information, a learning mechanism and a mechanism for deploying that knowledge. Currently, AI includes techniques such as machine learning, expert systems, neural networks and deep learning.

- **Machine Learning:** Numerical methods are used to give computers the skill to "learn" (e.g., incrementally advanced presentation) without being explicitly programmed. An AI program should focus on a specific task rather than attempting to be general.
- **Expert Systems:** provide solutions to problems within specialized domains. They address complications and make choices using fuzzy rules-based cognitive and wisely curated data bases, mimicking the thinking of human experts.
- **Networks of Neural Connections**: An observational computer learning from observational data is enabled by neural networks, a programming paradigm which is biologically inspired. Each node in a neural network allots a weight to its input based on its correctness or incorrectness in relation to the operation it is performing. These weights are added together to determine the result.
- **Deep Learning:** Deep learning comprises a larger domestic of machine learning devices which use learning data symbols rather than task-specific processes to gain insight into learning data. Image recognition can be made better than a human's ability with deep learning [16], and it is used for autonomous vehicles, diagnosis of medical conditions and for scan analysis.

8.3.2 Applying AI to Decision-Making

Research by progressive AI investigators in several real-time situations has also proved that AI mimics human decision-making in a wider sense. Making decisions involves reasoning and recognition, which remain key elements of the human decision-making process. Furthermore, they right that "good" decisions are considered by rational thinking, which includes weighing the alternatives and making the best decision [17].

Attempts are made to simulate human intelligence through AI. AI can help with cybersecurity. With the right training, AI systems can be trained to identify new types of malwares, generate alerts for threats and protect sensitive data for organizations [18].

Thousands of cyber threats are reported by companies every day, according to TechRepublic. Most companies do not have the expertise to deal with the volume of threats. In this case, some of these malicious threats will naturally slip by unnoticed and cause severe problems [18].

A modern cybersecurity solution based on AI will give businesses an edge online today. In order for security professionals to effectively protect their organizations from cyberattacks, they need the support of intelligent machines and advanced technologies. This chapter examines the benefits of integrating AI with cybersecurity.

8.3.3 An AI Approach to Cyber Security

There are many advantages and applications of AI in a variety of fields, cybersecurity being one of them. Figure 8.2, depicts the role of AI in cybersecurity. AI and machine learning can help keep up with cybercriminals, automate threat detection and provide better response than traditional software-driven or manual techniques [19], which have changed rapidly with fast-evolving cyberattacks and rapid proliferation of devices. These are some of the benefits of using AI:

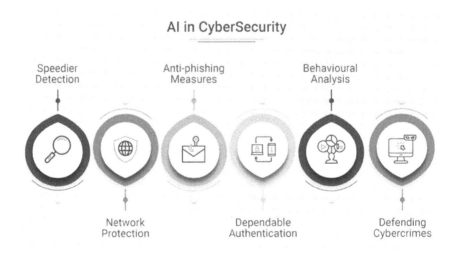

FIGURE 8.2   AI in cyber security.

1. AI Gains Knowledge over Time [18]

The term artificial intelligence refers to technology that is intelligent, and it helps to improve network security over time. In this technique, deep learning and machine learning are used to learn how a business network behaves over time. The algorithm identifies patterns in the network and groups them according to their significance. The system then identifies deviations from the norm and reacts accordingly.

Patterns learned by ANNs over time may eventually assist in improving security. Threats with characteristics similar to those recorded get blocked at an early stage. Hackers find it difficult to beat AI because AI is constantly learning.

2. Identifying Unknown Threats with AI [18]

The human mind is not capable of identifying every threat a company faces. Millions of cyberattacks are launched every year with wildly varying intentions. These malicious attacks can damage an organization's infrastructure severely. It is even worse when you don't detect, identify and prevent them from causing harm.

Using modern solutions to prevent attackers from trying new tactics, from sophisticated social engineering to malware attacks, is necessary. AI has proven to be one of the most effective technologies for identifying and preventing unknown threats.

3. AI Is Capable of Handling Large Quantities of Data [18]

An organization's network is very active. In fact, an average mid-sized company itself has high traffic. Data is transferred between customers and the business on a daily basis, so a lot of data is transferred to and from the business. Protecting this data is critical against malicious people and software. At the same time, cybersecurity personnel cannot monitor every packet for potential threats.

AI is the best way to identify threats masked as normal activity. Since it is an automated system, it can weed through massive amounts of data and traffic. Data can be transferred using AI-based technologies, such as a residential proxy. The system is also able to detect and identify any threats embedded within the chaos of traffic.

4. Improving Vulnerability Management [18]

Securing a company's network requires vulnerability management. As mentioned earlier, most companies deal with numerous threats every day. In order to remain secure, they need to detect, identify and prevent these threats. AI research can be used to analyze and assess existing security measures.

AI can help you assess systems much faster than cybersecurity personnel, thereby enhancing your problem-solving abilities. Business networks and computer systems are detected for weak points, helping companies focus on important security tasks. In this way, vulnerabilities are identified and security measures can be taken immediately.

5. Enhanced Security [18]

Throughout the life of a business network, the threats it faces change. The tactics of hackers constantly change. Organizing security tasks becomes more challenging in such an environment. At the same time, you may have to deal with phishing attacks, denial-of-service attacks or ransomware.

Although these attacks have similar potential, it is important to know what to do first. A greater threat to security is human error and negligence. To detect and prevent all types of attacks, you should employ AI on your network.

6. Reduce Duplication of Effort [18]

Attackers change their tactics frequently, as mentioned earlier. Security principles remain constant, however. Hiring someone to do these tasks may result in them getting bored. It might be impossible for them to perform a crucial security task due to fatigue and complacency.

AI, while imitating human qualities and leaving out the shortcomings, eliminates duplicative cybersecurity processes that could bore your cybersecurity personnel. Regularly checking for security threats and preventing them is an important part of this program. A deeper analysis is also carried out to determine if your network has any security weaknesses that could harm it.

7. Detects and Responds Faster [18]

A company's network can be protected from threats only by detecting them. The best solution would be to identify things like untrusted data as soon as possible. It will help you avoid irreparable network damage.

AI and cybersecurity go hand in hand. The integration allows threats to be detected and addressed in real time. The real-time detection and response to threats is possible through AI integration. It is not possible for humans to detect threats at the same time as AI.

8. Ensuring Authentication [18]

For accessing services or purchasing products, websites generally have a user account feature. Frequently, visitors are prompted to enter sensitive information in contact forms. Running such a site requires additional security since personal data and sensitive information is involved. Additionally, your visitors can browse your network safely thanks to the extra security layer.

Authentication is secured every time a user logs in. Identification is performed by various tools, such as facial recognition, CAPTCHAs and fingerprint scanners, among others. It is possible to detect if an attempt to log in is authentic or not by using the information collected by these features.

Credential stuffing and brute force attacks are used by hackers to gain access to company networks. As soon as an attacker gains access to a user account, your entire network is at risk.

8.4   BIO-INSPIRED COMPUTING

Biologically Inspired Computational Methods (BICMs) have recently emerged due to recent advances in computer technology. Recently, AI has been studying the application of bio-inspired computing [19,20] more and more. The technology exploits bio-inspired behaviors and attributes to address a range of academic and real-world environmental issues. ACO, Evolution Strategies (ES), Artificial Immune System (AIS), Particle Swarm Optimization (PSO) and GAs are some of the biologically inspired cyber security techniques. It is becoming increasingly accepted by scientists that computer malware can be classified using bio-inspired techniques. A lot of work was put into optimizing features and parameters of classifiers using these techniques. For example, the malware detection systems were improved by PSO and GA. Fuzzy logic was applied for detecting intrusions in another study. In order to predict network traffic behavior over a given period of time, we create a digital signature of a network segment using glow analysis. Moreover, a fuzzy logic approach was used to determine whether an instance on a network was abnormal. As a result of examining a university's network traffic, the accuracy rate was 96.53%, and the false notification rate was 0.56%.

8.4.1 ALGORITHMS BASED ON BIO-INSPIRED PRINCIPLES

Any given optimization problem can be solved by using bio-inspired algorithms which will find the best solution within the space of search at a much faster rate. Various traditional algorithms seek the optimal solution from the search space by following systematic procedures, which take a long time to reach convergence. Through bio-inspired algorithms, the disadvantages of traditional optimization algorithms can be overcome by looking at how certain species behave biologically in order to determine the optimal search strategy. Based on the evolution occurring in nature as a result of interactions between and within species, these algorithms are based on how species interact. Cooperation or competition is one example. Bio-inspired algorithms are equipped with the following capabilities:

- Applicable to numerous problems;
- Tuning the algorithm according to some parameters;
- Faster convergence to optimal values.

Both ACO and PSO are both bio-inspired algorithms for solving constraint-based optimization problems. These algorithms are inspired by ants colonies and bee swarms. Using data from bacteria, fruit flies, bats and cuckoos, a new class of bio-inspired algorithms was derived.

The Genetic Algorithm

GAs were first introduced by John H. Holland as an optimization tool during the 1960s. The GA selects from a people of potential answers individuals using genetic workers, namely limit and change. The evolutionary process is iterative until convergence criteria are met, and fitter individuals advance to succeeding generations. Iteration moves forward using the new population after each iteration is completed.

The Artificial Bee Colony

By analogy to honey bees, Karaboga's Artificial Bee Colony (ABC) algorithm uses bio-inspired parameters to simulate their foraging behavior [15]. A honey bee chooses a hive site, communicates, allots tasks between the bees, reproduces, forages, navigates and lays pheromones. Algorithms based on ABC emulate honey bee capabilities. The working principle of ABC consists of three groups. An employed bee occupies one half of the colony, while onlookers occupy the other. During each colony's active period the food source is assigned to a worker bee.

The ABC algorithm identifies possible food sources from the population of bees that is initially established. Following the identification of the candidate solution (food source), it is important to determine how valid it is (its suitability). The incumbent bees are able to discard an existing candidate solution if a better candidate solution is found to be superior in the subsequent stages. Onlooker bees share information with employees, and they attempt to advance the quality of the waste applicant keys. The candidate solutions will also be rejected from the population if the onlookers cannot improve their fitness. A scout replaces a rejected candidate solution with another probable one once the rejected solution is handled. The development endures till the best candidate key is known.

Algorithm for Fruit Fly

The Fruit Fly Optimization Algorithm (FFA) was introduced by Pan. Based on fruit fly biology, the algorithm optimizes the process. Fruit flies are excellent at locating their food using smell and sight [13]. According to biological sciences, this type of fly can smell food from distances of 40 km. The fly performs two stages of foraging in search of food. As part of the first stage, the flies are able to recognize the food based on the smell (osphresis organ), and then they get near the food using their effective vision (second stage).

Cat Swarm Optimization

Simulating cat behavior with Cat Swarm Optimization (CSO) is an optimization algorithm. Some applications in the last few years have been solved by CSO. The optimal solution can be obtained by depending on the time periods associated with the local search method during a latent dated for cats, but they are alert; tracing mode is used during the alert periods.

Moth Flame Optimization

The evening flight patterns of moths are similar to those of butterflies, and they orient themselves in the direction of the moonlight. Transverse orientation is something moths have developed in order to navigate at night. According to the mathematical model for the Moth Flame Optimization (MFO) algorithm, the candidate solutions are signified by moths, and the place of these moths in the space corresponds to variables in the problem. In this stage of the moth's development, the moth will be capable of flying in one, two or three dimensions.

8.5   EFFECTS AND CHALLENGES OF BIO-INSPIRED CYBERSECURITY

As AI consumes a massive amount of data artifacts, it improves its knowledge of bio-inspired security threats and risks. The AI technology analyzes threats like malicious files, suspicious IP addresses and insiders in seconds. Examples of data security challenges are shown in Figure 8.3. The use of AI will speed up the process of making critical decisions and dealing with threats. AI can be used to help security analysts in addition to reducing the time it takes to identify and fix threats, leading to a reduction in dwell time, reduced breach costs and improved security posture.

AI can be used to find significant advantages for institutions in cyber security, according to a recent review. Due to cyber security tools, two of three companies significantly improved their ROI. Using Amazon Web Services, Siemens AG, a world leader in electrification, automation and digitalization, built its Siemens Cyber Defense Center (CDC) on a self-evolving platform powered by AI. AI could estimate 60,000 possible attacks per unit time. Using AI enabled the capability to be managed by a team consisting of fewer than a dozen members without any adverse effects on system performance.

Through the use of AI, institutions are able to reapply past threat patterns in identifying new threats. By preserving time and effort, incidents can be identified and investigated earlier, and threats are remedied more quickly. About 64% of administrators report that AI reduced the cost of identifying and responding to breaches. Cyberattacks can be avoided by responding quickly. Organizations save on average 12% by responding quickly. Cyber security presents opportunities thanks to AI largely due to the rapid shift from the manual response, identification and

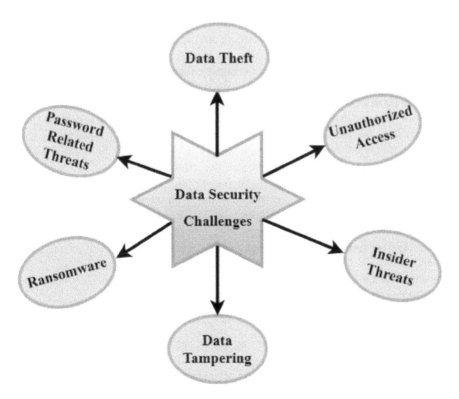

FIGURE 8.3 Data security challenges.

mitigation to automated mitigation. AI is capable of detecting novel and complex variants of attack extensibility.

The conventional approach focuses on proven intruders and intrusions and can fail to detect new intrusions and activities that are not expected. Smart technologies solved the shortcomings of early security technologies. For example, privileged intranet activities can be observed, and any expressive changes in privileged access operations can pose a security risk. AI provides the security teams with the edge they need to prevent threats from causing mishaps. With the aid of AI techniques, Dark Trace provides pattern recognition and detection services to the UK's manufacturing, retailers, energy and transportation industries. As cyberattacks become more complex and intruders develop new tactics, this is functional.

By creating self-regulating security systems, AI can handle large volumes of data, improve network security and identify attacks as well as react to breaches. Security groups may be thrown off balance when too many daily alerts are received. The automated detection and response to intrusions have reduced the efforts required by security experts, and they are typically more effective at identifying threats.

Whenever large amounts of security data are generated and sent daily on the network, network security experts have a difficult time tracking and identifying them quickly and reliably. By utilizing AI, it may be possible to detect and monitor suspicious activities more effectively. Using this approach, network security experts can respond to novel situations rather than having to resort to manually analyzing them. AI security systems are capable of learning to detect attacks more effectively over time: they can identify attacks based on application characteristics and network activity. AI security systems learn traffic patterns over time and set a threshold for normal activities. Any deviation from the norm is therefore considered an attack.

In a given optimization problem, bio-inspired algorithms can find an optimal solution faster by searching a search space for the optimal solution based on bio-inspired principles. In some existing search algorithms, an objective function is derived automatically from the hunt space, which takes a longer period to reach meeting. By analyzing the biological behavior of certain species in order to find the optimal search strategy, bio-inspired algorithms overcome the shortcomings of conventional optimization algorithms. Hence, nature-inspired algorithms are also referred to as AI and bio-inspired computing. Natural evolution is based on interactions between species and within species [17], these algorithms have been designed.

There may be competitive or cooperative interactions between and within the species. The capabilities of bio-inspired algorithms include:

- Suitable for a wide range of problems;
- Tuning the algorithm by adjusting a few parameters;
- Achieving optimum values with a faster convergence rate.

A number of bio-inspired algorithms were used until recently to explain constraint-based optimization difficulties, including ACO and PWO. A bio-inspired algorithm was created by analyzing the behavior of microorganisms, berry flies, bats and cuckoos.

8.5.1 AI APPLICATIONS IN CYBERSECURITY: CHALLENGES AND OPPORTUNITIES

Building an AI system requires a large number of input samples. The samples must be obtained and processed, which is time-consuming and requires numerous resources. In order to build and maintain the fundamental system, several resources, such as memory and processing power, are required. Using this technology requires the highest level of resources. False alarms are a common problem for the end client. Consequently, businesses lose efficiency as a result of procrastinating on crucial decisions. It is necessary to trade off minimizing false alarms by maintaining a high-security level during the fine-tuning process. Attackers can enter AI systems in a number of ways, including supplying adversarial inputs, stealing models and poisoning data.

The four components of AI systems are perception, learning, decision-making and action. In such sophisticated environments, the elements of the system must interact and be codependent (e.g., inaccurate perception can result in inconsistent decisions). Each element is also susceptible to specific attacks (for instance, perception is susceptible to a training attack, while decisions are vulnerable to classic cyberattacks). Keeping a system from misbehaving depends on consistency beyond logical reasoning: additives and uncertainty require bounds for every element. It is important to formalize verification of logical correctness, decision theory and risk analysis for both AI and ML elements.

It will require novel techniques to define the system requirements and to determine how to react to attacks. Digital security will be challenged by AI. As AI technology becomes more powerful, attackers are launching more sophisticated attacks. A major reason for this is that the cost to develop and adopt the technology is decreasing as improved AI solutions and machine learning tools become available. As a result, illegitimate users can access more sophisticated and adaptive vicious programs at lower costs. As a result, the task of fighting cybercrime has increased. Cyber security techniques using AI have the human element of complacency as one of their risks.

The employees of a cyber security department may be oblivious to prevention as an institution adopts AI and ML strategies. Since the importance of cyber security awareness was already discussed, it is not necessary to emphasize the high risks associated with complacent and uninformed employees.

8.6 CONCLUSION

Increasing security requirements and demands have accompanied the evolution of computing and communication capabilities. Data and software were protected from unauthorized access during the early days of computing by physical controls, which were physically isolated. It became necessary, with the advent of multi-user computing and computer networks, to devise mechanisms to control data and program exchange among a group of users. Distributed systems have further exacerbated these problems because they provide remote access for users and attackers alike. Boosting the performance of IT security teams is becoming increasingly challenging thanks to AI. Having a sufficiently secure enterprise attack surface is no longer possible with humans, and AI gives security professionals the tools to identify threats and perform analysis to minimize breach risk. Moreover, AI can assist in finding and prioritizing risks, directing incident response and identifying malware attacks beforehand.

Recent years have seen AI become a necessary technology to augment the efforts of human information security teams. AI allows cybersecurity professionals to better identify and reduce security risks as a result of a dynamic enterprise attack surface that humans cannot adequately protect.

Human–machine partnerships enabled by AI enable cybersecurity professionals to drive bio-inspired security by pushing the boundaries of knowledge, enhancing their lives and driving greater security than the parts alone.

Today's business environment makes it difficult for businesses to maintain a secure network and data. Using AI to strengthen your security infrastructure can help you move one step closer to being safer. The use of AI for business security has several advantages, and we anticipate that in the very near future, AI will be integrated into business security.

REFERENCES

[1] Ni J, Wu L, Fan X, Yang SX (2016). Bioinspired Intelligent Algorithm and Its Applications for Mobile Robot Control: A Survey. Computational Intelligence and Neuroscience 2016:3810903. https://doi.org/10.1155/2016/3810903.

[2] Demertzis K, Iliadis L (2015). A Bio-inspired Hybrid Artificial Intelligence Framework for Cyber Security. In: N Daras, M Rassias (eds), *Computation, Cryptography, and Network Security*. Springer. https://doi.org/10.1007/978-3-319-18275-9_7.

[3] Kadda B, Mustapha M, Abdelkrim L (2020). A Bio-inspired Algorithm for Symmetric Encryption. *International Journal of Organizational and Collective Intelligence* 10:1–13. https://doi.org/10.4018/IJOCI.2020010101.

[4] Ahsan MM, Gupta KD, Nag AK, Poudyal S, Kouzani, AZ, Mahmud, MAP (2020). Applications and Evaluations of Bio-inspired Approaches in Cloud Security: A Review. *IEEE Access* 8:180799–180814. https://doi.org/10.1109/ACCESS.2020.3027841.

[5] Mthunzi SN, Benkhelifa E (2017). Trends towards Bio-inspired Security Countermeasures for Cloud Environments. IEEE 2nd International Workshops on Foundations and Applications of Self* Systems (FAS*W), pp. 341–347. https://doi.org/10.1109/FAS-W.2017.170.

[6] Procopiou A, Komninos N (2019). Bio/Nature-Inspired Algorithms in A.I. for Malicious Activity Detection. In: E-SM El-Alfy, M Elroweissy, EW Fulp, W. Mazurczyk (eds), *Nature-Inspired Cyber Security and Resiliency: Fundamentals, Techniques and Applications*. IET.

[7] http://bsrg.tele.pw.edu.pl.

[8] Conti V, Ziggiotto A, Migliardi M, Vitabile S (2020). Bio-inspired Security Analysis for IoT Scenarios. *International Journal of Embedded Systems* 13: 221. https://doi.org/10.1504/IJES.2020.108871.

[9] Johnson A, Al-Aqrabi H, Hill R (2020). Bio-inspired Approaches to Safety and Security in IoT-Enabled Cyber-Physical Systems. *Sensors* 20:844. https://doi.org/10.3390/s20030844.

[10] Ogundele O, Alese B, Matthew O (2010). A Bio-Inspired Concept for Information Security Modelling. *IJGC* 1:53–67. https://doi.org/10.4018/jgc.2010010106.

[11] Hitaswi N, Chandrasekaran K (2016). A Bio-inspired Model to Provide Data Security in Cloud Storage. International Conference on Information Technology, pp. 203–208. https://doi.org/10.1109/INCITE.2016.7857617.

[12] Floreano D, Mattiussi C (2008). *Bio-Inspired Artificial Intelligence: Theories, Methods, and Technologies*. MIT Press.

[13] Rathore H, Jha S (2013). Bio-inspired Machine Learning Based Wireless Sensor Network Security. 2013 World Congress on Nature and Biologically Inspired Computing, pp. 140–146. https://doi.org/10.1109/NaBIC.2013.6617852.

[14] Rauf U (2018). A Taxonomy of Bio-inspired Cyber Security Approaches: Existing Techniques and Future Directions. *Arabian Journal for Science and Engineering* 43. https://doi.org/10.1007/s13369-018-3117-2.

[15] Suarez G, Gallos L, Fefferman N (2018). A Case Study in Tailoring a Bio-inspired Cyber-Security Algorithm: Designing Anomaly Detection for Multilayer Networks. *Journal of Cyber Security and Mobility* 8:113–132. https://doi.org/10.13052/jcsm2245-1439.815.

[16] www.balbix.com/insights/artificial-intelligence-in-cybersecurity.

[17] Paneerselvam S (2020). Role of AI and Bio-Inspired Computing in Decision Making. In: G Kanagachidambaresan, R Anand, E Balasubramanian, V Mahima (eds), Internet of Things for Industry 4.0. EAI/Springer Innovations in Communication and Computing. Springer. https://doi.org/10.1007/978-3-030-32530-5_8.

[18] www.cm-alliance.com/cybersecurity-blog/8-benefits-of-using-ai-for-cybersecurity.

[19] www.computer.org/publications/tech-news/trends/the-use-of-artificial-intelligence-in-cybersecurity.

[20] Johnson, V.T., Biologically Inspired Computational Methods(BICMs) in the structural design and damage Assessment of composites, PhD thesis, Indian Institute of Science, 1997.

9 Bio-Inspired Algorithm for Communication Network System Architecture and Protocols

Chitra P

9.1 INTRODUCTION

The bio-inspired domain [1] is distinguished within the current state of affairs. Organizations and societies are power-trained with the info explosion within the digital era. In some way, intelligent approaches are required to spot appropriate operating things. This chapter applies metaheuristic algorithms that investigate and stream a proper operating resolution to terribly complicated issues. Bio-inspired computing is to realize prominence at intervals of metaheuristics with intelligent algorithms which will learn and adapt to the mistreatment of organisms of a biological system. Some of the variations of nature-inspired algorithms can be observed in the Figure 9.1.

These approaches help reach progressive solutions for complicated issues. There have been complex issues like multidimensional hyperplanes, and the dynamic nature of the problems has incorporated some challenges.

Nevertheless, the growth across this scenario isn't easy to trace, thanks to entirely different algorithms presented. No similar study has tried to spot these algorithms completely, exploring and examining the compass of their liabilities. Only countable experimenters evaluated new algorithms to build new features and elevation. They have handled with limited visibility across bio-inspired algorithms [2].

9.2 SELF-ORGANIZATION: A TRANSFORMATION FROM NATURE TO ENGINEERING

This promising path appears to hold onto multiple rudiments of technology. 1st exploration of the organic pot and its doable edition to specialized answers originates in the 1960s to deliberate applying pot ways in multitudinous biological areas. They noticed the primary software in engineering generally. It has been proven that dispatches will profit from biologically specific mechanisms likewise.

DOI: 10.1201/9781003248545-9

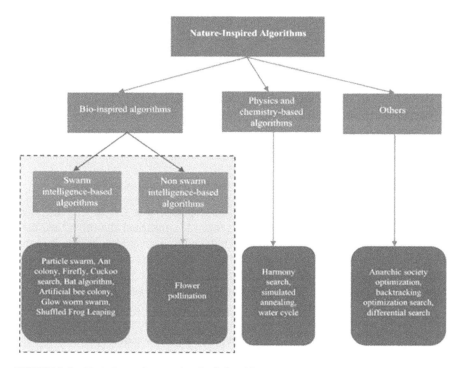

FIGURE 9.1 Variations of nature-inspired algorithms.

There are three key ideas of pot mechanisms comments circles, original area analysis and interplay among humans. Probabilistic ways that give measurability and some stages of certain elements might be discovered in nature and knitter-made to technology. This fashion pretensions conservative conception to help crimes way too constrained data regarding the organic styles or lacking correlations among the herbal and the specialized models. Supported this fashion, the cited mechanisms for the pot should be forced to be mentioned in redundant detail.

- **Feedback circles:** The process acts as an associate in tending digital contrivance for a given effect. Feedback is hired to control the device gets expeditiously to help against overreactions and misregulation. There is a resource of circle pictured in determine 3, the activation of the system step. The result incontinently that could suppress an environmental responsibility also it reduces the activation capabilities.
- **Native area:** The 2nd aspect is the original area. This method indicates that every subsystem blockish measures attempt and movement upon data that blockish degree maintains regionally. Any global control or reliance is prevented from changing tone-sufficient conduct bedded right into a global environment. The conception of victimization original area fully is pictured in our case through lacking outside control styles.

- **Relations:** Data switch among humans is pivotal to replacing the original area. There are styles to get similar relations, direct interplay or verbal exchange among linked subsystems and oblique data change through the atmosphere. This fashion is called stigmergy. The illustration in determines three consists of stigmatic relations. The device impacts the atmosphere (it produces many effects). This effect might be measured and incontinently grow or lower the device's activation capabilities.
- Probabilistic ways to help synchronization problems and increase the range of the software disciplines. Random options generally acquire measurability.

9.3   BIO-INSPIRED ALGORITHMS IN TECHNICAL SYSTEMS

The advancement of bio-inspired engineering depends on a variety of evaluation domains, mass intelligence, artificial intelligence (AI), inherited algorithms and natural system calculating methods, as well as cell and molecular biology-based methodologies. Then, a number of the suggested ways must be exemplified, while certain strategies are discussed in detail in this section. Massive brigades of nature have interacted with small insects like ants and have concocted ideas about place units as the basis for mass intelligence. There are some behaviours to be followed in those methods, such as the simple, disconnected, autonomous human composition of an elegant task. Similar precautions are required in various computer operations fields. Consequently, a shape for organizational structures is typed by mass genius [3–7]. A recent study provides similar methods for viewing aspect networks [8]. The method of critical evaluation employs a mammal device that was developed using a synthetic device (AIS). The prone system may respond to unknown attacks in a friendly manner. Therefore, it seems outrageous to employ specific procedures for affiliation and tone-mending activities in computer networks. A unit has numerous intentional infrastructures for an AIS. Examples of operations include unbiased verbal conversation and ad-hoc networking [9–12]. The contagion and intrusion-finding elements of the AIS method make up the instability scenario [13–15]. In nature, the elaboration device typically rests on the foundation of some techniques. Particularly, there are a few perspectives in their immediate neighbourhood that can teach the organism. The desire theme's (survival of the fittest) technique allows the elegantly equipped organisms to fully survive and procreate. For example, changes are felt through mutations. There is passed in a summary of natural method algorithms. A growing hand of the evaluation house searches for approaches that are based on molecular biology and the phone. Natural species have an individualized well system built within them. They are made up of cells and Hopkins-compliant organs. This physical structure is quite similar to computer networks, and it very closely resembles signalling networks. As a result, mobile and natural knowledge evaluation ensures high capabilities for computer networking generally and good networks.

There are several advantages to location-based services that successfully employ bio-inspired methodologies. We want to charge and investigate the limitations of bio-inspired systems. There are some discussions to be had between utterly unique claims in the herbal realm, and it is admirable that biology frequently fails in these

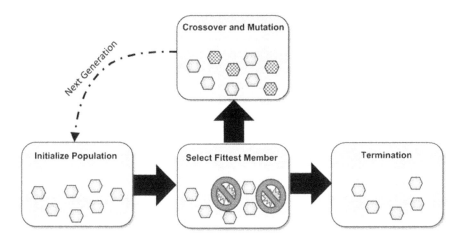

FIGURE 9.2   Bio-inspired algorithm using WSN.

discussions. Some natural systems lack proper documentation and may not have clearly defined drawback boundaries. Four networked bed systems are used as a location unit in various operational scenarios. Wi-Fi seeing problem networks (WSN) that cover a large geographic area were mostly used to study the region. Figure 9.2 depicts a bio-inspired algorithm using WSN.

Some of these challenges are significant when it comes to connecting numerous networked bed systems, specifically when they evolve to enable clear-cut WSN operation scenarios.

- **High-quality knots:** System networks are typically thought to be stationary or to have at least a basic topology in knot location. The subject of the most recent operational eventualities, like provision, is becoming quite extreme. On the other side, SANET is built with function dynamics and quality.
- **Network measurement:** In stark contrast to unique networks, a community on demand frequently has a significant number of bumps. Sub-networks in structured networks like the internet operate centrally and with canted affiliation. WSN and SANET are infrastructure-free networks that experience numerous dips in measurability.
- **Preparation viscosity:** When examining the state of affairs, the knot viscosity is extremely bad. WSN is frequently astoundingly high. This strategy may ruin home medium access control operation protocols and affect electricity prostration just for local discovery.
- **Energy restrictions**: Unlike established or mobile networks, which offer limitless power for calculation and communication, electrical restrictions are more stringent. Machine bumps typically run on batteries, and in some situations, it is impossible to recharge the power supply. We make a distinction between regenerative energy sources, such as those used in wearable detectors, replenishable energy sources, such as those used in remote, parlous tract sensors and

non-renewable electrical sources medium get admission to operation protocols
and have an effect on electricity prostration solely for regional discovery.

• **Energy constraints:** As an alternative to having limitless strength for calculation and communication, electricity constraints are greater rigorous than
established or cell networks. Generally, machine bumps are battery-operated,
and in bound cases, the recharging of the power pressure is not possible. We
distinguish between replenishable energy sources, e.g. for wearable detectors,
non-replenishable electricity sources, e.g. for sensors stationed in the remote,
parlous tract and regenerative energy sources.

• **Information/phrase emulsion:** Facts are described in the information/phrase
"emulsion" because of the cited electrical restrictions' necessity for aggregation methods. Every record packet that is being transferred through a WSN
is priceless. Collective statistics reduce electricity use and produce higher-
quality inventory. The need for affiliation mechanisms for better measurability
in WSN/SANET communication is frequently the same. The neighbourhood discovery, topological (re-)association and probabilistic methods are all
embodied in the abecedarian mechanisms. Since it is no longer possible to
optimize a world function, there is continually a significant disparity between
several objects.

9.4   NETWORKING INSPIRED BY BIO

The main section focuses on ideas related to bio-inspired networking. The evaluation
criteria and bio-inspired results are outlined in fresh detail and supported by a few
sophisticated methods. Many different engineering fields depend on the cooperative
efforts of many individuals, or impartial systems. The general public is informed
about microscopic insects like ants and concepts to solve related issues. Ants, for
instance, will obliterate difficult tasks with simple local solutions. The environment
needs to be changed for humans to carry out commercial responses. Finally, the ants'
productivity enables a better overall performance through a number of their conditioning, and all together, they are positioned as "grandmasters" in hunt and discourse.
The essential principle is upheld when all members of the herbal community who get
together to accomplish a shared goal adhere to practical rules that have an impact in a
significant transnational manner. The commonly observed was formerly investigated.

9.4.1   IMPORTANCE OF SWARM INTELLIGENCE

The answer to the present is straightforward currently, and we established this in our
previous marble example, that is assembling the answers (responses) from totally
different objects separately and so computing all responses as a full to an answer that
most closely fits our given downside. So here, with this approach, we have a tendency
to are having an additional optimized answer for a given downside which is the reason
why swarm intelligence came into the image; owing to this reason, we can use it in
numerous eventualities of life, e.g. statement, that policy is nice for the business, etc.
thus merely we tend are mistreatment the 'Brain of Brains' to achieve the answer for

a given downside. Suppose we are going to observe our surroundings (nature). In that case, we will be able to realize several samples of swarm intelligence like 'ant colony', 'swarm of bees',' flock of birds and truly, conjointly, the thought of swarm intelligence was taken from nature solely.

9.4.2 ANT COLONY OPTIMIZATION

If we are going to observe closely, then the ants conjointly follow the principle of swarm intelligence; for instance, to make the house, they collect mud particles from the environment separately and have a responsibility to make their home. They impart through signals and pheromones (ants use this for tracing different ants), and no matter what different ants do, a private is liable for solely its contribution to making the house. equally, once they explore for food, they initially search separately for food and exploit the pheromones behind and once they realize the food supply, then that ant communicates with different ants. So different ants will trace it and follow that path to achieve the food supply rather than simply indiscriminately looking for food in numerous locations.

9.4.3 SWARM OF BEES

Bees conjointly use constant principle for their survival: once they explore for a place like wherever they'll build their hive. The task of every bee is to think about many parameters that the hive which can be designed ought to air smart height to avoid predators, ought to be close to water resources, ought to be close to pollens (flowers to gather nectar), etc. then they use their pooled analysis. At last, an area is set wherever the hive would be designed considering all those parameters and that they reach the most effective answer for that downside.

9.4.4 ARTIFICIAL SWARM INTELLIGENCE

It is conjointly called Human Swarm. Here conjointly, the thought is that we tend to indiscriminately build a number of the persons collaborating in a very period system and tell them to seek out the answer for that individual downside separately. The ultimate answer is then computed when taking responses from every participant. Therefore the race murder is given that is additionally optimized compared to the answer taken from just one participant.

9.4.5 APPLICATIONS OF SWARM INTELLIGENCE

- Used in military services.
- NASA is generating the thought to use swarm intelligence for planetary mapping.
- Used in data processing. M. Anthony Lewis and St. George A. Bekey bestowed the thought that we will manage nanobots in our bodies to kill cancer tumours with the assistance of swarm.
- Used in business to achieve higher money choices etc.

9.5   ROUTING AND TASK ALLOCATION EXPLOITATION ATTRACTOR METHODOLOGY

In particular, the example of mass talent networking approaches chooses an attractor or topic for the routing and assignment allocation structures. The AntHocNet approach, which permits tone-organized routing in unexpected networks, is the foundation of this technique. Unintended networks advocate and make use of the trial-and-error method of seeking elegant solutions. The based response will be inferred from earlier (over difficult paths) communicated dispatches, which previously involved numerous literacy processes. The chapter's main focus is on how to successfully manage a knot during a straightforward job (whether encouraging a packet or commodity differently). The legal obligation of conducting business and learning about overpriced earlier. Additionally, the disadvantage is reduced if the knot fails for a particular task. Also, pays attention to the surrounding bumps to update its native properly. The posterior machine vicinity unit is taken into account in this formula. Every tangle of mates joins in on an endeavour to entice T as an accomplice. The knot computes a legal obligation for selecting scheme I while picking which task to carry out. Previously, the parameter was supplied to extend the exploitation in sophisticated methods. Every knot sets up τi with τ in it. However, τi is recalculated $\tau i = \min$; if the knot with success carried out the given undertaking i. Also, τi is decreased for unprofitable operations $\tau i = \min$. The one-of-a-kind formula, the corresponding computations related to in-depth evaluation will be planted. At some point in this chapter, a crew of trials was once carried out to exhibit the advantages of the attractor theme. The simulation setup is proven in parent five. Twenty-five bumps have been placed all through a grid on a playground of 500×500 m. Four special duties had been outlined to be carried out through these bumps. Anyhow, of the venture allocation, we might like to listen to the related route preference at some point in this network.

9.6   ARTIFICIAL SYSTEM

Artificial structures are inspired by educational scientific topics and used in complex strike fields as prone functions, principles and models. The first function of an artificial device (AIS) is to identify changes in the environment or deviations from the norm. The device place unit's attention skills (anomaly detection, noise tolerance), vibrancy, diversity, aptitude for supporting literacy and risk to studying compliance are its key impressing competencies.

The development of tone-optimizing and tone-literacy processes is enabled by these choices. The following will serve as an example of the section of the cranial device. It should guard the body from illnesses. Two prone reactions to this have been identified. The first step is to start a response to pathogens written in cursive. Contrarily, the susceptible secondary reaction, or immunological memory, takes note as soon as problems arise. The next time, it displays a specified response yet approves a hurried response (B-cells and T-cells). The complementarity between the listing place of a receptor-associated small amount of a depends on acknowledged as an epitome supports the susceptibility cognizance. Antigens may also have a variety of epitomes, whereas antibodies only have one type of receptor.

This tactic suggests that exceptional antibodies will acknowledge one problem. The device should be able to distinguish between tone and non-self cells. The device establishes several correctly amazing and dreadful options to prevent substance problems from causing mobile death. The AIS has a broad compass. Unit operations for AI, control, agent-specific grounded systems, fault and anomaly finding, facts mining (laptop literacy, sample recognition). The arrangement of the motes within the cerebral system determines the degree of list. An AIS must exist at equal distances. In general, antigens and antibodies are modelled after vectors, with Ab = Ab1, Ab2, ..., AbL> and Ag = Ag1, Ag2, ..., AgL> for place-based devices. Based on the current topography, several shape areas can be used.

The trait strings and unit real-valued vectors are real-valued shapes.

- A finite ABC of size ok was used to create a hamming shape area formed of trait strings.
- Emblematic shapes are occasionally made up of vibrant trait strings, like the "name", "colour", etc. The matching of antigens is based on this description. Other distance measures like performing Manhattan will additionally be used. The most operation in utilized knowledge and engineering is anomaly discovery. A sequence of compliance over time commonly signifies the typical gesture. The initial process relies on police work sundries, or anomalies will be considered as changing diversions of an attribute property in the system. For computer scientists, bearing on manner contagions and community intrusions is regarded as one of the most imperative anomaly discovery tasks. One of the most important AIS used to be bestowed in. To help the herbal system's operating concepts, frameworks for actus Reus discovery, assault, or infiltration have been established. The operation and operation of multi-robot systems have also been handled by AIS techniques in addition to community safety operations. While no longer a core operation, the collaborative method of robots building products in a partner setting is challenging to optimize. It has been demonstrated that AIS-related robotic exploitation solves several issues related to the growing trend of collaborative work done by humans.

9.6.1 Mobile Ad-Hoc Networks Misbehaviour Detection

Every knot in ad-hoc networks is a related end system, similar to a router. This gadget makes it possible to develop dynamic, on-demand community topologies that support cellular systems. Unintended cellular networks include numerous routing protocols that focus on route discovery and preservation (time, above, etc.). On the one hand, this dynamic function permits the exchange of delicate, cellular processes. On the other side, the same dynamics also make it possible to attack the subcaste of the routing protocol community. To rearrange the unintended community for specific services, similar assaults should be launched for provider refusal reasons. The frequency of false bumps serves as the third reason for actus Reus in unwilling networks. The gadget should be fallacious or inaptly carried out by way of the routing protocol. It works for a precise unintended routing protocol, DSR (dynamic pressure routing).

The routing protocol must be used incorrectly or inappropriately by the device. An artificial device has been used as the basis of an actus Reus discovery topic.

The unique paper outlines mapping the herbal gadget thoughts like tone, matter and protein to an unintended cell network. Also, the following method for actus reus discovery is bestowed.

- Cellular ad-hoc community of the whole body;
- Bumps carrying tone cells;
- Performing up bumps with non-self cells;
- Antibody A sample with a harmonious layout due to the fact of the compact illustration of a count;
- Negative selection antibodies region unit created all through partner offline studying section. This may additionally be wiped out a test bed with bumps stationed by way of a driver in a stationed system.

Since antigens symbolize traces of determined protocol events, comparable sequences would come lengthy for the duration of a brief quantum of your time. Thus, all paths should be limited by using furnishing a point in time for the commentary interval.

Antibodies have the harmonious structure as antigens (comparable to l3), besides they may have any variety of nucleotides acceptable. Associate protein fits companion remember if the protein consists of a one in every position, anywhere the difficulty consists of a one. This method has been nice with success. The fundamental evaluation standards for comparable discovery techniques place unit verify fantastic discovery fee and additionally the false-positive discovery rate, so {the vary the quantum the volume} of with success is recognized forward bumps and additionally the range of by accident misapplied bumps, severally. As proven in discerning seven, the strategy suggests a fairly encouraging result.

9.6.2 INTERCELLULAR INFORMATION EXCHANGE

Financial networking may benefit from looking into the organization and structure of animated problem verbal engagement. Biological principles serve as the cornerstone of all biological systems. A high level of data transfer specificity is used. In both biology and technology, notably in computer networking, we find several linked architectural forms. The original concepts identify diffuse communication in large-scale systems, as well as intra- and animate component communication pathways. It is possible to separate the following learning processes: pecuniary response to the inquiry, statistical path shortening and associated signal guiding to an appropriate location. This is so because biological systems resemble networks of linguistic interaction. Statistics will be divided into native statistics and remote statistics. Remote: a signal is released into the bloodstream, delivered to far-off cells and triggers a reaction in those cells, which then sends the signal or activates helper cells (e.g. the immune system). Particle-like signals, such as proteins and hormones, will manifest in response to discovered and adjusted environmental conditions, such as the atomic variety 20 concentration.

9.6.3 PROMOTERS AND INHIBITORS CREATING FEEDBACK LOOPS FOR POSITIVE ENVIRONMENTAL REMARKS

Electric powered circuit medium is a case study of the successful use of the defined conversation approach in WSN. Then, the pressure per unit place Angiotensin-grounded legislation device was orientated to model the operation circle for a restrictive provident approach in an organism. The excretory organ is working to produce the renin supermolecule in the situation of falling blood pressure. This supermolecule starts a cascade of many activations and changes. Thus, it encourages every other supermolecule (angiotensinogen) to change into a shorter one (now known as vasoconstrictor I), which is then reiterated to angiotonin.

This supermolecule is the last response to the countless things on highly specialized cells in multiple organs that are currently being used to extend the pressure per unit region to the normal position. A molecular remarks medium completes the entire mobile process at a constant time. Angiotensin helps to distinguish each receptor site unit. This device was tailored to find a clear-seeing component community by the employment of the latter two generalizations.

1. The viscosity of the optical problem community permits different remarks circles via the terrain immediately by the physical wonders that are to be controlled by the structure.
2. Circular communication lowers operational dispatches and enables flexible affiliation of unbiased structures. The process of conditioning in an optical component network calls for the statistics to alternate between a couple of bumps inside the network.

Similar to formal communication between nodes is necessary for at least two reasons. The operation records have been delivered to the correct location first, on the next part, the element must respond to the request by attesting to their signals. For such an operation, all commonly constructed community protocols abide by the same basic principles. An understanding packet intended for the factual objective is started to be transmitted. Up until a response, the packet is entered that confirms the team action, state statistics are accumulated at several community-based points.

Before the present, the paradigms for information transfer in optical factor networks were dynamic. Data-centric dispersion, underpinning-based adjustment to the trial-and-error elegant approach and in-network know-how aggregation and concealment are some of the fascinating aspects of directed prolixity introduced. A similar modification has been anticipated for the operation information influx on which we prefer to concentrate. It has been proposed that verbose verbal exchanges are perceptive. Priority is given to transferring the communications. The importance of the task at hand is illustrated by this priority. Supported by this precedent, the advertisement is distributed to a portion of the immediate neighbours and a correct decline portion of constantly useful bumps. Until the desired task is operational or the mission is exhaustively cancelled, this device remains intermittent. As a result, a randomness problem is applied to the distribution of functions or, more specifically, to the dissipation of facts. Superior machine reliability and strength, specifically in unreliable multi-hop precise Wi-Fi seeing aspect networks, are where the money is.

9.7   CONCLUSION

In conclusion, it should also be noted that numerous methods for bio-inspired networking are being researched and that we have already witnessed unusual impacts and operations. To address unresolved issues in networking discussion circles, the following mechanisms are tailored: native nation records for provident expertise emulsion, strength operation and clustering; weighted probabilistic strategies for task allocation, process-led discussion and traffic control. The multi-objective enhancement tool that balances the aforementioned trade-offs between a sure thing and energy comes into play eventually. The evaluation and development of communication and collaboration mechanisms between networked nested systems would be comparable. There are numerous items and numerous directions. However, comparable results can also be inferred. Bio-inspired networking is undoubtedly one method, notwithstanding its importance. The current evaluation criteria include allotted operation in SANET, handling and storing in WSN, mission allocation mechanisms and acceptable information dispersion.

REFERENCES

[1] Akkaya, K., and M. Younis (2004). 'Energy-aware routing of time- constrained traffic in wireless sensor networks', *Journal of Communication Systems*, Special Issue: Service Differentiation and QoS in Ad Hoc Networks, 17(6): 663–687.

[2] Akyildiz, I. F., and I. H. Kasimoglu (2004). 'Wireless sensor and actor networks: Research challenges', *Elsevier Ad Hoc Network Journal*, 2: 351–367.

[3] Akyildiz, I. F., W. Su, et al. (2002). 'A survey on sensor networks', *IEEE Communications Magazine*, 40(8): 102–116.

[4] Bentley, P. J., T. Gordon, et al. (2001). 'New trends in evolutionary computation', Congress on Evolutionary Computation, Seoul.

[5] Bekey, G. A., & M. A. Lewis (1995). Biologically inspired robot control. In *New Trends in Design of Control Systems* (pp. 379–383). Pergamon.

[6] Bonabeau, E., M. Dorigo, et al. (1999). *Swarm Intelligence: From Natural to Artificial Systems*. Oxford University Press.

[7] Culler, D., D. Estrin, et al. (2004). 'Overview of sensor networks', *Computer*, 37(8): 41–49.

[8] Das, S. K., N. Banerjee, et al. (2004). Solving optimization problems in wireless networks using Genetic Algorithms. In *Handbook of Bio-inspired Algorithms and Applications*, p. 219. CRC Press.

[9] De Castro, L. N., and J. Timmis (2002). *Artificial Immune Systems: A New Computational Intelligence Approach*. Springer.

[10] Di Caro, G., and M. Dorgio (1998). 'AntNet: Distributed stigmergetic control for communication networks', *Journal of Artificial Intelligence Research*, 9: 317–365.

[11] Di Caro, G., F. Ducatelle, et al. (2005). 'AntHocNet: An adaptive nature- inspired algorithm for routing in mobile ad hoc networks', *European Transactions on Telecommunications*, Special Issue: Self-Organization in Mobile Networking, 16: 443–455.

[12] Dorigo, M., V. Trianni, et al. (2004). 'Evolving self-organizing behaviors for a swarm-bot', *Autonomous Robots,* 17(2&3): 223–245.

[13] Dressler, F. (2005). Locality driven congestion control in self-organizing wireless sensor networks. 3rd International Conference on Pervasive Computing, Munich.

[14] Dressler, F. (2006). Self-organization in ad hoc networks: Overview and classification. University of Erlangen.

[15] Dressler, F., B. Krüger, et al. (2005). Self-organization in sensor networks using bio-inspired mechanisms. 18th ACM/GI/ITG International Conference on Architecture of Computing Systems, Innsbruck.

10 Genetic Algorithms for Wireless Network Security

Vijayalakshmi S and Savita

10.1 INTRODUCTION

Wireless networks use radio signal frequencies to connect between many computers and other devices. They are also known as Wi-Fi networks or WLANs and are becoming growingly popular because of their ease of setup and avoidance of cabling [1]. Wireless internet access is gradually becoming more prevalent in both office and public settings, as well as among home internet users. This modern era of innovation flexibility may also open the door to network security issues not just in the corporate world but also for residential users.

Metaheuristic algorithms have recently been used to solve real-world difficult problems in disciplines such as economics, technology, politics, governance and engineering. The essential components of a metaheuristic algorithm are intensification and expansion. To solve a real-life problem effectively, a perfect balance between such elements is required. The majority of metaheuristic algorithms are based on biological evolution, swarm behavior and the laws of physics. Wireless sensor networks (WSNs) are the most rapidly evolving technologies in data computation and information networking fields today. WSNs are composed of physically small sensor nodes that communicate with others mainly about their surroundings [2–5].

The main challenges in WSNs are safety, energy efficiency, size, expandability, energy efficiency, reliability, computing power and visibility and deployment. Security is a major issue in WSNs, and this is one of those challenges. Since the unguided information transmission medium is significantly more open to security assaults than the directed information transmission, remote organizations are more presented with various security chances. The significance of secure information transmission using an untrustworthy channel is developing constantly. To get remote sensor organizations, they should give these four security properties: honesty, secrecy, accessibility and genuineness.

Wireless networking has seen rapid growth, as evidenced by the widespread deployment of various wireless n/w of different sizes, like wireless personal area networks, wireless local area networks, metropolitan area networks and wide area networks. All mentioned wireless n/w can take many forms, including mobile networks, ad-hoc n/w

 DOI: 10.1201/9781003248545-10

and mesh n/w, as well as domain-specific networks like vehicular communication n/w and sensor technologies.

Wireless networks, on the other hand, lack physical security due to underlying communications being made possible by electromagnetic energy in open areas. Wireless n/w presents new challenges to the computers and network security communities. Many technical challenges are associated with the approach to strengthening wireless network security, which includes interoperability with existing wireless networks, computational complexity and feasible market values. There is a requirement to discuss wireless network protection as well as provide timely strong technical contributions.

Security processes are necessary for recent data communication standards over unprotected media like the internet. It is difficult to determine if a communication protocol satisfies the relevant security requirements, particularly in difficult scenarios like group communications in a WSN, in which a large number of entities may be involved.

A Genetic Algorithm (GA), first proposed by John Holland in 1970, is a metaheuristic optimization technique that tries to mimic the robust procedures utilized by numerous biological entities as part of normal evolution [6]. GAs have already been used effectively in a wide range of fields, including aviation industry, process technology, animation software, medicinal chemistry, telecommunications, software development and financial markets.

10.2   GENETIC ALGORITHM

With the growth and importance of the internet, the types and number of attacks have increased, helping to make intrusion detection an extremely important technic. To prevent computer systems from security breaches, various tools have been introduced and implemented such as security software, firewall, cryptography, security rules and password protection system. Even with our best attempts, a truly secure system is impossible to achieve. As a result, threat identification is becoming a prime method for monitoring n/w traffic and detecting network threats including unusual n/w behaviors, unapproved access, or malicious threats on systems [7].

A GA is a heuristic based on Charles Darwin's theory of natural selection [8]. This algorithm is modeled after the theory of natural selection, in which the best fit individuals are selected for reproduction to generate offspring for the coming generation. GAs extract the complex problem as an individual's population and iteratively produce generations to find the best fitness individual [9]. This concept can be used to solve a search problem. We define a set of solutions to complex problems and choose the best ones from among them. A GA considers different phases as given in Figure 10.1.

- **Initial population:** The process begins with a group of people known as a population. Every person is a solution to the issue the user wishes to solve. A person is defined as a set of parameters or variables called genes. To create a chromosome, genes are linked together in a string.

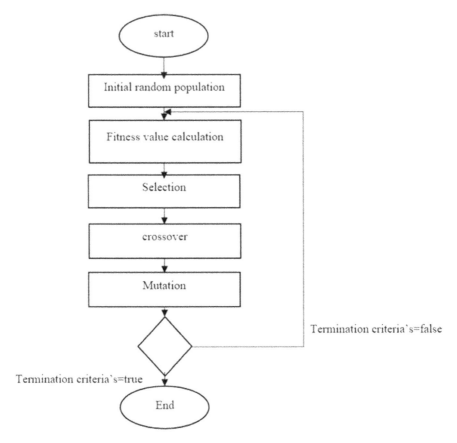

FIGURE 10.1   Genetic Algorithm flowchart.

- **Fitness function value calculation:** The fitness function defines how to fit a person (an individual's capacity to compete with others). It assigns a score value to every individual. The fitness score of an individual determines the likelihood that it will be chosen for reproduction.
- **Selection:** The idea behind the selection step is to select the best fit individuals from the population and allow them to transmit their genes to the future generation. The sets of individuals are chosen based on fitness levels. Individuals who have very high fitness have a better chance of being picked for reproduction.
- **Crossover:** Crossover is one of the most important stages of a GA. A crossover point from within the genes is chosen at random for every pair of parents to be mated.
- **Mutation:** Some of the genes in certain newly formed offspring may be subjected to a mutation with a low random probability. This indicates that some of the bits in the bit string can be switched.
- **Termination:** If the population has converged, the algorithm will be terminated. The GA is then said to provide solutions to the problem or issue.

10.3 WIRELESS NETWORK

"Wireless networking is a technique which allows two or multiple systems to connect by making use of basic n/w protocols except without using any cable. In a strict sense, a technique that accomplishes this could be referred to as wireless n/w." A wireless technique enables users to communicate as well as access data and applications without using wires. This allows for greater mobility and the capacity to develop applications in various elements of the building, city, or almost everywhere in the world. Wireless networks enable individuals to connect with email or access the web from wherever they want. WSNS has been an important aspect of communication in recent times, as well as a truly innovative paradigm change, allowing audiovisual communication among people and equipment from any location (Figure 10.1). It is bringing about fundamental changes in data networking, telecommunications and the creation of integrated networks. Due to modulation technique, adaptive modulation, info compression, wireless modems and multiplexing, it has created the network conveniently. Sensor nodes, smart buildings, remote patient monitoring and automated highways are just a few of the interesting applications it supports. The armed services, emergency services and enforcement agencies were among the first to use the wireless technique [10].

10.4 WIRELESS NETWORK EQUIPMENT

The main issue is equipment selection. As such, the durability, effectiveness and performance characteristics of the network as a whole are all dependent on the proper selection of system components. When selecting equipment, it is also essential to consider the future. Because electronic device technology is rapidly evolving, it is critical to include in the project device models that will ensure the efficient use of existing technology not only in present but also in the future. It allows future costs linked with n/w modernization to be ignored.

Wireless systems can be handled in one of three ways:

- **Wireless switch:** A wireless component and more than one wireless marker are present on the computer system. All installed wireless tools are enabled by default, and when a computer boots up, the wireless indicator glows blue. The wireless light represents the overall status of wireless devices rather than the state of a specific device. If the wireless light is colored blue, which means one wireless device is active. If all wireless devices are turned off and the wireless light is also turned off. Because all built-in wireless devices are turned on by default, wireless connectivity enables all devices to be automatically turned on and off.
- Some models use assistance software to control the devices.
- Operating systems allow users to manage integrated wireless systems and wireless connections.

10.5   NEED AND BENEFITS OF WIRELESS TECHNOLOGY

Wireless networks are one of the telecommunications industry's fastest-growing fields of technology. Wireless communication systems have gained widespread acceptance and popularity due to their numerous benefits over a wired network. Wireless networking has the potential to be a quick, simple and cost-effective alternative that operates between nodes and is carried out without using wires in our house or apartment. It also allows for the linking of buildings that are up to many kilometers off from one another. It provides consistent and effective keys to a variety of instant applications, so it is currently used across a wide range of platforms, including medical services, education, financial, hospitality, airports and general merchandise. Since it has a huge impact on the country, the use of wireless networks is increasing day by day [11]. As a result, its applications have grown considerably. Some benefits of using wireless n/w are:

- While working outside, the user can move around and connect to the wireless connection.
- The benefits of mobility and cost savings drove the need for wireless n/w. Costs are much lower because of wiring installed is minimal, if at all. The time required to deploy wireless n/w is significantly less than compared to wired networks.
- Anyone can send data all over the entire globe using satellites and other signals transmitted via wireless n/w.
- A wireless solution is ideal for places where wiring is banned or tough to set up, such as historical buildings or areas nearby rivers.

10.6   TYPES OF WIRELESS NETWORKS

Wireless networks can be classified in a variety of ways. Some wireless n/w are fixed, which means that antennas do not move. Other wireless networks are active, which means that the antenna can move at any time [12].

Mainly two kinds of wireless networks:

- An ad-hoc wireless n/w is made up of several computers, each of which has a wireless n/w interface card. Every computer can connect with another wirelessly enabled machine. They can start sharing devices such as printers, but they can't access wired LAN resources because at least one system uses special software to act as a bridge to the wired LAN which is later known as "bridging." Every device with a wireless interface can connect with another directly.
- An access point or base station, can be used in a wireless network. In this kind of n/w, the access point serves as a hub, connecting wireless computers. It can also connect (or "bridge") a wireless local n/w to a wired local n/w, authorizing wireless computers to access LAN assets like data centers or current network connectivity.
- **Wireless PAN:** The personal area is one type of wireless n/w in which all systems are connected within a small range (room)(up to 10 meters). WPAN requires very little infrastructure and has no direct contact with the outside

world. This enables the implementation of small, power-efficient, low-cost solutions for a broad variety of devices such as smartphones and PDAs. These networks rely on techniques like Bluetooth, Infrared Data Association, ZigBee and Ultra-Wide Band.

- **Wireless LAN:** Wireless development of local area n/w is known as a WLAN. Data is transferred between computer systems via radio signals sent over large areas such as homes, computer laboratories, offices, or schools. The IEEE 802.11 series standardizes wireless LAN protocols. Wireless LANs are intended to provide wireless access over a typical range of up to 100 meters. "wireless fidelity" or Wi-Fi standard, is broadly utilized for networking personal computers and the Internet. The Wi-Fi Alliance's Wi-Fi technology brand is being used to confirm products to set up interoperability that uses IEEE 802.11 standards.
- **Wireless MAN:** The third type of wireless network is Wireless Metropolitan Area Networks (WANs). WMANs are focused on the IEEE 802.16 standard, also known as Worldwide Interoperability for Microwave Access. WiMAX is an information and communication technology that enables a point-to-multipoint structure to deliver high-speed wireless signals over metropolitan area networks. This allows smaller wireless LANs to be linked via WiMAX to form a large WMAN. Thus, networking between city areas can be accomplished without the use of costly cabling.
- **Wireless WAN:** Wireless Wide Area Networks or WWAN usually extend over and above 50 km and use licensed frequencies. These networks can be maintained across large areas, such as cities or countries, by utilizing communications satellites or antenna sites managed by an internet company. There are primarily two techniques developed: digital cellular telephony and satellite systems [13,14].

Table 10.1 provides a brief overview of the various types of such networks. Each type of wireless network has functionalities that enhance other networks, allowing different network needs to be met.

10.7 TYPES OF WIRELESS NETWORK ATTACKS

Wireless networks are much more susceptible to threats, because of data processing and power restrictions, Many computers now come with network cards already installed. The ability to connect to a network while on the move is extremely useful. However, there are numerous security concerns with wireless networking. As security techniques age, they become easier to breach. To resolve this, network engineers or customers must stay informed of any new threats that emerge.

10.8 LIST OF ATTACKS IN THE WIRELESS NETWORK

Individuals and organizations should be familiar with the major types of wireless attacks: passive attacks and active attacks. Hackers who only intend to steal important information such as emails, identity, or login information but do not intend to exploit

TABLE 10.1
List of different wireless networks

N/W type	Range	Use	Standards	Connectivity types
Wireless personal area network	10 m	Specific network	802.15	Bluetooth
Wireless local area network	up to 100 m	Specific to building or office	802.11	Cellular
Wireless metropolitan area network	up to 10 km	City, or campus	802.16	WiMax
Wireless wide area network	More than 100 km	Regional or national cities	Rely on cellular technique	Long term evolution

any digital resources are recognized as passive attacks. Additionally, passive attacks do not generally leave evident tracks behind, which is much more harmful to users, as they may not realize it from the start, whereas active attacks are much more aggressive, in which the defendant is quickly aware of the breach being performed out and attackers that come under the category of active attacks generally have the purpose to straightforwardly find and decimate target network or system [15]. Some other attacks are listed below.

10.8.1 MITM ATTACK

MITM or Man in the mi attacks is active attacks wherein attackers listen in on the targets' connections and send messages among them. And the two victims think they are talking directly to one another, but the hacker controls the entire communication.

Man-in-the-middle attacks are simple when data packets are not encoded or when security mechanisms are inadequate. Some cryptographic processes, including endpoint verification, are used to resist this type of attack, especially to protect against MITM attacks.

Types of MITM Attacks

- **Captive portal:** Due to a lack of proper authentication and credential exchanges, a hacker may attack and steal critical info by creating a web page that looks similar to the one requested by the person. Hackers can even serve as a proxy, passing stolen data to the actual authentication mechanism. As a result, the hacker can access data. To resolve this, a certificate exchange should take place just before the conversation; the certificate clarifies the properties of authentication as well as the type of encryption that will be used on the data. Even the certificate exchange should be automated. As a result, there would be no need for separate certificate demands.

- **802.1X/EAP:** IEEE 802.1X is a port-based n/w access control IEEE standard (PNAC). It is an n/w protocol that is part of the IEEE 802.1 group. It gives devices that want to connect to a LAN or WLAN an authentication process. EAP means Extensible Authentication Protocol. IEEE 802.1X identifies the encapsulation process for the IEEE 802 extensible authentication protocol, also known as EAP over local area networks or wireless LANs. Many customers are not properly configured, leaving them prone to threats. This insecurity occurs as a result of failing to authenticate the RADIUS server. A model is developed to tackle the incorrect certificate exchange. In this framework, i.e., 802.1 X authentications, three parties are involved: a verification server, a supplicant and an authenticator. The supplicants are customer devices. The devices that want to link to the LAN or WLAN are known as supplicants [4]. And these systems provide the authenticator with their credentials.

A network device, such as an Ethernet or wireless access point, serves as an authenticator. A host that runs software that enables the RADIUS and EAP guidelines is used as an authorization server.

10.8.2 DENIAL OF SERVICE

DoS attack creates a network resource inaccessible to the targeted consumers. Threatening threats to data security. This may be one of the very well kinds of attacks, in which the attacker attempts to disable the service by accessing as much as it can carry. Multiple times that amount per minute and the text message-receiving service will either fail or slow down. DoS attacks can be carried out in a variety of ways. Dos attacks are divided into five main families:

- Physical n/w elements are disrupted.
- Router information is disrupted.
- Interruptions of state data, i.e., re-establishing TCP session settings.
- Utilization of computational resources, such as bandwidth, flash floods, etc.
- Restricting information exchange between the users and the defendant such that no communication is possible.

Jamming and flooding are two attacks that come under the DoS attacks category:

10.8.3 JAMMING ATTACK

The goal of jamming (also known as network interference) is to interrupt the network. Interruption is almost unpreventable due to the wireless functionalities. Mild interruption can be caused by Bluetooth headphones or maybe even a microwave oven. In most cases, malicious intruders integrate jamming technics with other techniques such as evil twinning. To protect your organization, you must invest in a spectrum analyzer, increase the power of existing APs or use different frequencies.

The transference of radio signals that disrupts communication by lowering the SNR (Signal to Noise Ratio) is known as jamming. Unintentional jamming occurs when an operator transfers a busy frequency without first determining whether or not something is in use. This is accomplished simply by producing Radio Frequency (RF) noise within the frequency used by wireless n/w devices. Microwave ovens, radars, monitors and other nearby devices that work on the very same frequency may be susceptible to communication jamming. Jamming threats are hard to detect.

Internal and external are two different jamming attacks. External jamming threats are those carried out by attackers who are not a member of or a part of the wireless network. Internal jamming attacks are carried out by the wireless network's nodes (intermediate nodes). Internal jamming actions are carried out by enemies who are informed of network secret documents and network protocol implementations. A paper has been written to address the solution to these internal jamming attacks.

10.8.4 FLOODING ATTACK

Flooding is a category of denial-of-service attack, and it can be verification flooding, De-authentication flooding and so on. In this threat, a continuous stream of a specific type of message is sent into the network. In authentication flooding, for example, the wireless network can be threatened by flooding with identity verification and affiliation frames at Access Points (AP).

As a result, the attacking machine will continuously parody its MAC address in an attempt to connect to the access point. At each attempt, the hacker will modify the MAC address, simulating the presence of multiple clients. As a result, this uses the processing power and memory of the access point (AC), rejecting service to other customers.

10.8.5 REPUDIATION

A repudiation threat happens when a person denies having performed a specific action or initiating a transaction. A customer can easily deny awareness of the transfer of funds or conversation and then assert that such transfer of funds or communication did not occur.

10.8.6 TAMPERING ATTACK

WSNs are extremely susceptible to physical threats because they are frequently installed in unprotected areas. A tampering threat will be launched after physically acquiring the node, to retrieve cryptographic content like encryption keys and program code saved inside a node, and it can be used to launch other sorts of threats such as changing routing information, generating redundant data packets, interfering routing facilities and so on, or to modify the collected node by installing additional code, causing abnormal behavior of the vulnerable sensor, controlled by the hacker. Destruction attacks involve removing the sensor from the network by ruining it, resulting in remote areas and, in extreme cases, the demolition of the entire network.

10.9 GA-BASED INTRUSION DETECTION IN MANETS

Mobile ad-hoc networks (MANETs) are much more vulnerable to security attacks, because of their complicated characteristics, such as a lack of clear defense boundaries, no centralized points and dynamic topologies. Because of the characteristics of MANETs, the identification of threats is more challenging than in traditional networks. In MANETs, one of the most serious attacks is distributed denial of service. This attack has the potential to reduce the accessibility of network services. Here GA can help to identify the DDoS attack very quickly in mobile ad-hoc n/w [16].

A GA is a very important method of searching that is based on natural genetics. Many problem areas (such as engineering and business) can benefit from the use of GA. GA employs three popular operators: selection, crossover and mutation. Individuals who are the best fit in the available population are selected. The primary record second half is combined with the secondary record first half in the crossover. Mutation haphazardly exchanges bits, i.e., 0 to 1 and vice versa. Figure 10.1 presents the basic flow of the GA.

The following steps are used in DoS intrusion identification:

- Data collection for DDoS attacks using QualNet simulator 6.1 and the AODV routing protocol.
- Have used a GA with such an appropriate fitness function on information (rules) to identify attack

GA approach of intrusion identification is divided into two stages. During the training stage, rules are generated using n/w audit data, and those rules with a corresponding fitness value are being used for intrusion detection. The highly effective features are used here to detect DDoS attacks. Table 10.2 lists the chosen features with explanations.

TABLE 10.2
List of features

Name of features	Description
No. req initiates	Total no. of PREQ initiates by node
No. req receive	Total no. of PREQ receive to node
No. req receive	Total no. of PREP received by node
No. rep from	Total no. of PREP sent by an intermediate node
No. err from	Total no. of PREP sent by a node
No. err receive	Total no. of PREP received by node
No. data pack initiates	Data packets sent by this node as the source of the data
Utilized battery	Calculates the amount of battery power used by this node to conduct any operation
Dropped data pack	Calculates the number of data packets that have not been forwarded by the next node

Each feature represents a chromosome gene. For attack detection, every rule is stated in an if–then clause. Every rule's fitness is determined by the specified fitness function. The fitness function is calculated as:

$$Fitness = x/X - y/Y$$

where
x = number of accurately detected attacks
X = total number of threats in the set of data used in the training stage
b = false-positive cases
B = number of normal connections in the dataset used.

The following steps are involved in the GA for intrusion detection:

1. Selection of DDoS attack features for data.
2. Data extraction using QualNet simulator 6.1 based on selected features.
3. Step 2 data is taken as a population in the approach
4. Apply GA
5. Determine the best fitness value for the GA.
6. Apply the chosen fitness function to the rules to discover the behavior, i.e., is normal and attack.

Fitness values are scored on a scale of [−1, 1], with −1 representing the lowest value and 1 representing the highest value. A high detection rate and a low false-positive rate result in the best fitness value. In contrast, a low detection rate and a high false-positive rate result in a low fitness value.

10.10   GA-BASED NETWORK SECURITY MODEL

Wireless access technology has become increasingly popular in recent years, because of the simplicity of functionality and installation of unbounded wireless links,. The configuration of wireless n/w is difficult because of its extremely interactive environmental conditions, which make input optimization a difficult task. Because of the dynamic, and frequently unknown, operational conditions, advanced wireless networking requirements increasingly depend on machine learning and artificial intelligence algorithms. GAs offer a well-established process of performing artificial intelligence works such as categorization, learning and utilization. GAs are quite good for their impressive generalization and flexibility, and they have been used in a wide range of wireless network configurations [17].

A fitness function is used to define a gene for an n/w packet, and a method for calculating fitness function is described. Basic attacks encountered include buffer overflow, array index out of bounds and so on. The emphasis is on the passive attack and active attack as well as brute force attack. There is an analysis of recent attacks and security. Finally, the best policy is discovered using a comparator. The primary goal is threat detection, time optimization, accuracy improvement and policy automation.

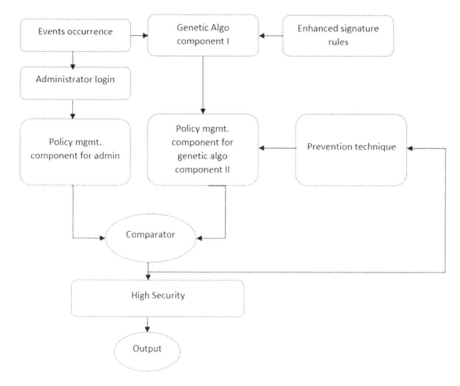

FIGURE 10.2   Genetic Algorithm-based framework for wireless network.

Figure 10.2 presents the basic framework for intrusion identification, optimization and accuracy in a wireless network.

- **Network event occurrence:** The administrator will choose the network incident or packets in this panel. Each network incident is analyzed here, and the network incident is passed to the GA-I.
- **Admin:** The user must be logged in as an administrator for Jpcap and WinPcap to identify packets; or else, no packets will be detected.
- **Policy Management Component for Admin:** In this panel, the Administrator chooses a policy and sends it to the selector or comparator.
- GA **Component I:** GA I was used to analyze packets. And also examined server-side data packets. The vector class is used and examined in n packets.
- **Component of policy management for GA component (GA-II):** GA-II is primarily used for policy shortlisting and protection. Types of threats and vulnerability verifications are discussed here.
- **Comparator:** This component compares two policy ideas administrator policy ideas and policy management points (GA-II). We are recycling policy by sending the comparator outcome to a network and selecting the best of the best policy.
- **Prevention technique:** In this component, the preventative measures process is utilized to infected connectivity terms, and the policy is passed to the Policy Management Point (GA-II).

- **High-security component:** Security has now been implemented in this factor for the finest of the best policy. When the users analyze a large number of packets over the network, the database is updated.

GA network security architecture consists of various subcomponents:

- **Gene developer:** Gene developer is used to receiving input in the form of a network packet. The properties can include the source and destination IP addresses, the destination port, packet size, and, in the event of a security breach, the level of threat and destruction caused, depending on the species of a security breach.
- **Operation unit:** Genetic actions such as crossover, mutagenesis and selection are applied to the administrator's initial population set in this component model.
- **Gene pool:** All of the genes picked during the genetic procedure relying on their fitness value score are saved in this portion, together with their best fitness, for reference purposes.
- **Comparator:** This component compares the gene created by the gene developer to the gene current in the genetic pool. If the gene is available in the gene pool, the component's outcome is transferred to the event action model. If the gene is missing, the fitness value of the gene is computed in the fitness calculator.
- **Fitness calculator:** The gene fitness is computed in this, and if the score is greater than the fitness function's threshold value, the gene is added to the gene pool, and the outcome is being sent to the n/w report generator. A GA-I for packet analysis and a GA-II is utilized here for policy choice and prevention.
- **Fitness function value:** Many parameters can affect the GA's effectiveness. One of the most critical parameters in GAs is the evaluation function. First, create a formula to determine whether a connection field matches the preclassified data set. The header fields of a chromosome are taken. A character, integer, double, or object can be used as the data type. If a specific packet has been matched to a set of rules and the difference is zero and one, the delta value can be calculated as:

$$M_v = \sum_{i=0}^{n} match * weight_i$$

where "n" presents the no. of genes found on each chromosome and the M_v is match value. In this case, a gene is a property that must be checked for in each network packet; ea network packet is equivalent to a chromosome.

10.11   CONCLUSION

In this chapter, we explained about the GAs in a wireless network. Wireless technology, which includes radio, mobile, infrared and satellite, is a method of transferring data from one location to another without the use of physical wires. Many businesses and industries are entering the wireless market. Airlines and hotel chains are two sectors of the economy that are most dedicated to utilizing wireless technologies for business travelers' communications needs. In addition to airports and hotels, several vertical market participants are taking full advantage of wireless networks. Most of these industries, such as delivery companies, community security, financial services, retail and surveillance applications, are still in the early stages of implementing wireless networks, but as time passes and supply and popularity grow, they will most likely implement wireless networking more deeply. With the emergence of these devices, it is essential to implement a security policy model to limit their possibilities for exploitation. Here we discussed the GA to detect all possible threats in wireless networks.

REFERENCES

[1] W. A. Arbaugh (2003). Real 802.11 Security: Wi-Fi Protected Access and 802.11i. Addison-Wesley.

[2] A. S. Jaradat and S. B. Hamad (2018). "Community structure detection using firefly algorithm." *International Journal of Applied Metaheuristic Computing*, vol. 9, no. 4, pp. 52–70.

[3] L. Tan, Y. Tan, G. Yun, and C. Zhang (2017). "An improved genetic algorithm based on k-means clustering for solving traveling salesman problem." *Proceedings of the 2016 International Conference on Computer Science, Technology and Application*, pp. 334–343.

[4] R. Matai, S. Singh, and M. L. Mittal (2012). "Traveling salesman problem: An overview of applications, formulations, and solution approaches". In: *Traveling Salesman Problem, Theory and Applications*. Intech Open, pp. 1–25.

[5] M. P. Durisic, et al. (2012). "A survey of military applications of wireless sensor networks." *Mediterranean Conference on Embedded Computing*, pp. 196–199.

[6] J. H. Holland (1992). *Adaptation in Natural and Artificial Systems*. University of Michigan Press.

[7] B. Shahi, S. Dahal, A. Mishra, S. V. Kumar, and C. P. Kumar (2016). "A review of genetic algorithm and application of wireless network systems." *Procedia Computer Science,* 78, pp. 431–438.

[8] S. Katoch, S. S. Chauhan, and V. Kumar (2021). "A review on the genetic algorithm: Past, present, and future." *Multimedia Tools and Applications*, 80(5), pp. 8091–8126.

[9] X.-S. Yang (2021), "Genetic algorithms." In *Nature-Inspired Optimization Algorithms* (2nd ed), ed. Xin-She Yang. Academic Press, pp. 91–100. https://doi.org/10.1016/B978-0-12-821986-7.00013.

[10] S. Khan, & A. K. Pathan (2013). *Wireless Networks and Security*. Springer.

[11] A. Prabhakar, A. Tiwari, and V. Pathak (2015). "The demand for wireless network and security in current research." *International Journal of Computers & Technology*, 14, pp. 5809–5813.

[12] H. Azizi (2017). "A brief review on wireless networks." *International Research Journal of Engineering and Technology*, vol. 4, no. 10, pp 329–333.

[13] N. N. Soni and A. M. Gonsai (2005). "Wireless network: Standards and its applications." 3rd Convention PLANNER. Assam University, Silchar, pp. 10–11 Nov., 2005.

[14] E. N. Enad and G. H. Muhanna (2013). "Computer wireless networking and communication." *International Journal of Advanced Research in Computer and Communication Engineering,* 2(8), pp. 3210–3216.

[15] T. Hussein Hadi (2022). "Types of attacks in wireless communication networks." *Webology,* 19, pp. 718–728.

[16] A. Chaudhary & G. Shrimal (2019), "Intrusion detection system based on genetic algorithm for detection of distribution denial of service attacks in MANETs." *Proceedings of International Conference on Sustainable Computing in Science, Technology and Management,* Amity University Rajasthan, India, pp. 370–377.

[17] L. M. R. J. Lobo and S. B. Chavan (2012). "Use of genetic algorithm in network security." *International Journal of Computer Applications,* 975, p. 8887.

11 Bio-Inspired Blockchain for Healthcare Workers
Insights on Covid-19

Siva Shankar Ramasamy, Ahmad Yahya Dawad, Naveen Kumar N and Chokkanathan K

11.1 INTRODUCTION

The duties of healthcare workers are changing era by era. Once the healthcare workers cared for the sick and ailing directly. Before the Covid pandemic we used to remember the healthcare workers as medical practitioners or doctors, nurses and lab technicians. After the Covid pandemic we came to realize and familiar with adding ward members, frontline workers, sanitary workers, medical suppliers, medical waste handlers are helping directly and indirectly by providing their service and support throughout the era. The World Health Organization (WHO) reminded every country to revisit the list and increase the count of workers to fight the global pandemic. Every country started acting towards the United Nation's Sustainable Development Goal (SDG) concerning health and well-being. They started to think and lay out the plans, people to work on them towards the ambitious targets. The expected results may rely on disease reduction, reducing the death rate and increasing the health equity within 2030. These plans shall not have compromises because the universal health coverage of United Nations (UN) General Assembly's plan by 2015 required this agenda for all the members in UN. Apart from health workers, the health systems require highly labor intensive, knowledge on every new step and timeline. The health workers play a major role in activating, monitoring and performing the health system functions. Due to a shortage of manpower, health workers are also trained to maintain the healthcare systems.

Even though health workers are cautious on the disease and hygiene, they are the most affected community during the pandemic. Those who work in frontline and primary healthcare are easily affected by the disease, work pressure and mental stress. Healthcare workers come forward to provide service only when provided with better equipment to protect themselves and patients too. The Indian healthcare system is vast and requires proper counseling and control during this pandemic situation. Being a healthcare worker is a challenging task. They have to take care of themselves, their family and their patients too. So their work–life balance should be managed. The government must provide flexible work hours to healthcare workers [1].

DOI: 10.1201/9781003248545-11

FIGURE 11.1   Distribution of employed and unemployed after technical education in the medical sector.

Source: Estimates from NSSO 2017–2018.

Figure 11.1 showcases the percentage distribution of various technical education in medicine. The employed and unemployed are also categorized. According to the UN, more than 60 million healthcare workers in frontline and supporting team are in demand globally. Deploying the healthcare workers is great task, but preparing them for a pandemic is a milestone.

Blockchain techniques have made it possible to store and handle information via a decentralized network of intermediaries. When the network of intermediaries structured more and the less the combined attitude of these intermediaries can be seen in this technology, without the need to trust any specific mediator [2]. The purpose of blockchain is to enhance the safety of health data by addressing questions about what use, why technical people need this assistance, which category of people need this support, how state-of-the-art blockchains are used to ensure the safety of medical data and so on [3]. Blockchain technologies thereby familiarize the concept of untrustworthy confidence, as consumers of an information system can trust the whole system without any special peer.

Blockchain has worldwide applications in healthcare. This type of technology helps to secure the transfer of medical records, unlock genetic codes and also manage the drug supply chain. The global blockchain healthcare market was expected to grow at a 72.8% CAGR from USD 53.9 million in 2018 to USD 829.0 million by 2023. This explains why blockchain technology is regarded as the next big thing in healthcare. According to an IBM Institute for Business Value report, between 2018 and 2020, 56% of 200 healthcare executives will have blockchains in production and on a large scale.

The Electronic Health Record (EHR) means the electronic medical history of patients that the provider maintains over time, and which may include all important clinical administrative data, including demographics, progress notes, problems and drugs. Proposes the implementation using Smart Contracts as an information mediator of large-scale information architecture for accessing EHR. The contribution of the author is the formulation and suggestion of a comprehensive blockchain based architecture addressing data privacy and accessibility concerns in health services [4].

The technological progress, there are many tools and techniques to enable the health industry to work efficiently and effectively. The flood of big data from IoT-based devices (the Internet of Things) which provide healthcare catalyzes the operation of this gadget further. For example, handwritten reports can be transformed into digital reports by IoT devices. They also offer a means to make it simple to save and share reports with various parties involved (e.g., patients, physicians, pharmaceutical service providers, health insurance workers and health administrators) [5]. EHR is a major component of health data [6]. It provides patient information for private medical diagnosis. In addition to EHR, several kinds of health data are available: (b) data from pharmaceutical and drug products containing information on manufactured and clinical trial medicines, or (c) information from health insurance that includes information related to a patient's health insurance policy, payment information and information concerning allergies and (d) data collected and used in health research, for example, cough sounds for identification of Covid-19 [7] and X-ray images for the categorization of pneumonia. Such huge data allows doctors to acquire a greater knowledge and offer better health services for their patients. Nonetheless, various stakeholders take advantage of different health data. An important problem with this health data is to maintain their security against several cyber threats [8]: (a) threats to health information (as EHR in hospitals are not well sheltered) and (b) how often the violation (such as Athena group hacking and (c) the accountability of performance for their success (such as the practice of personal website) has affected people and healthcare organizations [9]. All the above work focuses on the solutions for EHR data protecting in the area of healthcare data security. Pharmaceutical, administration and health insurance are also benefited since healthcare-related companies actively engage in the exchange, access and use of the created information. The safety of health data also includes information protection, such as data on medical diagnoses, insurance data, data on the pharmaceutical supply chain and biological research [10].

First, several nontechnical elements that make health information sensitive are discussed. Then, we offer an architecture capable of improving existing EHR systems. The aim is to ensure safety of patient information by avoiding access by other parties without authorization. Blockchain-based solutions can provide widespread access, protect data privacy, reduce curation and mediation costs and provide reliable information systems confidence. Blockchain technology is based on the concept that a distributed leader is a database that stores the history of transactions. Groups of agents are continuously audited (nominated according to different strategies, based on the application area). The audit results are saved in a block and transmitted to the network. Sequential blocks are attached to the ledger to create a connected chain. Efforts can readily be discovered to manipulate blocks or change their arrangement.

11.2   INSIGHTS OF BLOCK CHAIN IN COVID PANDEMIC

The study on blockchain and AI-based health systems is the latest. Researchers have developed several blockchain methods in order to overcome these challenges. The pandemic has not only had unintended effects at the global level but also has pushed health systems throughout the world to their limitations, such as the personal protective equipment (PPEs) and problems in diagnostics and monitoring of huge populations [11]. This epidemic caused several nations to shut down, keep locked and adopt social distance to prevent Covid-19 spread. This pandemic led us all into unexpected economic crisis. The new economic crisis brings the major industries such as Agriculture, automobile, aviation, regional markets. Indirect institutions are also affected such as supply chains, transportation, education and tourism as well [12]. The outbreak was officially announced in Wuhan, China by December 2019, the new coronavirus illness (Covid-19) has spread every state and country throughout the world. The world virtually saw the spreading and effects within few months. The broadcasting of the virus, the intensity and effects of this pandemic has become significant, because the World Health Organization (WHO) also declared the Public Health Emergency of International Concern (PHEIC) [13]. The current healthcare technology needs reliable data, which is vital if the new coronavirus is to be properly informed. Moreover, due to the inexactness and manual processing of huge amounts of data, the virus test method using medical instruments to identify coronaviral infections typically takes a few days to complete. Finally, it poses many privacy concerns for tracking or surveilling infected individuals or their connections [14]. These shortcomings highlighted by Covid-19 encouraged health organizations, in order to combat pandemic scenarios, to alter the existing digital healthcare infrastructure. In general, the digital healthcare ecosystem must allow clinical trials, frontline care, data monitoring, medical billing, telemedicine, pharmacy, therapy and discovery of strategy. Furthermore, a digital ecosystem to battle Covid-19 and future pandemics using digital platforms should be developed with a patient-centered and democratized focus [15]. Overall, the health system has worked in a closed ecosystem of siloed institutions, where the major stakeholder of the medical information was health professionals (i.e., physicians, radiologists, clinicians and researchers). The information flow is one way, i.e., a patient medical expert. However, data is increasing and moving across a closed healthcare system more quickly than ever before in the era of digital patient health records. The one-to-one flow of information gives way to a multitude of information [16]. Designed a clever contract-based, patient surveillance system for recording and sharing wearable device data with healthcare providers as events. This system's major objective is to remove third-party vulnerability and remote surveillance concerns [17]. Researchers have built a safe and trustworthy digital environment utilizing an intelligent contract-based medical system to avoid data violations in EHRs [18]. The authors of [19] suggested a system to store patient EHRs in a decentralized, patient-centered framework that allows patients to govern their data using a rules-based smart contract in order to achieve decentralized data management in medical care.

The rapidly growing parameter numbers, complicated structures and adequate data are needed to provide accurate, in-depth learning solutions to AI-based healthcare systems. The data is gathered and saved on the central server to find a global model from several sources.

11.3 BLOCKCHAIN IMPACT ON CLINICAL DATA

Medical care has become one of India's biggest areas, both as far as income and business. Medical services include emergency clinics, clinical gadgets, clinical preliminaries, reevaluating, telemedicine, clinical travel industry, healthcare coverage and clinical hardware. The Indian medical care sector is expanding at a rapid pace as a result of its expanding inclusion, benefits and consumption by both public and private players. The Indian medical care conveyance framework is divided into two major components: public and private. The government, or public healthcare system, consists of a few secondary and tertiary care institutions in major cities and focuses on providing basic healthcare facilities in rural areas through primary healthcare centers (PHCs). The majority of secondary, tertiary and quaternary care institutions are provided by the private sector, with a concentration in metros and tier I and tier II cities.

Blockchain, the innovation fundamental to the blast in cryptographic money, is presently being considered for a close utilization of clinical and well-being records. The security and uprightness of medical care information should be shielded from outer aggressors, yet additionally, from unapproved access endeavors from inside the organization or biological system (for example worker of the medical care supplier, or cloud specialist co-op). The assaults (for example spillage or change of information) can be arranged and unplanned, and associations might be rebuffed or expected misguidedly to take responsibility for such events, for instance under the Health Insurance Portability and Accountability Act [20]. There are four sorts of blockchains that we frequently know about (see Figure 11.2). These are private blockchains, public blockchains, consortium and hybrid blockchains [21].

FIGURE 11.2 Taxonomy of blockchain.

11.3.1 CATEGORIES OF HEALTHCARE DATA MANAGEMENT SYSTEMS AND ORGANIZATIONS

The health data is a reservoir of information that is useful to healthcare organizations and individuals. We give specifics of the data in the healthcare industry before we address blockchain implementation of healthcare data security. This section offers a brief overview of the various data categories related to the health sector and its management entities. The data systems work in the ground of medical care through the capabilities of generating, controlling access and storing personal health information. EHRs are the most popular and often created patient records. An EHR comprises personal information, indices of physiological health, medical history, laboratory findings and a patient's pharmaceutical prescription data. Health facilities including clinics and hospitals create EHR data based on diagnosis by medical experts and laboratories. Third-party specialists and suppliers usually administer EHRs, whereas health institutions and professionals are their customers [22]. The fundamental target of the HER is to focus on the total strength of the patient-going past normal clinical information gathered in the provider's working environment and a more extensive perspective on a patient's consideration [23–24].

11.3.2 BLOCKCHAIN IN PATIENT MONITORING

Indeed, even before the Covid-19, far off understanding checking frameworks got more well known unavoidably. Moreover, it tends to be described really during the 2020 changes to CPT codes that boost RPM into the consideration as one of the most productive Medicare care the board programs just as suppliers continually accepting innovation to support the wellness and well-being of their patients. Cloud Technology and IoT can help us to collect the clinical data in multiple aspects. Figure 11.3 illustrates the Digital gadgets are connecting almost all the human beings into one cloud. Many service providers are giving the applications for free and sharing that data to hospitals and governments also.

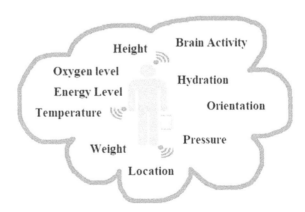

FIGURE 11.3   Remote patient monitoring through blockchain, IoT and cloud.

When the pandemic came into picture, remote monitoring and providing the data from remote locations received more focus. Because Patients were unable to move from one location to other location frequently. Entire government organization and healthcare system understanding the difficulty of the situation as well. So, government extended federal medical insurance inclusion of RPM administrations from beginning level to persistent or intense conditions, among different changes headed to utilize the RPM support enormously.

Though we can spend more on treating chronic health conditions, our healthcare industry is focused more on prevention than cure. Specialists feel that perhaps the most productive and splendid approach is to reduce down the expense through powerful avoidance. However, it is difficult to concentrate on the grounds that numerous Americans are as of now influenced a great deal by persistent infection. Remote physiologic monitoring system is greatly changed and expanded the health status to avoid critical and chronic conditions. This can confidently and substantially increase the savings and mitigate the emergency admissions and readmissions in the healthcare industry. This is the primary inspiration, why we have made this thorough checking framework for putting resources into a distant patient observing framework through programming just as associated patient gadgets. There are other valuable facts to understand about the Covid-19 and healthcare industry, particularly in this pandemic and we tried to cover them all [25].

11.3.3   BLOCKCHAIN AND PHARMACEUTICAL SUPPLY CHAIN

We can notice that there is a significant growth in the pharmaceutical industry in the recent past. At the end of 2019, $1.25 trillion is the total value of the global pharma market. It was an achievement when we compare it with the market value $390 billion in the year 2001. So we should understand the driving forces of the medical industry growth and influencing factors of this evolution.

A number of internal and external factors are shaping the global pharmaceutical logistics and supply chains. Their complexity will vary based on the parameters variations in the industry. For the last two or three decades most of the investment in pharmaceutical industry based on discovery, development and marketing of new drugs and therapeutics. Most expected challenges in the pharma industry are from supply chain management system.

11.4   SERVICES CONNECTED TO HEALTHCARE DATA

We have outlined several types of health data. Since health data extends beyond medical reporting and personal health data, doctors' diagnostics and medical tests also extend beyond connected services. These services are of a varied nature. They span from individual patients via diagnostics through to the deployment of health resources at the national and organizational levels. Furthermore, various healthcare data are a critical input in order to ensure service operations connected to health research programs, drug distribution and medical insurance processes (By 2022, the healthcare market could triple to Rs. 8.6 trillion (US$ 133.44 billion). In Budget 2021, India's public expenditure on healthcare stood at 1.2 percent of GDP [20]. Medical services, distribution services and commercial activities services are roughly grouped as medical services. We cover these services in depth here. In this section we discuss these services. The patient diagnosis and treatment plan are the most important healthcare service (medical service) based on healthcare data. Doctors associated or functioning alone with nurses provide these services primarily [26]. Through techniques such as medicine and operations the physicians require data from sources such as EHRs and PHRs to prescribe therapy.

11.4.1 CONNECTIONS BETWEEN THE NODES FOR THE CLINICAL DATA

Patient P needs some clinical information while having a clinical arrangement at Hospital H, yet the information was made during a past arrangement N among P and D, and the information is kept by Doctor D. The communication network between patients, doctors and hospitals is shown in Figure 11.4. In Blockchain, we can be able to link one patient to many hospitals as well. But when it comes to on hospital the patient will be linked to all the nodes in the hospital. Regarding clinical data, Patient's data will be in one hospital. When it comes to real-time utilization, one patient's information or clinical data shall be observed in different hospitals. In fact it shall be updated for the welfare for the entire society in this Covid pandemic.

A blockchain-based approach to data protection, reduction of curation and mediation costs and a reliability of information systems can enable wide-ranging accessibility. In the following sections we examine the associated tasks, data accessibility and privacy problems of blockchain based on a decentralized blockchain architecture with respect to the development and maintenance of a worldwide EHR system. In addition to the ethical concerns and openness, we explain some fundamental principles of this system and present an architectural blueprint that may embrace all of its qualities and concepts.

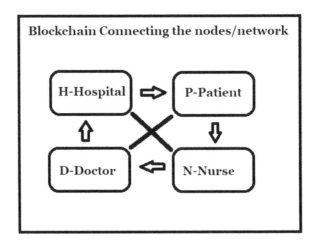

FIGURE 11.4   Understanding the connections within the nodes of clinical data.

11.5   DIGITAL TRACE ON HOSPITAL ZONES

11.5.1   Overall Global Architecture Blockchain-based EHR

Considering data accessibility, privacy, ethical problems and the importance of openness, we are introducing the EHR architecture, which can make interoperability on the well-being records conceivable and protected on a worldwide scale based on blockchain and smart contracts.

11.5.1.1   Blockchain Ledgers

A distributed ledger that can perform intelligent contracts. This component is responsible for recording health transactional references, such as health booking, clinical tests, prescription drugs, etc. Ledger wallets using Blockchain for data transactions is shown in Figure 11.5. Section 11.5.1 describes the structure for each transaction; in short, a block comprises monetary transactions in a cryptocurrency system. A block may include indicators of health information in a privacy layer for EHRs. For example, if a doctor at the Y hospital sees a patient X, an operation is attached to the headline stating that Y has access to the information of X.

11.5.1.2   Ledger Wallets

An electronic wallet is used to hold public and private encryption keys. The public key is the solution's user ID. The wallet will also save the email and password used

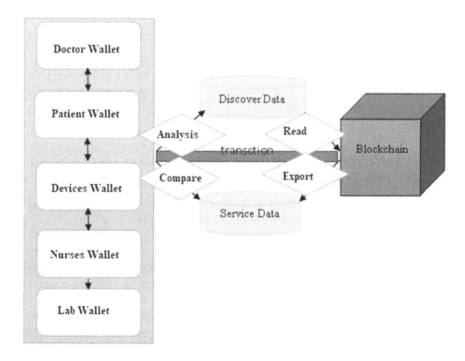

FIGURE 11.5   Ledger wallets in blockchain for Electronic Health Record environment.

for accessing the data service. The wallet is the fundamental system interface and access mechanism.

11.5.1.3 Digital Data

Digital data storage services required for the records of health. It is a cloud file system in this proposal where X belongs to every file, and it may be accessed using Y3. For example, utilizing major market clouds, such Google Drive, Mega Drive and Dropbox, this approach may be done. The service of data must offer cloud, access control and file access APIs to add and delete the read access to the files in order to be applied in our design.

11.5.1.4 Discovery of Data

For acceleration of the information search, the nonmandatory and auxiliary system. The data recorded in the blockchain is an index. The Discovery Department, for instance, presents a rundown of exchanges on the blockchain possessed by X with a patient X distinguished by his public key X+. It ought to likewise give an interface to discovering X and Y with an information document reference. This assistance can be completed using a NoSQL base that keeps a perspective on the blockchain (with conceivable consistency). This part has no security issues on the grounds that just the blockchain peruses and the aftereffects of questions can be checked essentially utilizing neighborhood duplicates of the blockchain. This part has no security issues in light of the fact that just the blockchain peruses and the consequences of inquiries can be checked basically utilizing neighborhood duplicates of the blockchain. The Discovery Service can likewise give fundamental expert pursuit administrations.

11.5.1.5 Using Framework

The blockchain maintains the history and links with the EHRs that provide full descriptions of each contact between patients and healthcare workers. The block also contains a hash of the medical record; thus, it is easy to verify the authenticity of the information.

11.6 VULNERABILITY OF HEALTH PROFESSIONALS TO COVID-19 KEY RISK REDUCTION STRATEGIES

All conditions imply critical danger to well-being laborers who have not undeniable degrees of clinical doubt in these patients, and who embrace sufficient security measures for patients who have uncommon indications of Covid-19 or exceptionally gentle general influenza like side effects. In tropics, in addition, febrile symptoms associated with the transmission of vectors and other diseases can be observed in individuals with coinfection with SARS-CoV-2. For instance, in Thailand, a patient with dengue disease was hospitalized and SARS-CoV-2 was also infected, with the healthcare worker responsible [27]. Healthcare personnel – and indeed patients who have been hospitalized to a health center for various reasons – are more vulnerable to "Super-Events" infection. In Wuhan, China, in one case, the healthcare staff and patients had a significant number of infections [28]. These infections have been identified to an abdominal patient who was hospitalized to surgery [29]. It takes funds that cannot be found in many Africa environments to trace and monitor super-spreading occurrences in hospitals. In healthcare institutions, the risks of infection by health workers can be minimized with appropriate measures [30]. This includes mainly the use of a cloth, gloves, face asking and a facial shield or a Goggle, personal protection equipment (PPE) [31]. The careful handling of this equipment continues to be a crucial defense but needs extensive training and oversight [32]. At the beginning of the epidemic, risk for infection may also be highest while healthcare personnel are still not aware of the usage of PPE. In high-income nations, there is severe PPE scarcity, and restricted supplies are likely to be given to low-income countries. Health professionals' risks of infection are among other things related to shift time and manual hygiene [33]. However, in some regions of Africa, water supplies for hand washing may be small or unavailable. The spectrum of cost-efficient cleaners that may be used for cleaning and disinfecting working surfaces and objects like stylos, stethoscopes and mobile phones in place of commercially made sanitizers is to be guided [34]. The likelihood of disease transmission to medical services work force in well-being foundations, including face veiling for patients with respiratory side effects and tissue patients, can limit an assortment of basic minimal expense therapies.

11.7 SUSTAINABLE DEVELOPMENT OF HEALTHCARE WORKERS AND POLICIES

Caring for patients with Covid-19 generates substantial mental strain, leading to high anxiety levels and posttraumatological stress disorders, particularly in the nursing community [35]. These circumstances affect medical professionals greatly but also hinder their capacity to make choices and to connect with patients with quality [36]. It should be remembered that the pressure at work has been increased by the exact same interruptions and uncertainties that are being faced by members of the broader public [37, 38]. Such psychological assistance may be important in many regions of the African continent, depending upon a huge number of HIV counselors or pensioners. However, the conflicting objectives of the health professionals may be hindered by formal organized interventions [39]. For example, counselors or beneficiaries visit medical care laborers resting submits in request to pay attention to issues or the accounts told by the representatives of their work. Casual methodology may turn out to be substantially more fruitful. Clinical help through informal communities, for example, the South African Vula stage, can assist with reducing pressure and spread it to different nations.

WhatsApp bunches among well-being specialists may offer clinical dynamic direction, yet in addition impart emotional wellness support messages. Normal correspondence among Ebola well-being experts guaranteed that new information could be conveyed between suppliers, especially when there were proof of holes in the infection [37]. Although health workers may accept a higher risk as a part of their chosen occupation, they may be extremely concerned that the virus may spread to children, families and friends, particularly elderly people or those with chronic health conditions and perhaps even their animals although there is limited proof that they suffer [40]. Healthcare workers may choose alternate housing to reduce the danger of transmission to a home. The now unoccupied student apartments or motels may be repropsed as locations of relaxation and isolation from their family for some time [41]. In addition, health workers may prefer to stay in hospitals for longer shifts throughout the week, instead of shifting shorter hours and returning every night. Protective steps might include separation of living spaces and toilets and routines when returning home after duty, for example take-off shoes, clothes removal and washing and bathing promptly.

11.8 CONCLUSION

Covid-19 pandemic has made many changes in socially, financially and the development that need to be done has been postponed across the world. It also took many lives irrespective of ages. It has become more dangerous as the days have passed. To maintain cleanliness healthcare workers has been helping a lot for the society. Healthcare workers played a major role in this pandemic. They are underserved and underresourced populations. They are risking their lives to maintain proper sanitation in our surroundings for the cause of people by taking less wages. Here blockchain has a wide scope of applications in medical services. This innovation helps the unreliable exchange of patient clinical records and furthermore deals with the medication inventory network.

These days as innovation creates many changes are accumulating in the field of medication as well. We have begun utilizing clinical sensors for healthcare observation reasons. This tremendous amount of information created by the sensors ought to be recorded and passed on to help the patients who are in basic circumstances. Patient's own data and healthcare records should be put away safely without losing the information. Blockchain innovation upholds enrolments of patients and specialists in a healthcare community to expand client cooperation in far-off understanding observing. It helps to observe patients at far-off places and alarms if there should be an occurrence of crisis. Utilizing the Blockchain innovation phony and security hack in medical services framework is decreased. The Blockchain can lessen the danger of extortion and information robbery as its innovation stores, scrambles and checks each and every piece of information. Its exchange costs are lower on the grounds that there are no outsiders repeated in the blockchain model.

Medical care laborers ought to be more cautious while serving society in a pandemic circumstance. At the point when medical care laborers display respiratory side effects, they ought not to give direct persistent consideration. They should cover and have to clean their hands as often as possible. They ought to be more cautious while managing Coronavirus patients. The government assumes a significant part in medical services financing by assembling the essential assets through open spending plans and another commitment instrument. The public authority proposes to give protection front of 50lakh per individual to bleeding-edge healthcare laborers – disinfection staff, paramedics and nurturers, and specialists who are neutralizing the COVID-19 disease and face the most noteworthy danger of getting the sickness. Roughly 22lakh healthcare laborers would be given protection cover to battle this pandemic. It will be essential to develop further following of financing for pandemic readiness. Use and offer specialized ability on fixed-cost things. Advance prescribed procedures in financing approaches and monetary reactions to the emergency. Reciprocal givers enjoy the benefit of having the option to depend on an assortment of organizations establishments common society and local gatherings, research focuses and so on Advancement finance establishments ought to likewise assume a part as mindful financial backers – embracing best practices in organizations they put resources into to slow the spread of infection. In this manner, medical care laborers, and innovative, cutting-edge laborers combined.

REFERENCES

[1] Anand, S., & Barnighausen, T. (2012). Health workers at the core of the health system: framework and research issues. *Health Policy*;105:185–91. http://dx.doi.org/10.1016/j.healthpol.2011.10.012.

[2] Fadhil, M., Owen, G., & Adda, M. (2016). Bitcoin network measurements for simulation validation and parameterisation. In Proceedings of the Eleventh International Network Conference, pp. 109–114.

[3] Pandey, M., Agarwal, R., Shukla, S. K., & Verma, N. K. (2021). Security of healthcare data using blockchains: A survey. arXiv:2103.12326.

[4] Da Conceição, A. F., da Silva, F. S. C., Rocha, V., Locoro, A., & Barguil, J. M. (2018). Electronic health records using blockchain technology. arXiv:1804.10078.

[5] Le, T. T., Andreadakis, Z., Kumar, A., Gómez Román, R., Tollefsen, S., Saville, M., & Mayhew, S. (2020). The Covid-19 vaccine development landscape. *Nature Reviews Drug Discovery*;19(5):305–06.

[6] Stafford, T. F., & Treiblmaier, H. (2020). Characteristics of a blockchain ecosystem for secure and sharable Electronic Medical Records. *IEEE Transactions on Engineering Management*;67(4):1340–62. https://doi.org/10.1109/TEM.2020.2973095.

[7] Brown, C., Chauhan, J., Grammenos, A., Han, J., Hasthanasombat, A., Spathis, D., Xia, T., Cicuta, P., & Mascolo, C. (2020). Exploring automatic diagnosis of Covid-19 from crowdsourced respiratory sound data. Proceedings of the 26th ACM SIGKDD International Conference on Knowledge Discovery & Data Mining, pp. 3474–84. https://doi.org/10.1145/3394486.3412865.

[8] Berenson, A. B., & Rahman, M. (2011). Prevalence and correlates of prescription drug misuse among young, low-income women receiving public healthcare. *Journal of Addictive Diseases*;30(3):203–215. https://doi.org/10.1080/10550887.2011.581984.

[9] Kumar, V., & Walker, C. (2017). Cyber-attacks: Rising threat to healthcare. *Vascular Disease Management*;14(3);51–54.

[10] Hardin, T., & Kotz, D. (2019). Blockchain in health data systems: A survey. Sixth International Conference on Internet of Things: Systems, Management and Security, pp. 490–97. https://doi.org/10.1109/IOTSMS48152.2019.8939174.

[11] Mandl, K. D., & Kohane, I. S. (2012). Escaping the EHR trap: The future of health IT. *New England Journal of Medicine;* 366(24);2240–42. https://doi.org/10.1056/NEJMp1203102.

[12] Kaye, A. D., Okeagu, C. N., Pham, A. D., et al. (2020). Economic impact of Covid-19 pandemic on healthcare facilities and systems: International perspectives. *Best Practice & Research Clinical Anaesthesiology*;35(3):293–306.

[13] Fernandes N. (2020). Economic effects of coronavirus outbreak (Covid-19) on the world economy. IESE Business School Working Paper No. WP-1240-E. https://papers.ssrn.com/sol3/papers.cfm?abstract_id=3557504 (accessed June 5, 2021).

[14] Wilder-Smith, A., & Osman, S. (2020). Public health emergencies of international concern: A historic overview. *Journal of Travel Medicine*;27;1–13.

[15] Ko, H., Leitner, J., Kim, E., & Jeong, J. (2020). Information technology-based tracing strategy in response to Covid-19 in South Korea: Privacy controversies. *JAMA*;323;2129–30.

[16] Reddy, S., Fox, J., & Purohit, M. P. (2019). Artificial intelligence-enabled healthcare delivery. *Journal of the Royal Society of Medicine*;112;22–28.

[17] Minor, D. (2018). Stanford Medicine 2018 Health Trends Report: The Democratization of Health Care. Stanford Medicine. https://med.stanford.edu/content/dam/sm/school/documents/Health-Trends-Report/Stanford-Medicine-Health-Trends-Report-2018.pdf (accessed June 5, 2021).

[18] Griggs, K. N., Ossipova, O., Kohlios, C. P., Baccarini, A. N., Howson, E. A., & Hayajneh, T. (2018). Healthcare blockchain system using smart contracts for secure automated remote patient monitoring. *Journal of Medical Systems*;42:1–7.

[19] Patel, V. (2019). A framework for secure and decentralized sharing of medical imaging data via blockchain consensus. *Health Informatics Journal*;25:1398–411.

[20] Healthcare Industry in India. www.ibef.org/industry/healthcare-india.aspx

[21] www.blockchain-council.org/category/infographics.

[22] Jabarulla, M.Y., & Lee, H.-N. (2020). Blockchain-based distributed patient-centric image management system. *Applied Sciences*;11:196.

[23] Evans, R. S. (2016). Electronic Health Records: Then, now, and in the future. Yearbook of Medical Informatics:S48–61.

[24] www.computer.org/publications/tech-news/research/blockchain-health-medical-records-cloud-security.

[25] www.prevounce.com/a-comprehensive-guide-to-remote-patient-monitoring.

[26] Shah, R., & Chircu, A. (2018). IoT and AI in healthcare: A systematic literature review. *Issues in Information Systems*;19:33–41.

[27] Joob, B., & Wiwanitkit, V. (2020). Covid-19 in medical personnel: Observation from Thailand. *Journal of Hospital Infection*;104(4):453.

[28] Ghinai, I., McPherson, T. D., Hunter, J. C., et al. (2020). First known person-to-person transmission of severe acute respiratory syndrome coronavirus 2 (SARS-CoV-2) in the USA. *Lancet*;395(10230):1137–44.

[29] Marchand-Senecal, X., Kozak, R., Mubareka, S., et al. (2020). Diagnosis and management of first case of Covid-19 in Canada: Lessons applied from SARS. *Clinical Infectious Diseases*;71(16):2207–10.

[30] Ni, L., Zhou, L., Zhou, M., Zhao, J., & Wang, D. W. (2020). Combination of western medicine and Chinese traditional patent medicine in treating a family case of COVID19 in Wuhan. *Frontiers of Medicine*;14(2):210–14.

[31] Cai, S. J., Wu, L. L., Chen, D. F., et al. (2020). Analysis of bronchoscope-guided tracheal intubation in 12 cases with COVID-19 under the personal protective equipment with positive pressure protective hood. *Zhonghua jiehe he huxi zazhi = Chinese Journal of Tuberculosis and Respiratory Diseases*;43:E033.

[32] Ran, L., Chen, X., Wang, Y., Wu, W., Zhang, L., & Tan. X. (2020). Risk factors of healthcare workers with corona virus disease 2019: A retrospective cohort study in a designated hospital of Wuhan in China. *Clinical Infectious Diseases*;71(16):2218–21.

[33] Chinazzi, M., Davis, J. T., Ajelli, M., et al. (2020). The effect of travel restrictions on the spread of the 2019 novel coronavirus (Covid-19) outbreak. *Science*;368(6489):395–400.

[34] Huang, J. Z., Han, M. F., Luo, T. D., Ren, A. K., & Zhou, X. P. (2020). Mental health survey of 230 medical staff in a tertiary infectious disease hospital for Covid-19]. *Zhonghua laodong weisheng zhiyebing zazhi = Chinese Journal of Industrial Hygiene and Occupational Diseases*;38:E001.

[35] Kang, L., Li, Y., Hu, S., et al. (2020). The mental health of medical workers in Wuhan, China dealing with the 2019 novel coronavirus. *Lancet Psychiatry*;7(3):e14.

[36] Catton, H. (2020). Global challenges in health and health care for nurses and midwives everywhere. *International Nursing Review*;67(1):4–6.

[37] Hu, Z., Song, C., Xu, C., et al. (2020). Clinical characteristics of 24 asymptomatic infections with COVID-19 screened among close contacts in Nanjing. *Science China Life Sciences*;63(5):706–11.

[38] Rose, C. (2020). Am I part of the cure or am I part of the disease? Keeping coronavirus out when a doctor comes home. *New England Journal of Medicine*;382:1684–85.

[39] Rodriguez-Morales, A. J., Cardona-Ospina, J. A., Gutierrez-Ocampo, E., et al. (2020). Clinical, laboratory and imaging features of COVID-19: a systematic review and meta-analysis. *Travel Medicine and Infectious Disease*;34:101623.

[40] Adams, J. G., & Walls, R. M. (2020). Supporting the health care workforce during the Covid-19 global epidemic. *JAMA*;323(15):1439–40.

[41] Zainab Kazmi, H. S., Nazeer, F., Mubarak, S., Hameed, S., Basharat, A., & Javaid, N. (2019). Trusted remote patient monitoring using blockchain-based smart contracts. 14th International Conference on Broad-Band Wireless Computing, Communication and Applications, pp. 765–776.

Index

Milton Keynes UK
Ingram Content Group UK Ltd.
UKHW031132141024
449569UK00006B/236